It's another great book from CGP...

This book is for anyone doing **GCSE Religious Studies**.

It covers all the important information and issues in a **clear** and **balanced** way, with plenty of advice for writing **top-notch answers** in the exam. There's even a section to help you score full marks for your **spelling**, **punctuation** and **grammar**.

What's more, we've included a **free** Online Edition of the whole book, so you can revise on a computer or tablet — wherever you are.

How to get your free Online Edition

Just go to **cgpbooks.co.uk/extras** and enter this code...

0307 9644 4096 9735

By the way, this code only works for one person. If somebody else has used this book before you, they might have already claimed the Online Edition.

CGP — still the best! ☺

Our sole aim here at CGP is to produce the highest quality books — carefully written, immaculately presented and dangerously close to being funny.

Then we work our socks off to get them out to you — at the cheapest possible prices.

Contents

The clouds on the pages of Sections 1-8 tell you whether the page covers:

 Christian views... ...Jewish views... ...Muslim views... ...or general views.

Published by CGP

Editors:
David Hickinson, Sharon Keeley, Luke von Kotze, Andy Park, Jo Sharrock, Julie Wakeling

Contributors:
Maria Amayuelas-Tann, Jill Hudson, Duncan Raynor, Paul D. Smith, Nigel Thomas

Bible / Qur'an References:

References from the Bible always go in the order: Book Chapter:Verse(s). So whenever you see something like: Mark 3:5-6, it means it's from the book of Mark, Chapter 3, verses 5-6.

Similarly, references from the Qur'an are shown with the Surah (Chapter) followed by the Ayat (Verse).

ISBN: 978 1 84762 300 3

With thanks to Mary Falkner for the proofreading.

Scripture quotations (marked NIV) taken from the HOLY BIBLE, NEW INTERNATIONAL VERSION ANGLICISED
Copyright © 1979, 1984, 2011 Biblica, Used by permission of Hodder & Stoughton Ltd, an Hachette UK company
All rights reserved.
"NIV" is a registered trademark of Biblica.
UK trademark number 1448790

Holy Qur'an quotations taken from the Holy Qur'an, Sahih International Version. www.quran.com

Hadith quotations taken from MSA West Compendium of Muslim Texts. www.msawest.net/islam

Quotation on page 38 © The Inter Faith Network for the UK. www.interfaith.org.uk

Quotation on page 39 taken from Decree Ad Gentes, II Vatican Council.

Quotations on pages 50, 57 and 103 taken from the Catechism of the Catholic Church.

With thanks to Enid Thompson for the church photos on page 78.

Photograph on page 93 reproduced by permission of Rex Features.

Every effort has been made to locate copyright holders and obtain permission to reproduce sources. For those sources where it has been difficult to trace the originator of the work, we would be grateful for information. If any copyright holder would like us to make an amendment to the acknowledgements, please notify us and we will gladly update the book at the next reprint. Thank you.

Groovy website: www.cgpbooks.co.uk

Jolly bits of clipart from CorelDRAW®
Printed by Elanders Ltd, Newcastle upon Tyne

Based on the classic CGP style created by Richard Parsons.

Photocopying – it's dull, grey and sometimes a bit naughty. Luckily, it's dead cheap, easy and quick to order more copies of this book from CGP – just call us on 0870 750 1242. Phew!

Reasons for Belief

General

Millions of people across the world believe in some kind of <u>divine being</u> or '<u>god</u>'. They believe for various reasons — for some people, it's based on <u>personal religious experience</u>, but for others it's more <u>indirect</u>. For many people, the fact that they're <u>brought up</u> in a religious environment leads to or supports belief in a god.

Religious Belief Can *Start* with Your Upbringing

1) Children generally <u>believe</u> what their parents tell them, and tend to <u>copy</u> their parents' behaviour.

2) So, if a child is brought up by <u>religious parents</u>, with an <u>upbringing</u> that's based on <u>religious teaching</u>, it's <u>more likely</u> that they'll <u>believe</u> in a god.

3) For example, most <u>Christian</u> parents will have their children <u>baptised</u> soon after they're born, take them to <u>pray</u> in church, send them to <u>Sunday school</u> to learn about the Christian faith and encourage them to be <u>confirmed</u> as Christians when they're old enough. They'll also take part in <u>religious festivals</u>, e.g. performing in a nativity play at Christmas. At home, church and Sunday school, there are <u>trusted adults</u> who set an example of belief in God, and can help a child to develop their <u>own faith</u>.

4) The same would apply if you grew up in a <u>religious community</u> or went to a <u>religious school</u> (e.g. a Roman Catholic school, a Jewish Cheder or a Muslim Madrasah) where life is based on faith in one particular religion.

5) Different religions have <u>different attitudes</u> towards raising children in their faith:

CHRISTIANITY

<u>Evangelical</u> Christians (see p.38-39) in particular stress this.

1) According to the New Testament, you <u>cannot</u> be 'born a Christian'.
2) It's said that God has no grandchildren. In other words, you can't rely on your <u>parents</u>' faith — you have to find your own. And your parents can't <u>force</u> you to accept Christianity — it's your decision.

I'm a Jew. / I'm a Muslim. / Um... I'll think about it later...

JUDAISM

1) Jews believe that if your <u>mother</u> is Jewish, you're Jewish — whether you like it or not.
2) However, practising Jews recognise the importance of encouraging their children to 'keep the <u>faith</u>'.

ISLAM

1) Muslims believe that everyone is <u>born</u> in submission to Allah.
2) They may walk away from Allah as a result of their <u>upbringing</u>, but this is not the way things were meant to be.
3) If someone embraces Islam later in life, he or she is said to be '<u>returning</u>'.

6) <u>Conversion</u> refers to the <u>first time</u> a person <u>becomes a follower</u> of a god (although it can also be used when someone <u>changes their faith</u>). They might say they've been '<u>saved</u>' or '<u>born again</u>'.

Religious Experiences *May Lead to Belief in a God*

There are <u>loads of ways</u> that people claim to <u>experience God</u>.

1) <u>Religious Scripture</u> — some people believe that <u>holy books</u> (e.g. the Bible) can reveal the nature of God.

2) <u>Prayer</u> — this is an attempt to <u>contact God</u> directly and can be thought of as a <u>conversation</u> with God.

3) <u>Miracles</u> — these are <u>amazing events</u> that <u>can't be explained</u> by the laws of <u>nature</u> or <u>science</u>.

4) <u>Numinous Experiences</u> — these are feelings of <u>awe</u>, in which a person can 'sense' the presence of God.

There's more about revelations on page 71.

BUT THERE ARE PLENTY OF SCEPTICS AROUND...

A <u>key concern</u> for <u>nonbelievers</u> is whether miracles and other religious experiences are <u>real</u>.

Sceptics argue that they're <u>just illusions</u> brought on by <u>religious hysteria</u> or a <u>desire to believe</u> in something. Or that events that <u>seem</u> miraculous can actually be explained by <u>science</u>.

I believe in Geoff — the god of biscuits...

What causes someone to believe in a god is different for everyone. Someone's upbringing often influences their belief, but people may <u>convert</u> because of religious experiences like miracles or feelings of awe.

Design and Causation

There are two main <u>philosophical</u> arguments for the existence of a god.
These are usually referred to as the <u>argument from design</u> and the <u>argument from causation</u>.

Design: "Someone Must Have Designed the Universe"

1) Many people are convinced of the existence of a god by 'design' arguments.

2) The idea here is that the <u>intricate workings</u> of the <u>Universe</u> (or of <u>life</u>) <u>can't</u> have come about by <u>random chance</u>. There must have been some kind of <u>designer</u> — and this designer was <u>God</u>.

3) Isaac Newton's <u>thumb theory</u> (because every <u>thumbprint</u> is intricate and <u>unique</u>, there must be a God) and William Paley's <u>watchmaker theory</u> (you <u>wouldn't think</u> an <u>intricate watch</u> you found was made <u>by chance</u> — so why believe the <u>world was</u>) are both design arguments.

4) Even Albert Einstein, one of the most prominent scientists of the twentieth century (and an agnostic — see below), said: "When I see all the glories of the cosmos, I can't help but believe that there is a <u>divine hand</u> behind it all."

5) Einstein might have been talking about design, but this might also be interpreted as a reference to a <u>numinous</u> experience — something that <u>inspires awe and wonder</u> at God's creation (see page 71).

Causation: "There Must Have Been a First Cause"

1) The Universe as we know it works on the principle of '<u>cause and effect</u>' — that is, <u>everything</u> that happens is <u>caused</u> by something else.

2) So an event happening <u>now</u> was caused by an <u>earlier</u> event, which <u>in turn</u> was caused by an even earlier event, and so on back through time.

3) If you trace this chain of cause and effect back in time, you find <u>two possibilities</u>:

   a) The chain goes back forever — i.e. the Universe has <u>always</u> existed, it's eternal.

   b) You eventually reach a starting point — an <u>uncaused cause</u> or '<u>First Cause</u>'.

     4) Some people argue that this 'First Cause' must have been <u>God</u>.

But Not Everyone is Convinced by these Arguments

1) These philosophical arguments convince <u>many people</u> of the existence of God.

2) However, <u>non-religious ideas</u> about the origin of the world might lead a person to become an <u>agnostic</u> (someone who doesn't know whether or not there's a god — strictly, someone who believes it's <u>impossible to know</u> whether there's a god or not) or an <u>atheist</u> (someone who <u>rejects completely</u> the idea of a divine being).

3) These ideas include the theory of <u>evolution</u> (often called <u>Darwinism</u>) and the <u>Big Bang theory</u> (<u>cosmology</u>) (more about those on the next page).

4) Cosmologists argue that the Big Bang theory offers an <u>alternative 'First Cause'</u>. According to the theory, both <u>space</u> and <u>time</u> started with the Big Bang. If this is true, then to ask what came 'before' the Big Bang or what 'caused' the Big Bang is <u>meaningless</u>.

Christians, Muslims and Jews have Similar Beliefs about God

Since Christianity and Islam both developed from Judaism, the <u>basic concept</u> of God (the Christian God, the Muslim Allah or the Jewish Almighty) is something that <u>all three faiths share</u>. God is believed to be:

<u>OMNIPOTENT</u>: all-powerful — nothing is impossible for God.

  <u>OMNISCIENT</u>: all-knowing — knowing everything that we do, think or feel, now, in the past and in the future.

    <u>OMNI-BENEVOLENT</u>: all-loving and all-compassionate — he wants only what's best for us.

Looks like the jury's still out on this one...

Philosophers have been arguing backwards and forwards about this sort of thing for thousands of years. But religion's a personal thing — Sam <u>gazes at the stars</u> and reckons there <u>must be a god</u> but Al <u>doesn't</u> believe <u>at all</u>. Whichever side you're on, you need to <u>learn these reasons</u> for believing (or not) for your exam.

The Origins of the World

No one saw exactly how the Earth came to be like it is... but science and religion both have their theories.

Scientific Arguments — There are Two Main Types

COSMOLOGICAL THEORIES — How the Universe came into being

Chief amongst these is the Big Bang theory. It says that the Universe began in an explosion of matter and energy. Matter from this explosion eventually formed stars, planets and everything else. The Universe still seems to be expanding today — important evidence for this theory.

EVOLUTIONARY THEORIES — How living things came to be like they are today

In 1859, Charles Darwin published 'On the Origin of the Species'. In this book he argued that all life on the planet originated from simple cells. Life evolved (gradually changed) over millions of years into a huge variety of forms. According to this theory, we evolved from apes — not from Adam and Eve.

These theories are at odds with many religious arguments. However, if you don't take everything in the Bible or Torah literally, scientific and religious ideas can exist in harmony. Science tells us how, religion tells us why.

Religions have their Own Ideas about all this...

Christian Ideas

1) Traditional Christian and Jewish teachings about Creation come from the same scriptures, and so are identical.

2) According to Genesis Chapter 1, God created everything. If the Bible is taken literally, the process took six days, and humankind didn't evolve from apes, but is descended from Adam and Eve.

3) However, some Christians view Genesis as a parable, or as a symbolic description of a more gradual evolution. So it's possible to believe in the Bible and science.

4) In 1996 the Roman Catholic Church accepted the Big Bang theory — definitely a significant acceptance of science.

> "In the beginning God created the heavens and the earth." Genesis 1:1 NIV

The Creation in Genesis Chapter 1

Genesis says things were created in the following order: on the first day light and darkness; on the second day the sky; on the third day oceans, land and plants on the land; on the fourth day the sun, moon and stars; on the fifth day creatures of the water and sky (e.g. fish and birds); and then on the sixth day, land animals and people. On the seventh day, God rested.

If you ignore the fourth day, this is pretty much the same order as scientists think things appeared. So the timescale is different (millions of years rather than six days), but the general idea is the same.

Jewish Ideas

1) Orthodox Jews, who see the Torah as the word of God and so literally true, would find it difficult to accept scientific arguments about creation.

2) Reform Jews might argue that Creation as described in the Torah is more a way for us to understand, not an explanation of, how it happened.

> Yeah, not bad. I reckon I deserve a day off.

Islamic Ideas

1) The Muslim creation story is very similar to that in Genesis. Muslims believe that Allah created the world and everything in it.

2) But descriptions of creation in the Qur'an aren't entirely at odds with science. In fact, scientific theories are supported by passages like this.

3) Islam differs from science when it comes to the creation of humans, though. The Qur'an states that Allah formed Adam from clay and breathed life and a soul into him — and that all humans descend from Adam.

> "Have those who disbelieved not considered that the heavens and the earth were a joined entity, and We separated them and made from water every living thing? Then will they not believe?" Qur'an 21:30

In the beginning, God created exams...

Albert Einstein once said that if you see something beautiful or amazing, you are seeing the work of God (see previous page). Yeah, well... what did thicky Einstein know... But whether the Universe came to be this way through chance or design is a key question in the science versus religion debate...

General & Christianity

Evil and Suffering

Loads of bad things happen in the world. People suffer from terrible <u>illnesses</u> and die in <u>pain</u>. Some people commit horrible <u>crimes</u> and other people <u>suffer</u> as a result. These issues often cause people to ask <u>why</u>. For religious people, the bigger question is: "Why is <u>God letting</u> this happen?"

Evil can be Either Human-Made or Natural

Evil and suffering can be divided into <u>two types</u>:

MORAL (HUMAN-MADE) EVIL

1) This is when suffering is brought about by the <u>cruel</u> actions of <u>people</u>.
2) This includes things like murder, war, rape and torture.
3) The person causing the evil is able to make a <u>choice</u> about what is morally <u>right or wrong</u>.

NATURAL EVIL

1) This kind of evil, and the suffering that comes with it, is <u>caused by the world</u> in which we live, and is <u>no-one's 'fault'</u>.
2) This includes things like disease, floods, earthquakes and hurricanes.
3) However, many <u>recent natural disasters</u> may have been caused by <u>human interference</u> in the natural world, raising the question of whether that makes those events human-made.

Evil can Lead People to Question their Faith

1) <u>Evil</u> and <u>suffering</u> may lead some people to <u>question</u> their belief in God — or even to <u>reject</u> their faith.
2) This might be because they can't believe that a God who is <u>good</u> would <u>allow</u> such things to happen, or because they feel that their <u>prayers</u> are <u>not being answered</u> (i.e. they think God <u>could</u> help, but <u>doesn't</u>).

ANSWERED AND UNANSWERED PRAYERS

There's more about prayer on pages 83 and 84.

Roman Catholics and Orthodox Christians often pray for a <u>saint</u> to intercede with God on behalf of someone who's suffering. These are called 'intercessory prayers'. In other Christian traditions, prayers of intercession for others are addressed <u>directly</u> to God, as are prayers for help in Judaism and Islam (called <u>du'a</u> in Islam).

Christianity, Judaism and Islam teach that <u>no sincere prayer</u> goes unheard or unanswered — if a prayer seems to be unanswered, it's just that we can't <u>understand</u> God's reply. Since no human can ever know <u>God's plan</u>, it's impossible to say what's really best for us. <u>Praying</u> for and <u>helping</u> those who suffer is seen as a key part of various <u>faiths</u>.

3) Other people might argue that God can't be very <u>powerful</u> if he is <u>unable</u> to prevent suffering (i.e. God <u>can't</u> help, even if he wanted to).

The Christian View — Adam & Eve, a Test of Faith...

1) <u>Christianity</u> and <u>Judaism</u> teach that evil <u>entered</u> the world as a result of <u>Adam and Eve</u> giving in to <u>temptation</u> in the Garden of Eden — this switch from a perfect world to one containing evil is known as '<u>The Fall</u>'.
2) After the Fall, every human being was born with a <u>flawed</u> nature, capable of causing suffering — this is the idea of <u>original sin</u>.
3) Christians believe God created humans with <u>free will</u> — it's up to us to <u>choose</u> whether we perform evil deeds or not, just as it was up to <u>Adam and Eve</u> whether to give in to temptation or not.
4) <u>Suffering</u> is often seen as a <u>test of faith</u> — <u>God</u> has his <u>reasons</u> (even if we <u>don't know</u> what they are). Christians believe that they should try to <u>help</u> people who are suffering — both <u>practically</u> and by <u>praying</u>.
5) Some (but not all) <u>Christians</u> believe in an <u>evil</u>, spiritual force known as <u>the Devil</u> or <u>Satan</u> who is <u>working against God</u>, bringing evil and suffering to humanity.

oops...

Christianity and Judaism <u>differ</u> in that Christians believe <u>Jesus</u> was put on Earth to <u>pay</u> for the sins of <u>all humankind</u>.

Not the cheeriest page in the book, for sure...

Eeek — we're into evil and suffering already. Many people have tried to work out exactly what evil is. Some argue that human-made evil is a psychological disorder that some people are more prone to than others.

Evil and Suffering

Judaism & Islam

The problem of <u>evil</u>, <u>why</u> people suffer, and <u>how</u> to deal with it. It's the sort of thing religion was <u>invented</u> for.

Judaism and Islam also say we have the Choice...

1) <u>Both</u> Judaism and Islam teach that <u>humankind</u> was created with <u>free will</u>.
2) Therefore, people can <u>choose</u> to follow God, or <u>choose</u> to do wrong.
3) Judaism and Islam also have <u>similar perspectives</u> on how to <u>deal with</u> suffering and evil.

Judaism says Suffering can have Positive Results

1) The <u>Book of Job</u> in the <u>Hebrew Bible</u> contains a key Jewish idea on evil and suffering. Job endures <u>terrible suffering</u> of all kinds and he <u>questions</u> God. In the end Job comes to the conclusion that God is <u>all-powerful</u> and knows what he is doing — and that suffering must be <u>accepted</u> because we can't really <u>understand</u> the world or <u>God's plan</u>.

2) Judaism teaches that we have <u>free will</u> and are able to <u>choose</u> what we do (like Adam and Eve — see p.4). But we are prone to making <u>mistakes</u>, which could lead to <u>suffering</u>.

> Bet you a fiver he'll crack...

3) Like many Christians, Jews may also <u>respond</u> to suffering and evil through <u>prayer</u>.

4) The <u>Jewish</u> approach to suffering often stresses the idea that <u>good</u> can come out of terrible suffering. Suffering can bring people <u>closer</u> to <u>each other</u> and <u>closer to God</u>. It also allows people to make <u>sacrifices</u> for other people and draw on their <u>inner strength</u>.

> Although Satan isn't a part of <u>modern</u> Judaism, he does give <u>Job</u> a hard time.

5) The following passage is taken from the <u>Midrash</u> (a collection of Rabbinical commentaries on the Tenakh, or Jewish Bible): "Not to have known suffering is not to be truly human." It suggests that suffering is simply a part of the <u>human experience</u> and, therefore, must be <u>accepted</u>.

The Qur'an says "We Will Surely Test You"

1) <u>Muslims</u> believe that evil is a <u>test</u> of <u>humanity's free will</u>. We have <u>free will</u> so can choose whether to <u>give in</u> to <u>temptation</u> or not. It's a <u>test of faith</u>.

2) Islam teaches that if we <u>choose</u> to act <u>against</u> the will of <u>Allah</u> we will have to <u>answer</u> for that wrongdoing on the <u>Day of Judgement</u>.

3) The following passage is taken from the Qur'an 2:155-156:

"And We will surely test you with something of fear and hunger and a loss of wealth and lives and fruits, but give good tidings to the patient, who, when disaster strikes them, say, 'Indeed we belong to Allah, and indeed to Him we will return.' "

> This is remarkably similar to the moral of the Book of Job, when you think about it.

4) The idea here is that <u>suffering should be accepted</u>. Muslims believe that, despite suffering in <u>this life</u>, there will be <u>joy in the next</u> as Allah is <u>compassionate</u>.

5) <u>Prayer</u> is one way of <u>coping</u> with evil and suffering. If people pray for <u>forgiveness</u> when they have <u>done wrong</u> they will be <u>forgiven</u>. One of the ninety-nine revealed names of Allah is <u>Al-Ghaffar</u> — <u>The Forgiver</u>.

> Remember — there are differences in belief and tradition within Judaism and Islam, as there are within all religions.

6) Muslims believe that those who are <u>suffering</u> should be <u>treated compassionately</u> by others. Many <u>Muslims work to help</u> those who are suffering.

7) However, there is a belief in a <u>devil</u> (called <u>Iblis</u> or <u>Shaytan</u>) who was <u>cast out by Allah</u> and tries to <u>lead people away</u> from him. <u>Some</u> Muslims would argue that Allah <u>allows Shaytan</u> to use this power to <u>test and tempt</u> us — we have the <u>free will</u> to resist.

"Will I be forgiven?" — "Best ask the Ghaffar"...

Christianity, Judaism and Islam all have pretty similar ideas about this stuff: 1) Suffering is often seen as a <u>test of faith</u>. 2) You should always try to <u>help others</u> who are suffering. 3) Evil is wrong, but if you <u>pray for forgiveness</u> after doing something wrong, God/Allah will be merciful and will <u>forgive you</u>.

General & Judaism

The Problem of Evil

What believers mean by the 'problem' of evil is <u>why</u> there is evil in the world and how we should <u>respond</u> to it.

There are <u>Different Ideas</u> about the <u>Problem of Evil</u>

CHRISTIANITY

1) Some Christians would argue that most evil comes about because of how we <u>humans</u> act. After the Fall (p.4) we have the <u>choice</u> to do evil — and it is our responsibility not to.

2) Some Christians think that evil is <u>necessary</u> for there to be free will — without the choice of doing wrong, what freedom is there? They believe that there has to be evil in the world for it to be <u>possible</u> for us to <u>do good</u> — really doing good things requires that we could have acted differently. If we could only do good, how virtuous would we really be?

3) Many Christians believe that all the suffering in the world will in the end come to good — that God has a <u>plan</u> in which we must have <u>faith</u>.

I'm part of the GRAND PLAN, darling.

JUDAISM

Most Jewish thought doesn't seek to explain the presence of evil, or try to explain away the problem of evil. Many Jews believe that evil requires a <u>human response</u> rather than a philosophical explanation — i.e. being available to help those people who are the victims.

ISLAM

1) Islam teaches that everything that happens is part of Allah's plan. Allah has <u>good reasons</u> for allowing evil, including natural evil, to occur — even if they aren't immediately apparent to us.

2) Evil also gives people the chance to <u>do good</u>. It's up to us to be good and help those in need. If we ourselves are afflicted by evil, Muslims believe we must meet it with <u>patience</u> and <u>faith</u>.

The <u>Holocaust</u> Caused Jews to ask "Where was God?"

1) Towards the end of the 18th century, <u>persecution</u> of Jews living in Europe, known as <u>anti-Semitism</u>, spread through many countries — especially France, Germany, Austria and Russia.

2) Later, during the 1920s, <u>Germany</u> faced huge economic problems. The National Socialist (<u>Nazi</u>) Party seemed to offer solutions. It pinned the blame for the country's problems on '<u>non-Aryan</u>' people (i.e. those who weren't considered 'pure Germans') living in Germany — especially the Jews.

3) In 1933 its leader <u>Adolf Hitler</u> became Chancellor of Germany, and laws began to be passed that gradually deprived the Jews of their citizenship rights. Eventually Hitler introduced the <u>Final Solution</u> — the plan to wipe out the Jews completely. <u>Six million</u> Jews died in the <u>Holocaust</u>.

The Holocaust posed very serious <u>spiritual problems</u> for Jews — they had to find answers to questions like:

> If God exists, and he is good, and all-powerful, how could he have allowed such terrible suffering?
> If we are the 'chosen people', how could God have let six million of us be wiped out?

Jews have come up with many <u>responses</u> to this type of question:

1) Some Jews have concluded that there is <u>no God</u>.

2) Some have concluded that if God does exist, he either <u>doesn't care</u>, or is <u>powerless</u> to intervene.

3) Some Jews say that the Holocaust, and all suffering, is a <u>test of faith</u> — if good people always got the best things in life, everyone would be good for the wrong reasons.

4) Some Jews say that God could intervene to stamp out evil if he chose to. However, he gave all human beings <u>free will</u> and refuses to override this even when it is abused. Also, it would be impossible for God to 'destroy all evil people' because <u>no-one</u> is completely evil or completely good.

5) Some Jews regard all those who died in the Holocaust as <u>martyrs</u> for the faith, and see their martyrdom as 'sanctifying the name of God'.

6) Some say the most important thing is to <u>keep practising</u> Judaism, or else Hitler will have won.

It'll be a problem for you too if you don't learn it...

Some really terrible things happen. It's no wonder that this stuff is a problem for religious believers. But most faiths try to tackle evil constructively and to help the victims of natural and moral evil.

The Media: Belief

Christianity,
Judaism, Islam
& General

The media, e.g. TV programmes, radio programmes and films, can have a big impact on people's beliefs.

A Christian Example: "Songs of Praise"

Dedicated religious programmes might affect people's attitudes to belief in God. One of the best-known is 'Songs of Praise', which features Christian hymns and focuses on a different community or theme each week.

SONGS OF PRAISE — SUNDAY EVENINGS, BBC 1

Positive effects on faith:
1) Viewers share other people's experiences of God and faith. This can help show the relevance of Christianity to people's lives, and make them feel part of a larger community.
2) The themes covered in the programme can lead to a deeper understanding of the Christian religion.
3) The programme is interactive — with hymn and prayer text on screen. This lets viewers take part in communal worship without having to go to church.

Negative effects on faith:
1) It's hard to feel personally involved in a service when you're watching it on TV.
2) The programme might be seen to trivialise the act of worship.
3) Some people find the traditional hymns boring and uninspiring.

BBC Radio 4 broadcasts religious programmes, including 'Sunday Worship' on a Sunday morning. There's also a Christian digital TV channel — GOD TV.

Christian leaders such as the Pope and the Archbishop of Canterbury often appear in the media giving their opinions on all sorts of issues. Their messages are sometimes presented out of context, though, making them sound more controversial. This makes for exciting headlines, but can give a very bad impression of Christianity.

Judaism is Sometimes Stereotyped by the Media

1) You don't tend to get regular, specifically Jewish programmes on national TV or radio, and this is a cause for some concern and frustration among the Jewish community in the UK.
2) Many feel that Jewish issues are not always dealt with fairly and that Jews are shown in a stereotypical way (e.g. passive victims in Holocaust films like 'Schindler's List', neurotic intellectuals in Woody Allen films like 'Annie Hall' or pushy, overprotective mothers in US sitcoms like 'Will and Grace').

In June 2008, BBC 4 broadcast an in-depth series of programmes called 'Jews' that looked at the history, religious practices and beliefs of different groups of Jews in Britain today. Programmes like this may help Jews to reconnect with their faith, as well as educating the non-Jewish community.

3) The UK's Chief Rabbi, Lord Jonathan Sacks is a regular contributor to BBC Radio 4's 'Thought for the Day'. He also writes occasional articles for national newspapers — usually The Times.

Islam has Been in the Spotlight Since 9/11

Since the rise of Islamic fundamentalism, Islam and its perceived link with terrorism have been all over the news. Programmes like Channel 4's 'Qur'an' (first shown in July 2008) have tried to show a more balanced view of Islam. 'Qur'an' looked at how different groups of people interpret the sacred text differently.

Some Other Muslim Programming:
• "Devotional Sounds: Islam" on the BBC's Asian Network radio station broadcasts religious music every Saturday and Sunday morning.
• Muslim clerics regularly contribute to Radio 4's "Thought for the Day".

An Atheist Viewpoint: "The Root of All Evil?"

1) Atheist programmes and literature might lead people to question the existence of God.
2) In January 2006, Channel 4 showed a two-part series by atheist Professor Richard Dawkins called 'The Root of All Evil?', related to his book 'The God Delusion'.
3) In these programmes, he argued that what he called 'a process of non-thinking called faith' has led to intolerance, violence and destruction whilst preaching peace and brotherhood.

I've told you before — The Simpsons™ is NOT a religion...

These are just examples, so don't worry if they're not the ones you've studied. Stick with what you've learnt.

Practice Questions

Makes you think doesn't it... Is there a God? Why is there suffering in the world?
Who actually watches Songs of Praise?

You need to have your own views on this stuff, but you won't get far in the exam if you don't know some religious teachings as well. So try these questions, and if there are any you can't answer, go back and have another look at the section. Then try the questions again until you can do them all.
(If you're struggling with the wordy questions, check out the exam help pages at the back of the book.)

Some questions will have extra marks available for spelling, punctuation and grammar (SPaG). The exam paper will say which ones, so make sure your answers to these are as well written as you can make them.

1) What is:
   a) conversion?
   b) omnipotence?
   c) omniscience?
   d) omni-benevolence?
   e) a numinous experience?
   f) atheism?
   g) agnosticism?
   h) moral evil?
   i) free will?

These "definition" questions are easy marks in the exam, so make sure you give a full definition. Try the glossary at the back of the book if you're struggling.

2) a) What is meant by a 'design argument' for the existence of a god?
   b) Give two reasons someone may have for believing in a god.
   c) State two things that Christians/Jews/Muslims believe about the nature of evil.
   d) Describe the difference between natural evil and moral evil.

Don't write an essay for these questions. Just make sure you get a couple of facts down for each.

3) For each of the following questions, give two reasons for your point of view.
   a) Do you think that religious experiences are real?
   b) Do you think God/Allah designed the Universe?
   c) Do you believe that good can come from suffering?
   d) Do religious programmes on the TV make people more likely to believe in God?

These questions are asking for your opinion as well as reasons to back it up. Give detailed reasons to make sure you get full marks.

4) For these questions, you need to express yourself as clearly as possible — make sure your writing is correct, accurate and well organised.
   a) Explain how a religious upbringing might lead to a belief in a god.
   b) Explain how Christians/Jews/Muslims respond to scientific theories about the origin of the world.
   c) Explain how Christians/Jews/Muslims respond to the problem of unanswered prayers.
   d) Explain the different ways in which Jews might respond to the Holocaust. (Judaism)
   e) Explain what Christians/Jews/Muslims might do to help people cope with suffering.
   f) Choose two television programmes, radio programmes or films and explain how they might affect a person's belief in God/Allah.

"Explain" means you have to say why people believe the things they do — not just what they believe. These questions test your 'clarity of expression' as well as what you know.

5) Read the following statements:
   a) "It is not possible to prove that God/Allah exists"
   b) "God created the Universe and everything in it in six days." (Christianity) (Judaism)
   c) "The presence of evil and suffering in the world shows that there is no god."
   d) "God/Allah cannot prevent suffering."
   e) "Evil is a test of our free will."
   Discuss each statement. You should include different, supported points of view and a personal viewpoint. You must refer to a religion in your answer.

More opinion questions — you get marks for each side of the argument. But this time, you have to give some religious views in your answer. If you don't refer to a religion somewhere, you'll lose a load of marks.

Life After Death

Every religion in the world has something to say about <u>death</u> — and what comes <u>after</u> it.

Life After Death — Some People Believe, Others Don't

1) Some people believe that when you die, that's it — your body decays and you <u>cease to exist</u>.
2) Others believe that, although your <u>body</u> may die and decay, your <u>soul</u> can live on — in other words, you move on to a different kind of existence. This is the basic idea of <u>life after death</u>.

Many Religions Teach that the Soul is Immortal

1) Most religions have a concept of <u>soul</u> — that part of a human being that isn't a part of the physical world.
2) Most religions teach that something happens to this soul <u>after death</u>:
   - Some religions teach that the soul is <u>rewarded</u> or <u>punished</u> for the actions of the person on Earth.
   - Others teach that the soul is placed into another body for another life (reincarnation).
3) Even some <u>non-religious</u> people believe in souls. The big differences between those things that are alive (like us) and those that aren't (like rocks) suggests to some people that there might be something special inside us that isn't just more 'stuff'.
4) The fact that people are <u>conscious</u> (aware) of themselves in a way that even other animals aren't is taken by many to suggest that this awareness must be separate from everyday matter.

Near-Death Experiences and the Paranormal

There are many reasons why people <u>believe</u> (or <u>don't believe</u>) in life after death.

Most <u>religions</u> teach that we all move on to an <u>afterlife</u> of some kind. For some people, this will be enough to make them believe in life after death — they have <u>faith</u> in what their religion teaches.

But even <u>non-religious</u> people can be convinced by things like <u>near-death experiences</u>, the <u>paranormal</u> and evidence of <u>reincarnation</u>:

NEAR-DEATH EXPERIENCES

A near-death experience usually involves an <u>out-of-body</u> experience when someone is close to death. While apparently physically dead, they glimpse what they believe to be an <u>afterlife</u>, or speak to long-dead family members.

Not everyone believes that these visions are real though. They argue that <u>hallucinations</u> could be a result of <u>chemical</u> activity in the <u>brain</u> when it's short of oxygen.

I believe science can explain the paranormal.

THE PARANORMAL

The <u>paranormal</u> (things science can't explain, which are thought to have a spiritual cause, e.g. ghosts) is sometimes used as evidence of life after death. Some people (<u>mediums</u>) claim they can talk to the dead.
Other people reckon these events have a <u>scientific</u> explanation — maybe we don't know what the explanation is yet, but there <u>will</u> be one. And some people don't believe these events happen in the first place.

EVIDENCE OF REINCARNATION

Some people claim to have evidence of <u>reincarnation</u> (having lived a previous life, died, and been reborn in a new body). Lots of research has been carried out with young children who claim to remember past lives, and the evidence has some people convinced. But sceptics suggest that the memories <u>aren't real</u> — that they must have been suggested to the children in some way.

I've got soul — and I'm super bad...

...said the twentieth-century theologian Mr James Brown. The idea of life after death is pretty central to most religions — they each have their own teachings on this stuff, as you'll see on the next few pages...

Life After Death: Christianity

Christianity

What people believe will happen to them after <u>death</u> can influence the way they <u>live</u> their lives.

Christians Believe in Heaven and Hell

1) Christianity teaches that the <u>soul</u> lives on after death (<u>immortality</u> of the soul), and that the body will be <u>resurrected</u> (brought back to life) for Judgement Day, just as Jesus was resurrected after his crucifixion.

2) Christians believe that God will judge you, and you'll go either to <u>Heaven</u>, or to <u>Hell</u>:

- Heaven is often portrayed as a place of great beauty and serenity, a <u>paradise</u> where you'll spend eternity with God — as long as you believe in <u>Jesus</u>, have followed his teachings and have lived a <u>good</u> life, that is. Those in Heaven are said to belong to the <u>Communion of Saints</u>.
- Hell, on the other hand, is often portrayed as a place of <u>torment</u> and <u>pain</u> — the final destination of <u>nonbelievers</u> and those who have led <u>bad</u> lives.

3) However, not all Christians believe that Heaven and Hell are <u>real</u> places — many Christians see Heaven and Hell as <u>states of mind</u>. In Heaven you'll be <u>happy</u>, and know God — in Hell you'll be <u>unable</u> to know God's love.

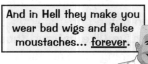

And in Hell they make you wear bad wigs and false moustaches... <u>forever</u>.

4) A few believe that those who God finds unacceptable will be <u>annihilated</u>. They had no interest in spiritual things when they were <u>alive</u>, therefore their spirits were never awakened and cannot survive death.

5) Roman Catholics also believe in a place, or state of existence, called <u>Purgatory</u>. Here <u>sins</u> are punished before the soul is able to move on to Heaven. This concept isn't in the Bible, so Protestants reject it.

"Whoever lives and believes in me will never die"

This is how the Christian Church sees <u>death</u> and <u>resurrection</u>:

1) Human beings <u>sin</u>, meaning that they don't live up to God's perfect standard. Because of this, they're not <u>fit</u> to be accepted into Heaven.

2) But Jesus <u>redeemed</u> his followers by <u>sacrificing</u> himself to pay for our sins. He <u>broke</u> the power of sin and death — his power and goodness were so <u>great</u> that after he was crucified, death couldn't keep hold of him.

3) Jesus promised that, just as he had been <u>saved</u> from death, anyone who <u>followed</u> him would find <u>salvation</u>.

4) Many Christians believe that even those who have led <u>sinful lives</u> may find salvation thanks to Jesus's sacrifice and God's saving power.

> "I am the resurrection and the life. He who believes in me will live, even though he dies; and whoever lives and believes in me will never die." John 11:25-26 NIV

The Idea of Heaven is Comforting to Believers

1) Pretty much everyone knows they're going to die one day — and for many it's a hard concept to grasp, and death is a <u>scary</u> thought. Many people get a lot of <u>comfort</u> from a belief in the afterlife.

2) Also, when someone you love dies, it's a lot nicer to think that they <u>still exist</u> in some form.

3) Belief in life after death is also important from a <u>justice</u> point of view. Lots of good people <u>suffer</u> greatly, and some, sadly, die young. At the same time, some <u>evil</u> people live out long lives and seem quite happy. It can make people feel a lot better if they believe that everything will be <u>evened up</u> after death.

4) So belief in Heaven and Hell might encourage some people to <u>follow Christian teachings</u> or do <u>good deeds</u> — they want to make sure they're well qualified for a good afterlife.

Get ready to do some soul searching...

It's easy to see how belief in an immortal soul can affect how people live their lives. If you knew your life would be judged on how you'd used it, chances are you'd think twice before doing something dodgy.

Life After Death: Judaism

It should come as no surprise at all to learn that Judaism has something to say about <u>death</u> as well.

Sheol — the Shadowy Destination of the Dead

1) Jewish teachings are largely concerned with the <u>earthly</u> life, and a person's <u>duties</u> to God and other people. According to the Torah, rewards for obeying God and punishments for 'breaking the covenant' are sent in <u>this world</u> (Leviticus 26:3-17). But Jews still have a firm belief in the <u>immortality of the soul</u>.

2) When the earliest Jewish scriptures were written, it was believed that after death <u>all souls</u> went to a place called <u>Sheol</u> — where the dead lived as shadows. Sheol was believed to be dark and cold, and your soul would stay there for <u>eternity</u>. This <u>wasn't</u> as a punishment — it's just what was believed to happen.

3) However, over time the Jews came to believe in the <u>resurrection</u> of the dead...

In the Messianic Age the Dead Will be Resurrected

1) Jews believe that the <u>Messiah</u>, a great future leader, will bring an era of <u>perfect peace</u> and <u>prosperity</u> called the <u>World to Come</u> (or <u>messianic age</u>). (Jews don't believe Jesus was the Messiah.)

"Multitudes who sleep in the dust of the earth will awake: some to <u>everlasting life</u>, others to shame and <u>everlasting contempt</u>." Daniel 12:2 NIV

2) It's believed that the <u>righteous</u> dead (both Jews and non-Jews) will be <u>resurrected</u> to share in the messianic peace. But the <u>wicked</u> dead won't be resurrected — they gave up their share in the World to Come by living sinful lives.

Okay, it was wrong. But everlasting contempt seems a bit over the top.

3) Orthodox Jews believe that the <u>physical body</u> will be resurrected, <u>intact</u>, in the messianic age. Because of this, the body shouldn't be cut after death (<u>autopsies</u> are frowned upon) and cremation is <u>forbidden</u>. A Jewish cemetery is called the '<u>House of Life</u>' (Bet ha-Chaim), which reaffirms the view that the body will be resurrected.

4) Reform Jews believe that the body is simply a <u>vessel</u> for the soul, and <u>reject</u> the idea of physical resurrection. So Reform Jews accept cremation and organ donation.

Modern Judaism Teaches of Gan Eden and Gehinnom

1) Modern Jews believe in an afterlife spent in places called <u>Gan Eden</u> ("Garden of Eden" or Paradise) and <u>Gehinnom</u> (a bit like Purgatory), but they don't tend to have firm beliefs on the <u>specifics</u> of the afterlife.

2) Some see Gan Eden as a <u>physical</u> place of lavish banquets and warm sunshine. But others have a more <u>spiritual</u> view of it — as a <u>closeness</u> to God. Similarly, there are different views of Gehinnom — a place of fire and physical <u>torment</u>, or a chance to see <u>missed opportunities</u> and the <u>harm</u> a person caused in life.

3) Only if you've lived a <u>blameless</u> life will you be sent straight to Gan Eden when you die.

4) Most souls are sent to Gehinnom for a period of <u>punishment</u> and <u>purification</u> first, which lasts no longer than <u>12 months</u>, before ascending to Gan Eden. Only the <u>truly wicked</u> never reach Paradise, but there are various ideas about what happens to them, e.g. they're annihilated, or they stay in Gehinnom forever.

Your Behaviour During Your Life is Judged

1) Many Jews believe that your <u>behaviour</u> here will determine what kind of <u>afterlife</u> you receive. This means that there's a strong emphasis on <u>moral behaviour</u> in this life — doing what is <u>right</u> even if it isn't easy or profitable for you.

2) However, some Jews would argue that being virtuous is its own <u>reward</u> — you should do good things simply because they are <u>good</u>.

Will there be exams in the next life?

Of the three religions in this book, Judaism has the least clear ideas about the afterlife. In some ways that makes it harder to learn — you have to know more points of view. But it gives you plenty to write about.

Life After Death: Islam

Islam has very definite teachings when it comes to life after death.

The Soul is the Real Person

It's free will that makes human beings different from angels — angels obey Allah perfectly.

1) Muslims believe that human beings are Allah's greatest physical creation. They also believe that humans are different from other animals, because we know we will die.

2) Islam teaches that every soul (ruh) is unique and has free will.

Muslims believe in predestination — Al-Qadr. Although we have free will, Islam teaches we cannot do everything we want — God is still in control. In recognition of this, Muslims will often say "insh' Allah" (if God is willing).

3) It is the soul that will be judged after death, as it is the soul that is our consciousness. Our body is thought of as a kind of 'vehicle for the soul'.

4) Muslims call life after death akhirah — it's one of the key Islamic beliefs. Not to have a belief in life after death would make this life meaningless for a Muslim.

5) Islam teaches that nothing that happens to us during our earthly lives is accidental — Muslims believe we are being tested, and that the way we act in life will determine what happens to us after we die.

6) A key teaching of Islam is that we remain in the grave after death in a state called barzakh (the 'cold sleep') until the Day of Judgement. On this day, Allah will judge everyone — not just Muslims.

The Soul Goes to al'Jannah (Paradise) or Jahannam (Hell)

1) Although the earthly life is short compared with the eternal, Muslims believe it's still very important. It's in this life that Allah tests us. On Judgement Day, it's too late to beg forgiveness for any wrongdoing.

2) Islam teaches that we are judged on:
   i) our character, ii) our reactions to good and bad events in our lives, iii) our way of life.

3) Muslims believe everything is the will of Allah — so there's no point moaning about your circumstances. We cannot know why things happen, or what Allah wishes us to learn from it. The important thing is that we react to it in the right way.

4) The reward for those who have followed Allah will be entry into al'Jannah (Paradise) — this is a place of peace, happiness and beauty. In fact, the Qur'an refers to al'Jannah as 'gardens of delight', filled with flowers and birdsong.

5) For those who don't believe in Allah, or have committed bad deeds, the reward is Jahannam (or Hell). The Qur'an describes Jahannam as a place of scorching fire, hot winds and black smoke. Here, those who have ignored Allah's teaching and failed to act righteously will be punished for eternity.

Allah is merciful and compassionate, but at the same time, he's a tough judge. Basically, if you're a good Muslim, you'll go to Paradise. But if you're a bad Muslim or a non-Muslim, you deserve Hell, but you might get lucky and be sent by Allah to Paradise if he's feeling merciful.

6) But Allah is also merciful, so many of those who have lived sinful lives may not be sent to Jahannam.

Being Obedient to Allah is Vital for a Muslim

'Islam' literally means 'submission' or 'obedience' to Allah. And there are certain day-to-day rules that Allah expects you to follow if you want to show that you're being obedient. The key to getting to Paradise for a Muslim is obedience. The reasoning is as follows...

1) Allah expects obedience, and obedience is a Muslim's duty.
2) If a Muslim does his or her duty, that person will please Allah.
3) If a person pleases Allah enough, they will be sent to Paradise after they die.
4) And if Allah is not pleased with someone, they will be punished after they die.

So this is vital stuff. How a Muslim lives in this life will determine where he or she ends up in the afterlife.

Stop moaning about your exam — it is the will of Allah...

Yep, it's true. Don't be put off by the long and difficult words on this page — just get learning and your RS revision will fly by. There's only another few pages to go in this section... well... nine... (but who's counting...)

Abortion

Abortion is a subject that people often hold very strong views about.
And as you'd probably expect, religions have strong views about it too.

Abortion — Terminating a Pregnancy

1) Abortion is when a foetus is removed prematurely from the womb, before it is able to survive.

2) Abortion has been legal in England, Scotland and Wales since 1967. It can take place until the 24th week of pregnancy, as long as two doctors agree that it's required. They must consider the quality of life of the woman, the unborn child, and any children the mother may already have.

> There are complicated arguments for and against abortion...
>
> i) The 'pro-choice' argument says that a woman has the right to choose what happens to her body (and since the foetus isn't independent of the woman, this argument says it must be considered part of the woman).
>
> ii) But is it right to consider the foetus part of the mother when it's genetically different?
>
> iii) Although many people are generally against abortion (seeing it as the taking of a life) they will agree that in certain circumstances, abortion should be permitted, e.g. if the mother's or child's health is at risk, if a woman has become pregnant through rape, or if a mother is too young to cope with a child.
>
> iv) The question of when life actually begins is important here, too. Is it at conception (as the Roman Catholic Church says)? Or at birth? And is a foetus an actual person, or just a potential person?

The 'Sanctity of Life' Argument

Probably the most important biblical passage regarding the Sanctity of Life argument is the sixth of the Ten Commandments, "You shall not murder." Exodus 20:13 NIV

1) Christianity, Islam and Judaism teach that all life is created by God. As God's creation, all life belongs to God and is therefore holy. This is the 'sanctity of life' argument.

2) Based on this, many religious people believe that we don't have the right to interfere with when life ends, or to prevent the beginning of a new life.

Many Christians see Abortion as Undesirable

1) Abortion is a very complicated and emotional issue, but generally speaking, Christianity teaches that abortion is undesirable. However, the Roman Catholic Church goes so far as to say that abortion is murder.

"Abortion has been considered to be murder since the first centuries of the Church, and nothing permits it to be considered otherwise."
Pope Paul VI (Leader of Roman Catholic Church, 1970)

2) Not all Christian churches see it in such 'black-and-white' terms, however. The Church of England believes that abortion is permissible in certain circumstances, while the Religious Society of Friends (the Quakers) argues that the life of the unborn child cannot be valued above that of the woman.

3) Indeed, many Christians argue that allowing a woman to choose is a way of showing Christian compassion — whether they agree with the choice made or not.

4) Although the Bible doesn't actually mention abortion, other Christian writings (e.g. the Didache, a 2nd century manual of Christian teaching) are quite specifically against it.

It's tricky, emotional stuff...

There are no easy answers. So learn the stuff on this page, and be ready to give both sides of the argument.

General & Christianity

Euthanasia and Suicide

Another couple of very <u>complicated</u> subjects...

Euthanasia is often called Mercy Killing

<u>Euthanasia</u> means killing someone <u>painlessly</u> to relieve suffering, especially from an incurable illness. It's often called <u>mercy killing</u>.

1) There are two forms of euthanasia — <u>voluntary</u> euthanasia and <u>non-voluntary</u> euthanasia.

2) <u>Voluntary euthanasia</u> is when an ill person <u>actively requests assistance</u> to die, or refuses treatment which is keeping them alive, i.e. the person <u>decides</u> that they want to die and <u>seeks</u> help to achieve this.

3) <u>Non-voluntary euthanasia</u> is when the patient is <u>unable</u> to make such a request, and the decision is made by someone else — usually doctors and family members.

4) <u>Suicide</u> is when someone takes their own life — usually because of depression or illness. <u>Attempted suicide</u> used to be a <u>crime</u> in the UK, but it's now seen as a sign that someone needs <u>help</u>.

5) <u>Assisted suicide</u> is when a doctor provides someone with the means to end their <u>own</u> life, usually by prescribing a <u>lethal dose</u> of medication.

Euthanasia is Illegal in the UK

1) Euthanasia and assisted suicide are <u>illegal</u> in the UK, but euthanasia is <u>allowed</u> in certain circumstances in Albania, Belgium, Luxembourg, and the Netherlands, and assisted suicide is legal in Switzerland.

2) The charity 'Dignity in Dying' believes that many people would be grateful for 'the mercy of a painless death', and many people want assisted suicide <u>legalised</u> in the UK. In the 2005 British Social Attitudes Survey, <u>80%</u> of people said that they were in favour of letting terminally ill patients die with a doctor's help.

3) Legalisation would mean that scarce medical <u>resources</u> could be saved for people who could be cured.

4) A few doctors have even admitted to helping patients to die, sometimes by giving a patient an <u>excess of painkillers</u>, which can ease suffering but can also lead to eventual <u>death</u> — this is known as '<u>double effect</u>', which is legal so long as the intention was to relieve pain.

5) However, there is a concern that if euthanasia were legalised, some elderly people may feel under <u>pressure</u> to end their life, even if they don't want to.

"Your Body is a Temple of the Holy Spirit"

1) The passage in the subheading (from 1 Corinthians NIV) suggests that God lives <u>within</u> each of us. Life is considered a <u>sacred</u> gift, and so both <u>euthanasia</u> and <u>suicide</u> are seen as <u>wrong</u> by many Christians (see page 13 — the 'Sanctity of Life' argument). However, some argue that Jesus's resurrection proves that death is not the end, and that earthly life isn't always the most important thing.

2) <u>Roman Catholics</u> are the most strongly opposed to euthanasia. They believe that anything that intentionally causes death is 'a grave violation of the law of God'. So even those who are unlikely to recover consciousness should be kept alive.

3) To Roman Catholics, <u>suicide</u> is considered so <u>grave</u> a sin that suicides aren't given a Christian <u>burial</u>. However, some Christians point out passages in the <u>Bible</u> that describe suicide (e.g. King Saul's death in 1 Samuel 31:4-5) without calling it a sin.

4) Many Christians suggest that the easing of suffering in <u>euthanasia</u> is a way of demonstrating <u>Christian compassion</u>, and that the use of '<u>extraordinary treatment</u>' (e.g. life-support machines) to keep a person alive is not always the best approach.

5) Most Anglican denominations agree that terrible distress should not be suffered <u>at all costs</u>, and that death may be considered a <u>blessing</u>. They argue that a person's <u>quality of life</u> must also be considered.

6) Local churches often have links with <u>hospices</u>. A hospice is a place where <u>terminally ill</u> people can be cared for, and can discuss any fears that they may have about death.

I told you it was complicated...

While religions provide clear guidelines on many matters, there doesn't seem to be much clear-cut teaching on medical ethics. It comes down to interpreting scripture and tradition to try to find what's right.

Abortion, Euthanasia and Suicide

Abortion, Euthanasia and Suicide — The Jewish View

1) As a general rule, Judaism is <u>opposed</u> to abortion, euthanasia and suicide — the passage on the right is often used to support this view.

> "There is no god besides me. I put to death and I bring to life" Deuteronomy 32:39 NIV

2) However, Judaism does not teach that the life of an unborn child is more <u>valuable</u> than that of the mother. Many Jews accept that, in certain cases, abortion should be allowed. Most rabbis allow abortion if pregnancy becomes physically or mentally <u>dangerous</u> for the woman concerned, or if the child is likely to be severely <u>disabled</u> and unable to lead a full life. But it cannot be carried out simply for <u>convenience</u>.

3) <u>Reform</u> rabbis are more likely to allow abortion than Orthodox ones.

Only God can Decide when we Die

1) Jewish teaching is <u>opposed</u> to the practice of euthanasia — life is seen as a <u>gift from God</u> and is therefore <u>sacred</u>. We do not have the right to decide when a life should end.

2) The same thing applies to <u>suicide</u> — most Jews see it as such a great <u>sin</u> that those who take their own lives are not buried in the same part of the cemetery as other Jews.

3) However, most Jews who are suspected of having committed suicide are given <u>standard funeral rites</u>, as they are often judged to have been <u>disturbed beyond being responsible</u> for their actions.

4) The <u>relief</u> of pain and suffering is a key part of Jewish teaching. So although euthanasia is seen as wrong if it involves <u>actively</u> doing something to cause someone's death, it may be possible to <u>withhold treatment</u>, if this treatment would cause further distress.

5) The words of Rabbi Moses Isserles are sometimes used to argue that it may be reasonable to switch off a <u>life-support machine</u> that's keeping someone alive.

> "If there is anything which causes a hindrance to the departure of the soul... then it is permissible to remove it."

Abortion, Euthanasia and Suicide — The Islamic View

Muslims believe that Allah created the world and everything in it. Our lives are <u>sacred</u> (see the 'Sanctity of Life' argument on p.13). This means that abortion and euthanasia are <u>generally</u> seen as wrong.

1) The passage on the right sums up Islamic teaching on <u>abortion</u>. But there are circumstances in which it is <u>permissible</u>.

> "And do not kill your children... We provide for them and for you. Indeed, their killing is ever a great sin." Qur'an 17:31

2) When the <u>mother's</u> life is in danger, abortion is <u>lawful</u>. The <u>potential</u> life in the womb is not as important as the <u>actual</u> life of the mother.

3) Within the <u>first 120 days</u>, abortion can also be allowed if the baby would be born with a serious <u>defect</u> (though not all Muslims agree with this). After 120 days, abortion is <u>only</u> allowed to save the <u>life</u> of the mother.

4) Some Muslim women argue that they should be free to <u>choose</u> what happens to their bodies. Those that disagree claim that in the Qur'an it says that unborn children will want to know <u>why</u> they were killed.

Allah knows Why we Suffer...

1) Euthanasia and suicide are seen as <u>wrong</u> by most Muslims, because our lives are <u>Allah's</u>.

2) Muslims believe that Allah has a <u>plan</u> for every living person — he has decided how long each of us will live on this Earth, and we do not have the right to <u>interfere</u> with that plan.

3) Islam teaches that life on Earth is a <u>test</u>. Allah knows why we suffer, and we do not have good reason to end our own lives, no matter how bad that suffering is.

4) Instead, those who are suffering should turn to <u>Allah</u>, <u>pray</u> and 'patiently <u>persevere</u>' — Allah is <u>merciful</u>, and all will be revealed on the Day of Judgement.

5) However, in cases where a patient has a terminal illness, with <u>no hope</u> of improvement, Islam allows doctors to stop '<u>unnecessary</u>' treatment.

Allah even has a plan for you, Norman Shuffleploppy.

Good lord — it's not like maths, is it...

I mean, in maths, things are true or false, right or wrong, black or white... with this it's all <u>shades of grey</u>.

Wealth, Poverty and Disease

Wealth is basically <u>money and possessions</u>. Wealth is a big issue for religious people, because it's not very evenly distributed in society — some people are rolling in it, while other people are left struggling in <u>poverty</u>.

Being Wealthy isn't a Bad Thing in Itself

1) None of the three major religions teach that <u>wealth</u> is bad.
2) There are people in the Bible who are <u>both</u> wealthy and faithful to God, e.g. <u>Joseph of Arimathea</u> was a rich council member who retrieved the body of Jesus from the Roman authorities and arranged his burial.

> "...there came a rich man from Arimathea, named Joseph, who had himself become a disciple of Jesus." Matthew 27:57 NIV

3) And there are plenty of examples from the <u>Jewish</u> books of the Kings, e.g. <u>King Solomon</u> was one of the great kings of Israel, who built the Temple in Jerusalem: "King Solomon was greater in riches and wisdom than all the other kings of the earth." (1 Kings 10:23 NIV)
4) Muslims believe that all wealth <u>belongs</u> to Allah, and that personal wealth is a <u>gift</u> from Allah.
5) So in all three religions, it's not wealth, but a <u>love of wealth</u> that's a problem:

> "No one can serve two masters... You cannot serve both God and Money." Matthew 6:24 NIV

> "...those who hoard gold and silver and spend it not in the way of Allah — give them tidings of a painful punishment." Qur'an 9:34

> "Whoever loves money never has money enough..." Ecclesiastes 5:10 NIV

> "...the love of money is a root of all kinds of evil." 1 Timothy 6:10 NIV

There are Many Causes of Poverty and Hunger

<u>Poverty</u> leads to great <u>suffering</u>. So its causes and effects are of great concern for religious people.

1) The <u>Brandt Report</u> in 1980 identified an imbalance between the <u>developed</u> and the <u>developing</u> worlds. The developed world contains around 25% of the world's <u>population</u> but around 80% of the <u>wealth</u>. Little has changed since 1980. Some religious people believe that the <u>greed</u> of people in developed countries <u>leads</u> to poverty in developing countries.
2) Direct causes of poverty in the developing world include <u>rapid population growth</u>, <u>war</u>, and the sale of <u>raw materials</u> at low prices. This poverty often leads to <u>hunger</u>, because people can't afford to buy food.
3) <u>Famine</u>, an overall lack of food in an area, is often caused by <u>war</u> or <u>climate</u>. War stops people from working on farms, because they're either <u>involved</u> in the fighting or <u>sheltering</u> from the violence. <u>Droughts</u>, <u>floods</u> and other extreme weather conditions can <u>destroy</u> crops and ruin the <u>fertility</u> of the soil.
4) <u>Hundreds of thousands</u> of people die of <u>starvation</u> every year.
5) In the UK, causes of poverty range from <u>unemployment</u> to <u>gambling</u> and <u>alcoholism</u>. The poorest people become <u>homeless</u> and are dependent on charity for food and shelter.

Poverty and Disease Often Go Together

1) <u>Poverty</u> and <u>disease</u> are very closely related. The <u>effects</u> of poverty, e.g. <u>malnutrition</u>, <u>poor sanitation</u>, lack of proper <u>healthcare</u>, etc. leave people more <u>susceptible</u> to disease — particularly children. The World Health Organisation estimates that around <u>a third</u> of all deaths worldwide are poverty related.
2) At the same time, disease <u>weakens</u> people, making it <u>harder</u> for them to work their way out of poverty.
3) <u>Education</u> also has an effect on patterns of disease. For example, sexually transmitted diseases like HIV and syphilis can be controlled by educating people about <u>safe sex</u> and avoiding <u>promiscuity</u>.
4) <u>Religious organisations</u> like <u>Christian Aid</u>, <u>Muslim Aid</u> and the Jewish charity <u>Tzedek</u>, aim to provide <u>immediate help</u> for the sick and starving, as well as long-term projects to help whole communities get themselves out of poverty. (More about that on the next three pages.)

Money makes the world go round, the world go round...

People used to believe that disease was sent by God as a punishment for sin. This attitude still existed as recently as the start of the AIDS epidemic. Since the disease first took root in the gay community, some religious people believed that AIDS was a punishment for the 'sin' of homosexuality.

Money and Charity: Christianity

Christianity

Basically, Christianity teaches that you shouldn't be <u>selfish</u> with your money.

It's What You Do With Your Money that Counts

1) Christians believe you should only <u>earn</u> money in <u>moral ways</u>.
2) Occupations that many Christians consider immoral are those that <u>exploit</u> or <u>harm</u> other people (e.g. weapons trading or working with oppressive regimes), are damaging to the <u>environment</u>, or are <u>sexual</u> in nature.
3) Also, you mustn't <u>use</u> your money in ways that might <u>harm</u> you or others.
4) This means that many Christians (especially Methodists) disapprove of <u>gambling</u> (playing games of chance for money). Gambling can be <u>addictive</u>, and profits are made at the <u>expense</u> of others.
5) Christians also disapprove of the practice of <u>usury</u> — charging high rates of interest on loans. This is seen as <u>profiting</u> from someone else's <u>poverty</u>.

The Roman Catholic Church and, to a lesser extent, the Church of England are very <u>rich</u> institutions — this is a <u>worry</u> for some believers.

Christians have a Duty to be Charitable

1) Jesus taught that the most important commandments were to <u>love God</u> and to "<u>love your neighbour</u> as yourself</u>" (Mark 12:31 NIV). For Christians, <u>charity</u> means putting this love into practice:

"If anyone has material possessions and sees his brother in need but has no pity on him, how can the love of God be in him? ...let us not love with words or tongue but with actions and in truth." 1 John 3:17-18 NIV

2) Christians believe they have a <u>duty</u> to care for other people, and use many <u>sources of authority</u> to stress this. The Bible contains many passages encouraging <u>charity</u>.

"The man with two tunics should share with him who has none, and the one who has food should do the same." Luke 3:11 NIV

"Go, sell everything you have and give to the poor, and you will have treasure in heaven." Mark 10:21 NIV

"I was hungry and you gave me something to eat, I was thirsty and you gave me something to drink... whatever you did for one of the least of these brothers of mine, you did for me." Matthew 25:35-40 NIV

3) In practice, 'charity' is any sort of <u>help</u> that's <u>freely given</u>. This could be a donation of <u>time</u> (e.g. visiting the sick or elderly), <u>effort</u> (e.g. working on a building project) or <u>material things</u> (e.g. giving money). A number of <u>Christian charities</u> exist — working both in the UK and globally, e.g. <u>Christian Aid</u>:

CHRISTIAN AID

Christian Aid was set up after World War II to help <u>refugees</u>. It now has over 40 member organisations in the UK and Ireland, and works <u>globally</u> to relieve poverty. It raises money through <u>donations</u>, <u>events</u> and <u>collections</u>.

Most of Christian Aid's work is in <u>development</u> — they believe the <u>best</u> way to help people is by 'helping them to help themselves'. They set up projects in the developing world, drawing on the skills of <u>local people</u>.

Development projects set up by Christian Aid aim to help with problems such as poor <u>sanitation</u>, <u>education</u> and <u>healthcare</u>, as well as encouraging the use of <u>birth control</u>. The organisation also aims to change <u>government policy</u> to help reduce the suffering of the world's poor, e.g. through <u>debt relief</u>, and <u>fair-trade</u> products.

4) Some <u>religious orders</u> (communities of monks or nuns) are dedicated to relieving suffering amongst the starving, poor and sick. One example is the <u>Order of the Missionaries of Charity</u>:

MOTHER TERESA

Mother Teresa was an Albanian Roman Catholic nun who devoted herself to the <u>destitute</u> and <u>dying</u> in <u>Calcutta</u>, India. She founded the <u>Order of the Missionaries of Charity</u>, whose nuns now work amongst the poor all over the world. She said that it isn't <u>what</u> you do for God that counts, but <u>how much love</u> you pour into it. She won the Nobel Peace Prize in 1979, and died in 1997 at the age of 87.

Feel the luuurve...

Christians don't have any strict rules about how much of their income they should give to the poor (although many use 10% as a guideline). Donations are left to the conscience of each individual Christian. Jesus emphasised that you should give charitably out of <u>love</u>, rather than because society expects it of you.

Money and Charity: Judaism

Judaism

Judaism teaches that it's our <u>duty</u> to look after those less fortunate than ourselves.

Jews must Deal Fairly and Honestly

1) Although Judaism doesn't teach that everyone should <u>try</u> to be wealthy, it does suggest that extreme poverty will make <u>others</u> responsible for you — so all Jews should aim to <u>work</u> and <u>earn</u> a living.

2) But the <u>love of wealth</u> may turn you from God — so you should <u>neither seek nor shun</u> wealth.

3) Unfairness and dishonesty in business are <u>condemned</u> — you're answerable to <u>God</u> for any wrongdoing.

> "Hear this, you who trample the needy and do away with the poor of the land... skimping the measure, boosting the price and cheating with dishonest scales... The LORD has sworn by the Pride of Jacob: 'I will never forget anything they have done.'" Amos 8:4-7 NIV

4) All money must be <u>morally earnt</u>, so any occupation that's <u>harmful</u> in any way is forbidden. Jews particularly frown on work that is damaging to <u>God's creation</u> (e.g. unsustainable tree felling or bullfighting).

5) It's also <u>strictly forbidden</u> for one Jew to charge <u>interest</u> on a loan to another Jew (Leviticus 25:37) — a practice called '<u>usury</u>'. This rule <u>doesn't apply</u> to loans made to <u>non-Jews</u>, however: "You may charge a foreigner interest, but not a brother Israelite..." (Deuteronomy 23:20 NIV).

6) Although <u>gambling</u> is generally frowned on, <u>occasional</u> lighthearted games for small stakes are allowed. For example, it's traditional to play a gambling game called <u>kvitlech</u> (similar to blackjack) at Hanukkah.

7) Jews try to avoid talking about or handling money on the <u>Sabbath</u> — the day of rest.

Judaism says, "Do not be hardhearted or tightfisted..."

1) This passage from Deuteronomy sums up Jewish teaching on <u>charity</u>:

> "If there is a poor man among your brothers in any of the towns of the land... do not be hardhearted or tightfisted toward your poor brother." Deuteronomy 15:7 NIV

2) Also, Maimonides said that the best way to give was "to help a person help themselves so that they may become <u>self-supporting</u>".

Maimonides was an important Jewish Rabbi and philosopher.

3) There are two main ways of giving to charity — <u>Tzedakah</u> and <u>Gemilut Hasadim</u>:

<u>TZEDAKAH</u>: Tzedakah is <u>financial</u> aid — even the poorest in society are expected to contribute 10% of their wealth. All wealth belongs to <u>God</u>, and not giving to the poor deprives them of what they're owed.

<u>GEMILUT HASADIM</u>: This means, literally, the 'giving of loving-kindness' and refers to any <u>kind</u> and <u>compassionate actions</u> towards others.

4) Many Jewish homes have <u>collection boxes</u> (called <u>pushkes</u>) in which money for charity can be placed. Children are <u>encouraged</u> to use these boxes — maybe donating some of their pocket money each week.

5) <u>Donating clothing</u> to people who need it, <u>feeding</u> the hungry, <u>visiting</u> someone who's sick and burying the <u>dead</u> are all considered Gemilut Hasadim. The most important thing is, that whatever you're giving, you don't expect anything in <u>return</u>.

6) There are <u>Jewish charities</u> that have been set up to help the poor:

TZEDEK (JEWISH ACTION FOR A JUST WORLD)

Tzedek is a Jewish charity set up in the UK that works with poor people of all races and religions, 'providing direct support to small scale sustainable self-help development projects for the relief and elimination of poverty'.

Their focus is on helping <u>local projects</u>, e.g. health and agriculture training schemes, that improve a community's ability to get itself <u>out of poverty</u> and achieve a <u>better standard of living</u>.

Not many Jews in Yorkshire then — sorry, sorry...   ...I'll get my coat

Judaism teaches that God has provided the world with everything we need, so that there should never be any poverty or hunger. Jews believe that the poverty that does exist is caused by the greed of others.

Money and Charity: Islam

Islam

In Islam, the principle is much the same as Christianity and Judaism — <u>greed</u> and <u>waste</u> are frowned upon.

Gambling and Charging Interest are Absolute No-Nos

1) Islam forbids using money in ways that might <u>damage</u> yourself or others — it's a basic principle of Shari'ah (Islamic law) that a Muslim should <u>not</u> harm others.

2) Islam forbids <u>alcohol</u>, so Muslims consider it <u>immoral</u> to make money from alcoholic drinks.

3) Islam also stresses the importance of <u>sexual modesty</u>, so <u>making money</u> from sex is forbidden (either directly, e.g. in prostitution or indirectly, e.g. through sexually-suggestive advertising).

4) If you <u>win</u> money by <u>gambling</u>, it's only because someone else has <u>lost</u> it.

5) Shari'ah also forbids any financial deals involving the charging of <u>interest</u>. This is to prevent rich people making more money at the <u>expense</u> of poorer people, and to make sure wealth is spread more <u>fairly</u>.

Charging interest (particularly a high rate of interest) is called 'usury'. The Arabic word for it is riba.

6) This means Muslims can't use most Western bank accounts. Also, Muslim <u>businesses</u> must be run differently from others, because the Western economic system depends on lending money and charging interest. Some <u>Islamic banks</u> exist to get around this.

Charity is One of the Five Pillars of Islam

1) Muslims believe that possessions ultimately belong to <u>Allah</u>.

2) Islam teaches that you should act <u>responsibly</u> and help those in need.

3) As in Judaism, there are two main ways to help the disadvantaged — <u>Zakah</u> and <u>Sadaqah</u>:

> <u>ZAKAH</u>: This is one of the <u>Five Pillars</u> of Islam — 2.5% of your yearly savings should be given to the needy, no matter how rich or poor you are.
>
> <u>SADAQAH</u>: This is <u>additional</u> aid — maybe financial donations or an act of compassion and love.

4) <u>Zakah</u> is the <u>Third Pillar</u> of Islam. The Five Pillars are a guide to living a good Muslim life — they're <u>practical</u> ways of showing obedience to Allah. Zakah is also a way of <u>redistributing</u> wealth.

- The money donated is collected by a local <u>mosque</u>. It's then <u>redistributed</u> to needy Muslims, or used for religious purposes, like running Muslim schools.

- It's a sign of <u>concern</u> for others and encourages <u>unselfishness</u>.

5) This <u>Hadith</u> (saying of the Prophet Muhammad) sums up the importance of Zakah pretty clearly:

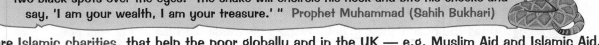

> "Whoever is made wealthy by Allah and does not pay the Zakah of his wealth, then on the Day of Resurrection his wealth will be made like a bald-headed poisonous male snake with two black spots over the eyes. The snake will encircle his neck and bite his cheeks and say, 'I am your wealth, I am your treasure.' " Prophet Muhammad (Sahih Bukhari)

6) There are <u>Islamic charities</u>, that help the poor globally and in the UK — e.g. Muslim Aid and Islamic Aid.

MUSLIM AID

Muslim Aid provides <u>disaster relief</u> and <u>development aid</u> around the world.

They aim to provide not only <u>initial emergency aid</u> after a war or natural disaster, but <u>ongoing help</u> to get people back on their feet. This help includes building <u>new permanent housing</u>, <u>sanitation</u> and <u>schools</u>, and offering <u>small interest-free loans</u> to help start-up businesses.

ISLAMIC AID

Islamic Aid is an international organisation dedicated to reducing <u>poverty</u> and <u>deprivation</u>.

In the UK, they work to improve the lives of Muslim <u>immigrants</u>, e.g. by raising awareness of 'ghettos'.

Don't gamble on this in the exam — get it learnt...

Muslim businesses still need money to start up, and this can be a problem without business loans. Often, a Muslim will look for an <u>investor</u> instead, who becomes part of the business rather than just a lender.

General

The Media: Life and Death

There are a lot of <u>sensitive issues</u> in this section, and many people feel very strongly about them.

The Media Sometimes <u>Criticises Religious Views</u>

1) Life and death issues are <u>important</u> to everyone, so they tend to crop up <u>a lot</u> in the media — from <u>in-depth documentaries</u> to <u>soap operas</u>.

2) But the media is often accused of <u>insensitivity</u> to religious views — so the big question is this: "Should the media be <u>free to criticise</u> what religions say about matters of life and death?"

Arguments For

- <u>Freedom of speech</u>. This is the most <u>fundamental</u> one. In the UK, we have the <u>right</u> to freedom of opinion and expression — as long as anything said about a person is <u>true</u>.

- <u>Education</u>. By covering all views on topics like euthanasia and abortion, the media can help to educate people about their <u>options</u>, and the <u>implications</u> of their choices.

- <u>Constructive questioning</u> can help deepen a person's faith.

Arguments Against

- <u>Insensitive coverage</u> of these issues can be seen as <u>causing unnecessary offence</u>.

- <u>Unbalanced coverage</u>, e.g. the media is sometimes accused of having a <u>pro-choice bias</u> when it comes to abortion coverage.

- <u>Exaggerated</u> or <u>untrue</u> representations of beliefs can damage a person's faith or give religion a '<u>bad name</u>'.

3) TV programmes, newspaper articles and films are sometimes <u>censored</u> (bits of material are cut out).

4) This can happen if they contain material that's thought to be <u>obscene</u> or excessively <u>violent</u>, or if they cover <u>subjects</u> that society considers <u>unacceptable</u>.

5) Religious groups might also try to suppress material that they feel puts a '<u>wrong</u>' or '<u>dangerous</u>' message across, e.g. <u>glamorising</u> abortion or suicide.

Example: "Million Dollar Baby"

1) Some religious people question whether life and death issues are treated <u>fairly</u> by the media.

2) A good example is the 2004 film "<u>Million Dollar Baby</u>", which tackles the issue of <u>euthanasia</u>.

> <u>What it's about</u>: A boxing coach (a Catholic) takes on a female boxer ("Million Dollar Baby") and guides her up through the ranks. An illegal move by an opponent leaves her <u>paralysed</u> from the neck down with <u>no hope</u> of recovery. She asks her coach to <u>help her to die</u>, which he does in the end. (Oh yes — it's a cheery film...)
>
> <u>The issue</u>: Does the coach show <u>love</u> by helping his student to die at her request and with dignity, or is it <u>murder</u> and a mortal sin?

<u>How the film tackles it</u>:

1) The coach spends a long time talking to his <u>confessor</u> and wrestling with his <u>conscience</u>.

2) In the end, by helping "Boxing Baby" to die, the trainer <u>goes against his religion</u>.

3) The film deals with <u>beliefs</u>, <u>relationships</u> and <u>people</u> very <u>sensitively</u>.

4) It gives <u>no clear-cut answers</u> — the viewer is left to decide whether the coach should be <u>condemned</u> by God.

<u>How the film was received</u>: The film was <u>critically acclaimed</u> and won four Academy Awards. But anti-euthanasia campaigners, including the bioethicist <u>Wesley J. Smith</u>, criticised the film for <u>encouraging</u> the euthanasia of disabled people.

There's nothing like a nice cheery end to a section...

For some religious people, their religion is such a big part of their identity that they see any criticism of it as a personal insult. But does protecting them hinder other people's right to free speech? It's a complex issue...

Practice Questions

You're right... there's some heavy stuff in this section. And a lot of it makes it on to the telly pretty frequently in one way or another. When it comes to the exam, all this extra knowledge from the newspapers and the TV is useful. But there's no getting away from the fact that you also need to be able to present the religious viewpoints — even if it's only to say why you disagree with them.

So try your hand at these questions. And keep trying them until you can do them all without breaking into even the mildest of sweats. Don't forget, there may be marks for good spelling, punctuation and grammar.

1) What is:
   a) a near-death experience?
   b) the paranormal?
   c) resurrection?
   d) reincarnation?
   e) immortality of the soul?
   f) akhirah? (Islam)
   g) barzakh? (Islam)
   h) al'Jannah? (Islam)
   i) abortion?
   j) euthanasia?
   k) assisted suicide?
   l) usury?
   m) Tzedakah? (Judaism)
   n) Gemilut Hasadim? (Judaism)
   o) Zakah? (Islam)
   p) Sadaqah? (Islam)

Don't hang about with these — a one-line answer will do.

2) a) State two things that Christians/Jews/Muslims believe about Heaven/Paradise.
   b) State two things that Christians/Jews/Muslims believe about Hell.
   c) What is meant by the 'sanctity of life' argument?
   d) Describe some of the common causes of hunger/famine.
   e) What sorts of occupation might a Christian/Jew/Muslim consider to be immoral?

Don't worry too much about connecting your points for these quick questions — just get the facts down.

3) For each of the following questions, give <u>two</u> reasons for your point of view.
   a) Do you think there is a life after death?
   b) Do you agree with abortion?
   c) Do you agree with voluntary euthanasia?
   d) Do you think it matters how people spend their money?

Don't worry if you haven't got a strong opinion on these. Just pick <u>an</u> opinion and justify it.

4) For these questions, you need to express yourself as clearly as possible — make sure your writing is correct, accurate and well organised.
   a) Explain how non-religious experiences might lead to a belief in life after death.
   b) Explain how and why different believers of <u>one</u> religion may differ in their beliefs about life after death.
   c) How might a Christian's/Jew's/Muslim's belief in the afterlife affect how they live?
   d) Explain why many Christians are against euthanasia. (Christianity)
   e) Explain how one religious charity is working to reduce world poverty.
   f) Explain from <u>two</u> different religious traditions, beliefs about giving money to charity.

In these questions, you'll be marked on the quality of your English as well as the content of your answer — so watch your grammar and technical terms.

5) Read the following statements:
   a) "Everyone's soul will be rewarded or punished in the afterlife."
   b) "Only Christians/Jews/Muslims will enjoy eternal life."
   c) "Abortion is wrong in all circumstances"
   d) "Only God/Allah should be allowed to decide when we die."
   e) "Religious people shouldn't be wealthy."
   f) "Religious people have a responsibility to relieve world poverty."
   g) "Religious views on matters of life and death are sacred, and the media shouldn't be allowed to criticise them."
   Discuss each statement. You should include different, supported points of view and a personal viewpoint. You must refer to a religion in your answer.

You should aim to give well structured, balanced arguments for each of these. See p.119 for help.

Christianity,
Judaism, Islam
& General

Attitudes to the Family

As the saying goes, "you can choose your GCSEs, but you can't choose your <u>family</u>". Or something like that...

Marriage in the UK — Times are Changing

1) The number of marriages taking place in the UK each year has been <u>decreasing</u> for at least thirty years.

2) At the same time, it's become more popular (and acceptable) for couples to <u>cohabit</u> (i.e. live together) — either <u>instead</u> of getting married, or as a '<u>trial marriage</u>' before doing it for real. (However, government statistics seem to show that a marriage is more <u>likely</u> to break down if the couple <u>lived together</u> first.)

3) In most cases, cohabitation still involves <u>commitment</u>. When you commit to a relationship, you promise to <u>stay together</u> and be <u>faithful</u> to each other — so you're no longer free to do whatever you please.

Family Life in the UK is also Changing

1) There used to be two basic types of family that 'society' and the Christian Church considered 'ideal' — the <u>nuclear</u> family, and the <u>extended</u> family.

2) A <u>nuclear</u> family consists of <u>parents</u> and <u>children</u>. An <u>extended</u> family is where three or more <u>generations</u> live together or as close neighbours.

3) In reality, families can have very different structures — e.g. <u>single-parent</u> families and <u>re-constituted</u> families (where divorcees with children <u>re-marry</u>, or find new partners).

4) Family life is changing in the UK — and one of the most important changes in the past 30 years has been the growth of <u>single-parent</u> (or '<u>lone-parent</u>') families. This is partly due to more children being born outside marriage, but it's also because more than 1 in 3 marriages now end in <u>divorce</u>.

Family is Important to Christians, Jews and Muslims

The Importance of the Family to Christians

1) <u>Family life</u> is seen as very important by most Christians — it's believed to be better for a child to have a <u>father</u> and a <u>mother</u> present (ideally the child's <u>biological</u> parents), so that he or she grows up with one <u>role model</u> of each sex.

2) Ideally, a stable family can give a child a sense of <u>identity</u> and a feeling of <u>security</u>, teaching him or her how to <u>behave</u> in different social situations, and how to give and receive <u>love</u>.

3) Many Christian churches offer help in raising children through <u>Sunday schools</u>. These schools aim to teach Christian <u>morals and ideals</u> through the study of Bible stories.

The Importance of the Family to Jews

1) Family life is also very important to Jews, as it's through the family that the Jewish <u>religion</u> and <u>customs</u> are passed on. Children take part in <u>Shabbat rituals</u> (the special meals and prayers of the day of rest) at home from an early age.

2) At a Jewish school called a <u>Cheder</u>, children learn <u>Hebrew</u>, and study the <u>Torah</u> and <u>Talmud</u> (see p.75).

The Importance of the Family to Muslims

1) Muslims believe that a stable family life teaches people to be <u>kind</u>, <u>considerate</u> and <u>affectionate</u> towards others, and that it's the <u>duty</u> of the <u>father</u> to raise his children as Muslims.

2) Local Mosques often have <u>schools</u> (<u>Madrasahs</u>) to help teach children the ways of Islam. There they learn <u>Arabic</u> so that they can read and understand the <u>Qur'an</u>, and are taught from the <u>Hadith</u> and the <u>Sunnah</u> (see p.76).

Famililililililily — it's... erm... an extended family...*

So family life is changing, but it's still really important. And even though marriage might not be such a big deal these days, still about 50% of women and 40% of men in the UK marry before they're 30.

    * Sorry, but it was either that or the "nuclear family" joke — take your pick.

Marriage in Christianity

Marriage — a pretty big thing in anyone's life. Including yours if you get a question about it in the exam.

Courting is a Bit Like Dating

1) The Bible doesn't say anything about how to find someone to marry, because in biblical times marriages were arranged. However, modern Christians believe that everyone has the right to choose who they marry.
2) Many Christians find a partner by courting (dating). Couples don't usually have sex during the courtship period because sex before marriage is forbidden by God.

A Christian Wedding has Legal, Social and Religious Features

Most Christian weddings take place in church. The details will vary according to tradition and denomination, but all combine legal, social and religious features:

Hymns symbolise the couple starting their life together with the help of God and the religious community.

Guests symbolise the involvement of the community. The opening statement often explains the purpose of marriage.

These are a traditional part of Christian worship. They remind the couple of the seriousness of their vows.

The couple declare that there's no reason why they can't marry (and the congregation are asked if they know of any reason why they shouldn't). They then take vows in front of witnesses, which indicates the seriousness and sacredness of marriage.

Order of Ceremony

Hymns

Opening statement and welcome to friends and family

Prayers and readings

Declarations and vows

Exchanging of rings

Signing of the register

The rings are a physical symbol of the vows and of lifelong commitment.

Signing the marriage register is a legal requirement in the UK.

A Roman Catholic wedding may also include nuptial mass (Holy Communion).
In an Orthodox wedding, crowns are placed on the heads of the bride and groom.

Church Weddings are Less Popular than they Used to Be

1) In the past, most people married in church. However, now only around 1 in 3 weddings is in a church.
2) The number of weddings being held in non-religious venues, like hotels or castles, is increasing. Many people also choose to get married abroad, often somewhere hot and sunny.

You can't get married absolutely anywhere — the place has to have a special licence.

3) The ceremony will be a civil ceremony — it'll have absolutely no reference to religion.
4) Many Christians choose to marry in church so the wedding takes place 'in front of God'.
5) The Church of England used to have strict rules about which church you could marry in — you had to have lived in the parish or worshipped there regularly. These rules were relaxed in 2008 to make it easier for couples to choose the church where they wanted to get married.

Dum dum de derrrr, dum dum de derrrr...

The number of marriages in the UK is falling, but that doesn't make it a less popular topic with the examiners. Make sure you learn what happens during a Christian marriage ceremony, and what each bit symbolises. When that's done, try to think of some reasons for and against getting married in a church.

Marriage and Divorce: Christianity

All Christians see marriage as a <u>lifelong commitment</u>, but they don't all agree on what to do if it <u>breaks down</u>.

Christians say Marriage Should be Forever

1) The Christian faith values marriage very <u>highly</u> — the joining of husband and wife in <u>holy matrimony</u> reflects the union of Jesus with his followers.

"...a man will leave his father and mother and be united to his wife, and the two will become one flesh." Mark 10:7-8 NIV

2) Jesus taught that marriage should be a <u>lifelong</u> union — marriage is seen as a <u>covenant</u> or <u>contract</u> between two people, involving <u>commitment</u> and <u>responsibility</u>. Christianity teaches that the purpose of marriage is for two people to offer love and mutual support and for <u>procreation</u> (to have children).

3) The Church recognises that not everyone is called to marriage (e.g. Roman Catholic priests) and from these people it demands <u>celibacy</u>.

> **CENTRAL BIBLICAL TEACHINGS ON MARRIAGE**
> 1) Marriage must be <u>faithful</u>.
> 2) Marriage must be <u>worked at</u> — you have to keep on <u>forgiving</u>.
> 3) Marriage reflects Christ's love for his followers.

The Bible gives Advice on Having a Successful Marriage

1) <u>Faithfulness</u> in marriage is so important that it's one of the <u>Ten Commandments</u>. A married person <u>mustn't</u> have sex with anyone else — that would be <u>adultery</u>.

"You shall not commit adultery." Exodus 20:14 NIV

2) The Bible also says that marriage involves <u>submission</u> (devoting your life to the other person).

3) Many Christians believe that it's best to marry <u>another Christian</u>, or you'll be pulling in opposite directions.

Yokes were used to attach two working animals together.

"Do not be yoked together with unbelievers." 2 Corinthians 6:14 NIV

In Ephesians 5:21-33, wives are encouraged to <u>submit</u> to their husbands, and husbands to <u>love</u> their wives, laying down their lives for them as Christ laid down his.

Christian Churches have Different Attitudes to Divorce

1) The <u>breakdown</u> of a marriage is seen by all Christians as a <u>tragedy</u>. However not all Christians agree about whether divorce is <u>permissible</u>, or even <u>possible</u>.

> The <u>Roman Catholic Church</u> states that it is actually <u>impossible</u> to divorce. Marriage is a <u>sacrament</u> — God has made the couple into one flesh, and this cannot be undone. However, a marriage can be <u>annulled</u> — annulment means that it was never a <u>true</u> marriage in the first place. This can happen if:
> i) either partner did not <u>consent</u> to the marriage or didn't <u>understand</u> what marriage is about,
> ii) the couple didn't or couldn't have <u>sex</u>, or one partner <u>refused</u> to have children.

> The <u>Church of England</u> states that divorce is <u>possible</u> and accepts that some marriages fail. Divorced people can only re-marry <u>in church</u> if they can find a minister willing to marry them, but this doesn't satisfy every member of the Church.

> <u>Nonconformist</u> Churches (e.g. Baptists and Methodists) will generally re-marry divorcees, but an <u>individual minister</u> can refuse to do so if this goes against his or her own conscience.

2) Jesus himself was <u>anti-divorce</u>, but <u>pro-forgiveness</u>.
In Mark 10:2-12 Jesus says that Moses allowed divorce because of people's 'hardness of heart'. But he says that marriages were meant to last for life, and if a divorcee re-marries it's the same as committing adultery.

In John 8:1-11, Jesus freely forgives a woman caught in the act of adultery. But he tells her, 'Go now and leave your life of sin' (NIV).

Matthew 19:8-9 says that divorce and remarriage are only permitted to someone whose partner has been unfaithful.

3) But some Christians view an <u>unhappy</u> marriage as a <u>waste</u> of two lives, and so see divorce as preferable. It's also argued that parents <u>fighting</u> can harm the emotional wellbeing of children <u>more</u> than a divorce.

Don't let all this trouble and strife get you down...

Divorce is an issue that you might feel very strongly about — but make sure you learn the full range of views.

Marriage and Divorce: Judaism

Traditionally all Jews have been <u>expected</u> to marry and have at least two children — ideally a boy and a girl.

Marriage Matters in Judaism

1) To Jews, marriage is an <u>emotional</u>, <u>intellectual</u> and <u>spiritual</u> union. It is seen as the proper context for <u>sex</u> (seen as natural and God-given) and having children (<u>procreation</u>), but is also for <u>companionship</u>.

2) It's the Jewish custom for parents to arrange for their children to meet suitable partners. To help in this it was common to use a 'shadchan', or <u>matchmaker</u> (and it still is among the ultra-Orthodox).

> Nowadays there are shadchan services available via the <u>Internet</u>.

3) Although 40% of UK Jews 'marry out' (i.e. marry non-Jews), those who take their religion seriously find this <u>worrying</u> — children of 'mixed marriages' are less likely to be brought up as <u>observant</u> Jews. Some Jews see this as a threat to Judaism's survival, and even a 'posthumous victory to Hitler'.

Kiddushin is the First Part of the Marriage Ceremony

'<u>Kiddushin</u>' is the first part of the Jewish marriage ceremony, and is usually translated as 'betrothal'. The word comes from a root meaning <u>sanctified</u>, which reflects the <u>holiness</u> of marriage.

Different Jewish communities celebrate marriage in different ways, but there are some <u>common features</u>.

1) The ceremony takes place beneath a <u>chuppah</u>, a wedding <u>canopy</u> — this is a piece of cloth supported by four poles. It is thought the cloth represents <u>privacy</u>, and the open sides <u>hospitality</u>.

2) Usually, the bride will <u>circle</u> the groom <u>seven times</u>.

3) The groom gives the bride a <u>ring</u> and makes the <u>betrothal declaration</u>: 'Behold you are consecrated to me with this ring according to the laws of Moses and Israel.' This <u>completes</u> the kiddushin.

4) Then the <u>ketubah</u> (marriage contract) is read out. The traditional ketubah sets out the woman's right to be <u>cared for</u> by her husband and her entitlements in the event of divorce (a bit like a modern prenuptial agreement). Reform Jews have rewritten the ketubah to be a <u>mutual statement</u> of love and commitment, more like Christian marriage vows.

5) The <u>sheva brachot</u> or <u>seven blessings</u> are said — normally by a rabbi, who usually conducts the service.

6) The groom <u>breaks</u> a glass with his foot in memory of the destruction of the <u>Temple</u> in Jerusalem by the Romans in 70 CE. It's said that there can never be complete joy for the Jewish people until the Temple is restored — this is why it's remembered.

7) After the service there will be a festive meal and dancing, and shouts of 'mazel tov!' (good luck, best wishes). Among some Orthodox Jews, the men and women dance <u>separately</u>.

Divorce is a Last Resort

1) Judaism accepts that some marriages don't work out, and that it's better for a couple to divorce than to stay together in bitterness. But divorce is a very <u>last resort</u> after all attempts at <u>reconciliation</u> have failed.

2) Traditionally, a woman cannot <u>initiate</u> divorce, but a divorce does require the wife's <u>consent</u>.

3) In Reform synagogues, if the husband will not grant his wife a certificate of divorce, a 'Get', the <u>Bet Din</u> (Jewish court) can do so, freeing her to re-marry.

4) In Orthodox synagogues, women who want a divorce but whose husbands will not grant one (or who aren't around to grant one) are known as '<u>agunot</u>' — chained women.

Go on, learn it all — and I'll give you a Scooby-snack...

Rrrokay... Christian, Jewish and Muslim teachings about marriage and morality <u>have a lot in common</u>. This isn't so surprising — all three religions share the same <u>Near Eastern background</u>. And can I just say how nice it is to have a few <u>happy</u> pages after some of the previous section in this book. (Apart from the divorce bits, that is.)

Marriage and Divorce: Islam

Islam

Marriage is very important in Islam. Muslims are advised to marry, and Muhammad himself was married.

Marriage is Recommended for Three Reasons

1) Marriage provides companionship.

2) Marriage provides a secure environment for having children (procreation) and bringing them up as practising Muslims.

3) The sexual instinct is very strong and needs to be carefully channelled.

See page 27 for more about marriage in Islam.

"...He created for you from yourselves mates that you may find tranquillity in them; and He placed between you affection and mercy..." Qur'an 30:21

"Whoever among you can marry, should marry, because it helps him lower his gaze and guard his modesty." Prophet Muhammad (Sahih Bukhari)

Choosing a Partner is often your Parents' Responsibility

Practising Muslims generally want their children to marry other Muslims. Islam affects a Muslim's whole life, and being married to a non-Muslim could create tension, especially with bringing up children.

1) Most Muslims believe it's unwise for young men and women to mix freely, and 'dating' is discouraged or even forbidden.

2) In most Muslim communities, parents search for suitable partners for their children — i.e. Muslims often have 'arranged marriages'.

3) However, as marriage is a contract, both partners must consent to it.

4) Parents also have a responsibility to help if the marriage begins to go wrong.

The Marriage Ceremony — Customs Vary

The marriage ceremony is different in different Islamic cultures, but there's always a religious ceremony (witnessed by Allah) and a public one (witnessed by the community). They usually go like this...

1) A nikah (contract) is drawn up in advance by the families of the bride and groom, and a mahr (dowry) paid by the groom to the bride.

2) An imam (leader of prayers) is often present (though this isn't compulsory).

3) Vows are exchanged, and a marriage declaration is made by each partner. A Hadith (prophetic saying) or a khutbah (speech) may also be said.

4) There will be a big feast afterwards, though the men and women may enjoy this separately.

Divorce is the Last Resort

1) Divorce is permitted, but only as a very last resort. If things aren't going well, an arbiter from each family should be appointed to try to sort things out.

2) Muslims see reconciliation as particularly important when the couple have children.

3) But, in Islam, marriage is a contract and like any other contract it can be ended.

4) When the man says 'I divorce you' three times, the marriage is said to be over. However, there's often a period of three months after the first of these declarations. This allows time for reflection, and also to ensure that the woman is not pregnant.

5) A woman can divorce a man in this way (divorce 'by talaq') if it was written into her marriage contract. Otherwise she has to apply to a Shari'ah court for a divorce 'by khul'.

6) After divorce, both men and women are free to re-marry.

"Of all the lawful acts the most detestable to Allah is divorce." Prophet Muhammad (Sunan Abu Dawud)

This kind of divorce isn't legal in the UK, as Islamic law isn't part of the British legal system.

But I never said I wanted to study a foreign language...

There are quite a lot of Arabic words in these Islam sections — and they're in the syllabus too, so you need to know 'em. The same goes for the sections on Judaism — they contain quite a bit of Hebrew. So if your RS teacher never told you what you were letting yourself in for, it's too late to complain now.

Religious Attitudes to Sex

Christianity, Islam and Judaism have all formulated laws concerned with <u>sex</u>. But this doesn't mean that religious people think there is anything <u>wrong</u> or <u>dirty</u> about having sex — quite the <u>opposite</u>.

Christianity, Islam and Judaism have a Lot in Common...

The three faiths have a lot in common when it comes to <u>sex</u>.

1) <u>Traditionally</u> all three religions teach that the only right context for sexual activity is within <u>marriage</u>.

2) But nowadays you'll find <u>liberal</u> Christians, Jews and Muslims who'll tell you that this belief is outdated. ➤

3) 'Orthodox' members of all three faiths say that certain <u>moral principles</u> never change, however.

> They might argue that when the <u>scriptures</u> were written, contraception was <u>unreliable</u> and the danger of unwanted pregnancy very <u>great</u>. But modern methods mean this isn't the case any more. Also, allowing sex before marriage gives young people a chance to <u>explore</u> their sexuality and channel their sexual urges. It's argued that <u>sexual frustration</u> is a bad reason to get married.

4) All three religions teach that couples <u>should</u> wait until they are <u>married</u>, rather then having <u>pre-marital sex</u>. In fact, it's very important to most <u>Muslims</u> that people, especially girls, remain <u>virgins</u> until marriage.

5) The Christian Church teaches that the total giving of self in sex shouldn't be treated <u>casually</u> — self-control and sexual restraint are considered important. Christians are urged to keep sex within <u>marriage</u> for <u>positive</u> reasons more than <u>negative</u> ones — marriage is believed to give sex a <u>special</u> status.

6) <u>Promiscuity</u> (having many sexual partners) is seen as wrong in all three religions — in Christianity it's seen as <u>dishonouring</u> yourself.

...but they're Not Identical

1) Judaism and Christianity are <u>monogamous</u> — <u>adultery</u> is forbidden by one of the Ten Commandments.

2) Islam permits, but doesn't encourage, <u>polygamy</u>. A man may have up to four wives, but only if he can support them and treat them equally.

> <u>Muhammad</u> actually had <u>eleven wives</u> during his lifetime — although not all at the same time.

Homosexuality — Scriptures say it's Wrong

Homosexuality means being attracted to members of the same sex.

1) Homosexuality is seen in other species, and many non-religious people see it as a <u>natural alternative</u> to heterosexuality.

2) But the scriptures of all three religions <u>seem</u> to say that homosexual sex is <u>wrong</u> — although the relevant passages are interpreted <u>differently</u> by some people.

> "Because of this, God gave them over to shameful lusts... Men committed indecent acts with other men, and received in themselves the due penalty for their perversion." Romans 1:26-27 NIV

3) Some (including some priests) argue that the scriptures were written against a very different <u>cultural background</u> from ours, so we can't apply their standards today.

4) Christianity and Judaism no longer <u>condemn</u> homosexuality, but it isn't seen as the <u>ideal</u> and many still view homosexual <u>sex</u> as a sin. So many religious gays opt for <u>celibacy</u> (they don't have sexual relationships).

5) <u>Civil partnerships</u> became legal in the UK in December 2005. They give homosexual couples the same rights as <u>married</u> couples concerning things like custody of children.

6) <u>The Church of England</u> doesn't allow same-sex partnerships to be <u>blessed</u> in a church. However, there have been some cases where vicars have <u>gone against</u> this rule and blessed the unions of homosexual couples anyway.

7) <u>Reform</u> Jews don't usually condemn homosexuality, and even allow <u>commitment ceremonies</u> for homosexuals — these can take place in a synagogue. They also allow homosexuals to become <u>rabbis</u>.

8) Homosexuality is strictly <u>forbidden</u> by Islamic Shari'ah law (see p.61), so in many <u>Muslim</u> countries it's still <u>illegal</u>. In some countries, e.g. Iran and Saudi Arabia, homosexual acts between men carry the <u>death penalty</u>.

9) As with other religions though, some <u>moderate Muslims</u> believe that the traditional teachings on homosexuality cannot be applied to <u>modern society</u>.

Oranges are not the only fruit, but that's all you're allowed to eat, apparently...

Oooh, here we go again... courting controversy. Whatever you think about this stuff yourself, <u>you need to know what the religions teach</u>. Then you can agree or disagree with them all you like — it's up to you...

Contraception

Hmmm... another tricky topic...

Contraception — Preventing a Pregnancy

1) Contraception (or birth control) is anything that aims to prevent a woman becoming pregnant (conceiving).

2) Contraception can be temporary (e.g. the contraceptive pill, condoms) or permanent (sterilisation).

3) The Roman Catholic Church believes that preventing conception is against 'natural law' and that the use of any artificial contraception is a grave sin. Indeed, it teaches that humans have an obligation to 'be fruitful and increase in number'. Many individual Roman Catholics disagree with this, especially because of recent concerns about AIDS. The Church does allow natural family planning though — by only having sex at the times during a woman's cycle when she's less fertile.

Be fruitful and increase in number...

4) Other Christian Churches have different views on the matter. The Anglican, Methodist and Presbyterian Churches are in favour of contraception, suggesting that it lets parents plan their family in a responsible way.

5) Many Christians believe that contraception should be a question of individual conscience.

Jews Generally see Contraception as Bad

1) Judaism traditionally teaches that a child is a gift from God, and contraception interferes with God's plans to bless couples with children.

2) Most Orthodox Jews only accept contraception if pregnancy could be physically or psychologically harmful to the mother or an existing child.

3) Reform Jews are happier with the idea of contraception for family planning — leaving the decision of whether or not to use it to individual conscience. (Having said that, not wanting to have children isn't a good enough reason to use contraception for many Jews.)

4) Sex should be as natural as possible, though, so hormonal contraceptives like the contraceptive pill are generally preferred to barrier methods like condoms. But their use may be encouraged by some as a means of preventing the spread of HIV and other STIs (sexually transmitted infections).

Islam Teaches that Life is a Sacred Gift from Allah

1) The Qur'an encourages procreation, and Muslims believe that conception is the will of Allah. So although contraception isn't specifically mentioned in the Qur'an, it's often seen as unwelcome.

"...He gives to whom He wills female [children], and He gives to whom He wills males ...and He renders whom He wills barren..." Qur'an 42:49-50

2) Most Muslims feel that it's the right of both husband and wife to try for children, so both partners must agree to any contraception.

3) Different Muslims have different views on contraception, e.g. in Iran, contraception for family planning is actively encouraged. But more conservative scholars and clerics have campaigned against contraception.

In most Muslim countries, contraception is permitted if:
i) there's a threat to the mother's health,
ii) it could help a woman who already has children,
iii) there is a greater than average chance of the child being born with disabilities,
iv) the family is too poor to raise a child.

4) Only 'reversible' methods are allowed, though — permanent sterilisation and vasectomies are frowned on.

Nothing's ever simple is it...

People interpret their religion's teachings in different ways, so it's difficult to give a clear-cut overview of what a religion teaches. These are very 'human' topics, and people are very different. But all these different opinions about various issues makes for plenty to say in the exam.

Section Three — Marriage and the Family

The Media: Marriage and Family

It's <u>another</u> media page — 'is nothing sacred!', I hear you cry. Erm... apparently not... no.

Soaps Tackle some Difficult Issues

1) In recent years, soap operas like 'Eastenders' and 'Hollyoaks' have covered (amongst other things) <u>homosexuality</u>, <u>rape</u>, <u>prostitution</u>, <u>celibacy</u>, <u>incest</u>, <u>marriage</u> and <u>infidelity</u> (although rarely in the same episode).

2) Even though soaps are often seen as a form of <u>escapism</u>, they let us see how a variety of characters deal with issues and emotions that we could <u>all</u> face at some point in our lives.

3) However, characters are sometimes criticised for being <u>stereotypes</u>. They can easily cause <u>offence</u> to people.

Don't you gow blaymin' 'er — you's ve one what ran off with moi bravva woile oi was still in 'ospital 'avin' me leg amputated after you burned the 'ouse down... again... and it caved in on me woile you was daan ve pab, off your 'ead — even though you was pregnant wiv' moi best mayte's kid...

Films are Classified and there's a Watershed

1) <u>Films</u> are <u>classified</u> — some are only deemed suitable for people over a certain age. They may be <u>censored</u> too (see p.20), e.g. if they're too sexually explicit.

2) In the UK there's a television '<u>watershed</u>' at 9 p.m. After this time, programmes are aimed at <u>adults</u>, and it's up to <u>parents</u> to decide whether children watch or not.

3) Many people, both religious and non-religious, object to <u>sex</u> and <u>adultery</u> being explicitly portrayed — they feel that this might promote <u>promiscuous behaviour</u> as 'the norm'.

Reflection or Cause...
Some people think that the sex and 'immorality' that we see on TV just <u>reflects</u> what already happens in society. But others say that showing these things has a direct <u>influence</u> on society.

An Example from Film: "Four Weddings and a Funeral"

'Four Weddings' was first released in 1994. It covers lots of <u>different issues</u> to do with marriage and family:

> <u>What it's about</u>: It's a romantic comedy, but it asks lots of important questions about love, relationships and commitment. The plot centres around Charles, a single thirty-something, and his on-off relationship with Carrie, an American woman he meets at the film's first wedding. (If you haven't seen it, this is the perfect excuse.)
> <u>The issues</u>: Promiscuity, marriage and divorce, homosexuality, committed cohabitation.

Promiscuity:

The central characters are "<u>serial monogamists</u>" — they've had a string of <u>different</u> sexual partners. Carrie admits to having had <u>33 different sexual partners</u>. Some Christians might see this as <u>sexually irresponsible</u> and <u>emotionally empty</u>. But the film doesn't <u>encourage</u> this behaviour — Charles is shocked.

"Flee from sexual immorality... he who sins sexually sins against his own body. Do you not know that your body is a temple of the Holy Spirit..." 1 Corinthians 6:18-19 NIV

Marriage and divorce:

During the film, Carrie marries 'the wrong man' (a rich politician), which very soon ends in <u>divorce</u>. And Charles <u>nearly</u> marries 'the wrong woman' in a Church wedding. His brother stops him, because he knows Charles doesn't love her. This illustrates the importance of marrying for <u>love</u>.

Homosexuality:

For most of the film, the happiest, most <u>committed relationship</u> we see is that between Charles's two <u>gay</u> friends Gareth and Matthew. Their relationship is shown as a '<u>marriage</u>', which ends suddenly when Gareth <u>dies</u> of a heart attack. The film <u>challenges</u> the idea that homosexual relationships are less committed or <u>loving</u> than heterosexual ones.

Committed cohabitation:

At the end of the film, Charles and Carrie decide to stay together and have <u>children</u>, but <u>not</u> get married. Religious <u>liberals</u> accept cohabitation in a stable and loving relationship, but hope that it will be a '<u>prelude</u>' to marriage. Roman Catholics and many other religious <u>conservatives</u> believe that when you decide to commit to someone it should be <u>inside marriage</u>, and both partners should be open to having and raising <u>children</u>.

Eastenders — real life stuff or total pap? Cast your votes...

Sex, marriage and divorce are part of a lot of people's lives, so it's no wonder they're in the media a lot.

Practice Questions

Ding dong, ding dong, ding dong, ding dong... ah, don't you just love weddings. But as with most 'religion and life' topics, it's not all champagne and roses. All three religions teach that marriage involves commitment and faithfulness, and that it's something that has to be <u>worked</u> at...

Speaking of working, here are some questions to test your knowledge. If you can't do them, go back and read through the pages of this section again until you can. Remember your spelling, punctuation and grammar — some questions will offer extra marks for these in the exam.

1) What is:
   a) a nuclear family?
   b) cohabitation?
   c) procreation?
   d) adultery?
   e) mahr? (Islam)
   f) the ketubah? (Judaism)
   g) kiddushin? (Judaism)
   h) promiscuity?
   i) a civil partnership?

You need to make sure you can define all the key terms in the section. If you don't <u>learn</u> the definitions (and they're all in the <u>glossary</u>), you're throwing away some easy marks.

2) a) Describe two features of a Christian/Jewish/Muslim wedding ceremony.
   b) Describe Christian/Jewish/Muslim views on civil partnerships.
   c) Describe Christian/Jewish/Muslim beliefs about sex before marriage.
   d) Why might a religious person object to how sex is portrayed in a television drama?

These are quick questions — just get a couple of points down and move on.

3) For each of the following questions, give <u>two</u> reasons for your point of view.
   a) Do you think marriage is important?
   b) Do you think divorcees should be allowed to re-marry in a place of worship?
   c) Do you agree with contraception?

These are pretty big questions, but remember you only need to <u>state</u> an opinion and give <u>two good reasons</u> for holding it. You don't have to write an essay.

4) For these questions, you need to express yourself as clearly as possible — make sure your writing is correct, accurate and well organised.
   a) Explain how the structure of families in the UK has changed over the last thirty years.
   b) Explain why most Christians/Jews/Muslims value marriage highly.
   c) Explain how a Christian/Jewish/Muslim marriage ceremony reflects religious teachings.
   d) Explain Christian/Jewish/Muslim teachings about divorce.
   e) Explain why some Christians/Jews/Muslims may be against the use of contraception.

If you're studying more than one religion, see if you can answer these questions for <u>both</u> religions — it's good practice.

5) Read the following statements:
   a) "Religion can help keep a family together."
   b) "Marriage is important."
   c) "Getting a divorce is better than living in an unhappy marriage."
   d) "Religious couples should keep sex within marriage."
   e) "Homosexuality is wrong."

   Discuss each statement. You should include different, supported points of view and a personal viewpoint. You must refer to a religion in your answer.

This type of question is worth plenty of marks in the exam. So take your time, structure your answer carefully, and give as many different sides of the argument as you can.

Prejudice and Equality

General

The world we live in is full of people from different <u>religious</u>, <u>racial</u> and <u>cultural</u> backgrounds. And the way each religion deals with this is important, as it can help or hinder the building of <u>communities</u>.

Prejudice *has Many Causes*

It's worth being very clear about what a few words mean...

Justice	the principle of <u>fairness</u> — both <u>legally</u> and more <u>generally</u>.
Equality	being <u>equal</u>, and being <u>treated equally</u>.
Community	the <u>people</u> living in a certain place, or a group of people with the <u>same</u> religious or cultural <u>characteristics</u>.
Prejudice	<u>judging</u> something or someone with no good reason, or without full knowledge of a situation.
Discrimination	<u>unjust treatment</u>, often resulting from prejudice.

1) Prejudice has many <u>causes</u>, and is often the product of <u>early influences</u>.
   It tends to be the result of <u>widely held</u> (yet <u>inaccurate</u>) beliefs of a particular community or family.

2) <u>Discrimination</u> comes in many forms... <u>Individuals</u> may discriminate by being <u>violent</u> and <u>abusive</u>.
   Whole <u>societies</u> may discriminate by passing <u>laws</u> which prevent certain people from doing certain things.

Racism *is One Form of Prejudice*

It's a sad fact that some people are prejudiced against anyone from a different <u>cultural</u> or <u>religious</u> background, or simply because of the <u>colour</u> of their skin.

1) There have been many instances of <u>racial discrimination</u> in the UK in recent
   years — usually as a result of <u>ignorance</u>, <u>misunderstanding</u> or <u>segregation</u>.
   At times these have culminated in <u>rioting</u> or <u>murder</u>.

   Racial segregation is when people of different races do their daily activities separately — either because they're forced to, or because it's the social norm.

2) Racism is often based on <u>stereotypes</u> — fixed and standardised images of groups of people, which can be used to promote <u>negative</u> thoughts and actions.

3) The <u>media</u> has an important role to play. Television and newspapers can <u>educate</u> — or help fuel <u>negative</u> stereotypes (see p.40).

4) More than <u>80%</u> of all hate crime (crime driven by <u>prejudice</u>) is <u>racially</u> motivated.
   These racist crimes lead to further <u>segregation</u> and increased <u>hostility</u> within communities.

The Government *Tries to Promote Community Cohesion*

1) The UK is a <u>multi-ethnic</u>, <u>multi-faith</u> society (see p.38), so it can be hard for members of a community to feel they have much in common — they can lack '<u>community cohesion</u>'.

2) This is particularly true of places where there are lots of people from <u>ethnic minorities</u>.

3) The Government is trying to promote the idea of '<u>Britishness</u>' as something that goes beyond racial and cultural differences to help <u>tie</u> communities together.

4) The <u>Race Relations Act (1976)</u> is part of this. It makes it <u>illegal</u> to discriminate on the grounds of race, colour or nationality, or to publish anything likely to <u>cause</u> racial hatred.

Sex Discrimination — *it's also Illegal*

Most societies have historically been <u>male dominated</u>, and have only started to change relatively <u>recently</u>.

1) Up until the middle of the <u>20th century</u>, it was seen as a woman's role to stay at <u>home</u> and take care of the <u>family</u>. But during World War II, women had to take on <u>traditionally male</u> roles, e.g. factory work, while the men were away fighting. After the war, many women didn't want things to go back to the way they'd been.

2) In 1975 the <u>Sex Discrimination Act</u> was passed by Parliament. This made it <u>illegal</u> to discriminate against people on account of their <u>gender</u> (<u>sexism</u>) — especially in the fields of employment and education.

Community cohesion — you could always try superglue...

This is <u>difficult</u> and <u>emotive</u> stuff, but like all Religion and Life topics, it's not supposed to be easy...

Attitudes to Equality: Christianity

Christianity

For Christians, the <u>Bible</u> has plenty to say on the subject of equality...

The Bible has Plenty of 'Anti-Prejudice' Stories

1) The idea of 'do to others what you would have them do to you' is a fundamental part of Christian teaching (sometimes called the 'Golden Rule').

2) Generally Christians believe that everyone was created <u>equal</u> by God, and so they try to <u>avoid discrimination</u> and <u>promote equality</u>. They look to the example of Jesus, who told <u>stories</u> about equality, and acted true to his own teaching by <u>mixing</u> with a variety of people himself.

3) One of the most famous stories in the New Testament is the Parable of the <u>Good Samaritan</u> (Luke 10:25-37) where one man comes to the aid of another simply because he is <u>suffering</u>.

> **The Parable of the Good Samaritan**
> A man is beaten up and left half-dead by robbers. First a priest and then a Levite (the Levites were a Jewish priestly tribe) walking down the road see him, but carry on walking. But a Samaritan (considered an enemy by the Jews) bandages the man, puts him on his donkey, takes him to an inn and sees that he is looked after.

4) But there are plenty of other biblical verses preaching <u>equal treatment</u> for all — these two are from the New Testament.

> "...there is no Greek or Jew... barbarian, Scythian, slave or free, but Christ is all, and is in all." Colossians 3:11 NIV

> "My brothers... don't show favouritism. Suppose a man comes into your meeting wearing a gold ring and fine clothes, and a poor man in shabby clothes also comes in. If you show special attention to the man wearing fine clothes... but say to the poor man... 'Sit on the floor by my feet,' have you not... become judges with evil thoughts?" James 2:1-4 NIV

Quite right too.

5) And <u>Deuteronomy</u> (a Book of Law in the <u>Old Testament</u>) includes these...

> "Do not take advantage of a hired man who is poor and needy..." Deuteronomy 24:14 NIV

> "Do not deprive the alien or the fatherless of justice..." Deuteronomy 24:17 NIV

By the way, 'alien' means 'foreigner' here.

Many People have Fought against Prejudice

1) Most Christians would argue that we should <u>avoid</u> prejudice on the basis of race, gender, religion, age, disability, colour or class. The Bible has plenty of <u>specific teaching</u> on these matters.

> "...loose the chains of injustice and untie the cords of the yoke, to set the oppressed free... Then your light will break forth like the dawn..." Isaiah 58:6-8 NIV

2) There are many examples of <u>individual Christians</u> struggling against injustice — e.g.:

<u>DIETRICH BONHOEFFER</u> was a German Christian who felt the church had a duty to speak out against the Nazis' treatment of the Jews. He later became involved in an active conspiracy against the Nazi Party and was hanged in a concentration camp.

<u>ARCHBISHOP DESMOND TUTU</u> and <u>BISHOP TREVOR HUDDLESTON</u> were active in the fight against apartheid in South Africa (see next page).

<u>DR MARTIN LUTHER KING</u> was a Baptist minister who dedicated his life to trying to change the way black people were treated in the USA. He organised peaceful marches, rallies and boycotts, and in 1965 blacks were given equal voting rights with whites. King was assassinated in 1968 aged only 39.

The Good Samaritan — what a nice bloke...

This is a serious issue that often makes it into the <u>news</u>. And it's one that you might have <u>personal</u> experience of — and if you do, you can use that experience to help answer an exam question on it. But be careful not to just <u>rant</u> on about yourself — you'll need to refer to the religious teachings as well.

Attitudes to Equality: Christianity

Christianity

Most Christian Churches Work to Promote Racial Harmony

1) Leviticus 19:33-34 contains some basic teaching on the way people from different races and cultural backgrounds should be treated.

> "When an alien lives with you in your land, do not mistreat him... Love him as yourself..." Leviticus 19:33-34 NIV

This story's actually about foreigners living in Israel, but Christians argue that it also applies to the modern world.

2) There's a story about Simon Peter in Acts that's also relevant.

> Acts 10:1-35 tells a story about Simon Peter. He is told by God not to consider impure anything that God has made. So when Cornelius, a Roman soldier, sends for Peter, Peter goes willingly, even though it is against the law for Jews to associate with non-Jews. Peter says, "...God does not show favouritism but accepts men from every nation..." (NIV)

3) The parable of the Good Samaritan (see previous page) is an example of Christian teaching on the treatment of people from other cultures. The Samaritans were a mixed race who suffered a great deal of discrimination at the time Jesus told the story.

4) More recently, Dr George Carey (the former Archbishop of Canterbury) spoke about the fundamental Christian belief that racism is wrong, that everyone is created in God's image.

> "Racism has no part in the Christian Gospel... it contradicts our Lord's command... It solves no problems and creates nothing but hatred and fear." Dr George Carey

Not really what we were after, guys...

5) But although Christians generally work to improve racial harmony (people of all races living and working together peacefully), there have been occasions when this hasn't been the case...

> The Dutch Reformed Church of South Africa (DRC) believed that God had divided mankind into different races and made white people superior. This idea became law in the system of apartheid.
>
> Trevor Huddleston (an English bishop working in South Africa) argued that apartheid was against God's will. For nearly 50 years, he struggled against it using non-violent methods, until apartheid eventually ended in 1992.

Sex Discrimination — Not So Clear

1) The Bible gives different messages on the subject of sex discrimination. In the New Testament, women are found among Jesus's followers and he treated them equally — remarkable for the time.

> "I do not permit a woman to teach or to have authority over a man; she must be silent. For Adam was formed first, then Eve... it was the woman who was deceived and became a sinner. But women will be saved through childbearing..." 1 Timothy 2:12-15 NIV

2) But this is taken from St Paul's letter to his assistant Timothy:

3) Although in Galatians 3:28 St Paul writes, "There is neither... male nor female, for you are all one in Christ Jesus." (NIV)

Women in the Christian Church

There's evidence from the Bible that women, as well as men, taught and led congregations in the very early Christian Church, e.g. Phoebe (Romans 16:1-2), Priscilla (Acts 18:26, 1 Corinthians 16:19, Romans 16:3), Mary, Tryphena and Tryphosa (Romans 16:12).

But for much of the Church's history, women haven't been allowed to be ordained as priests. The reasoning being that Jesus only called men to be Apostles.

Over the last 50 years, this has started to change — women can now be ordained as ministers in most Protestant denominations and as Anglican priests, but not as Roman Catholic or Orthodox priests.

Racism — still a big issue today, unfortunately...

In the UK prejudice against Muslims has increased in recent years. This has led to further mistrust and calls for segregation from some, and an increased desire for tolerance and integration from others.

Attitudes to Equality: Judaism

Judaism

Like Christianity and Islam, <u>Judaism</u> teaches that God created people <u>equal</u>.

The Hebrew Bible Preaches Tolerance

<u>Racism</u> is disapproved of in Judaism. The Hebrew Bible (the Old Testament) has a lot to say on the matter.

1) The Book of Genesis suggests that all of humanity comes from the <u>same source</u> and is, therefore, <u>equal</u> before God.

> "Adam named his wife Eve, because she would become the mother of all the living." Genesis 3:20 NIV

2) Other messages of <u>tolerance</u> can be found in Deuteronomy 23:7, and Leviticus 19:33-34 (see p.33).

> "Do not abhor an Edomite, for he is your brother. Do not abhor an Egyptian, because you lived as an alien in his country." Deuteronomy 23:7 NIV

3) Deuteronomy 23 contains a discussion of who should be called 'the Lord's people'. This could be taken as meaning we should show <u>tolerance</u> for other nationalities. However, the same chapter does contain references to certain people or nations who should be <u>excluded</u>.

4) The Jewish people are sometimes called the '<u>chosen people</u>'. This doesn't mean they think they're <u>better</u> than anyone else — simply that God gave them additional <u>responsibilities</u>.

5) The stories of <u>Ruth</u> and <u>Jonah</u> (both in the Hebrew Bible, i.e. the Old Testament) could also be used to promote <u>social</u> and <u>racial</u> harmony.

The Story of Jonah...

Jonah was told to preach to the people of Nineveh, who had <u>upset God</u>. When he preached God's message, the people of Nineveh were humble and repentant, which pleased God, and so God <u>spared</u> the city, <u>upsetting</u> Jonah. But God said he was right to spare the city, and that Jonah was wrong to be upset. The message is, "If God can love and forgive, we should be able to live with others too."

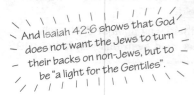

First I get thrown off the boat, then I get eaten by a big fish. This must be a Monday.

Before he got to Nineveh, Jonah was swallowed by a big fish and stayed there for 3 days.

And Isaiah 42:6 shows that God does not want the Jews to turn their backs on non-Jews, but to be "a light for the Gentiles".

The Story of Ruth...

Naomi and her husband leave Judah because of a famine — they end up in <u>Moab</u>. Naomi's sons marry Moabite girls — but soon after, Naomi's husband and sons <u>die</u>. <u>Ruth</u> (one of Naomi's daughters-in-law) stays very <u>loyal</u> to her <u>Israelite mother-in-law</u>, and becomes devoted to God. This bloodline eventually produces <u>King David</u>. The message is, "Good things happen to those who are nice to people from other lands."

"Male and female he created them" — Genesis 1:27 NIV

1) The above passage is sometimes read as meaning that men and women are seen as <u>equals</u> before God, although <u>different</u>, and with different <u>responsibilities</u>. (God did create two different <u>sexes</u> after all, so he can't have wanted us all to be identical.)

2) Some people involved with the <u>feminist</u> movement (fighting for women's rights) argue that the expectation for women to become wives and mothers is <u>unfair</u>, and has <u>hindered</u> women's progress.

3) Judaism doesn't suggest that women should <u>not</u> be able to follow their chosen career. However, there is still a belief that motherhood is a <u>privilege</u>, and women should devote some of their life to it.

4) But there are definitely differences of opinion on this. <u>Orthodox Jews</u> aim to uphold many of the ancient Jewish <u>traditions</u>, and so would be more likely to suggest that women should remain at home as <u>mothers</u> and <u>wives</u>.

There are also rules governing <u>SYNAGOGUE WORSHIP</u>. Usually ten <u>men</u> (called a minyan) are required for a service, and it is <u>men</u> who read from the Torah. Also, men and women in Orthodox synagogues have <u>separate</u> areas for prayer.

<u>Reform Jews</u> don't accept all these rules, however — women can form a minyan, and even become rabbis.

5) However, <u>Reform Jews</u> are willing to <u>interpret</u> traditional teachings so that they are, perhaps, more relevant to the <u>modern age</u>. For this reason they're less strict when it comes to the roles of men and women.

I don't believe the Jonah story — it all sounds a bit fishy...

Jews have suffered from a great deal of racism and persecution over the years. By far the most extreme form of social injustice was the <u>Holocaust</u> in World War II, when discrimination became <u>government policy</u>. It serves as a reminder to everyone of how much suffering can arise from racial hatred.

Attitudes to Equality: Islam

Islam is truly <u>international</u> — with followers from many countries, and many ethnic and cultural backgrounds.

Islam *says* People are Created *Equal, but not Identical*

1) Islam teaches that all people were created by Allah, and were created <u>equal</u> (although not the <u>same</u>). He intended humanity to be created with <u>differences</u>. But this just means we're all individuals. Hurrah.

> "And of His signs is the creation of the heavens and the earth and the diversity of your languages and your colours..." Qur'an 30:22

2) Muslims all over the world are united through the <u>ummah</u> — the community of Islam. The ummah consists of <u>all</u> Muslims, regardless of colour, nationality, tradition (i.e. Sunni or Shi'ite) and so on. This can help promote racial and social harmony, as no one is <u>excluded</u> or <u>discriminated</u> against in theory.

Most Muslims in the UK are from ethnic minorities, and so they're more likely to be subjected to <u>racially motivated</u> attacks, abuse and murder than their white neighbours.

As a result, a number of peaceful <u>pressure groups</u> have been established — some working within Muslim communities, others working with the Government or with other faith groups.

3) <u>Hajj</u> (pilgrimage to Makkah) especially demonstrates <u>equality</u>. Those on pilgrimage all wear simple white garments, showing <u>everyone's</u> equal before Allah — wealth, status and colour don't matter.

4) The fact that <u>all</u> Muslims should <u>pray</u> five times a day at set times, and face Makkah whilst doing so, also demonstrates <u>unity</u> and <u>equality</u>. Men and women often pray <u>together</u> at home — however, they must pray in <u>separate groups</u> in the mosque.

The Qur'an teaches that Men and Women are Equal

1) Men and women have an <u>equal obligation</u> to Allah in terms of prayer, fasting, pilgrimage and charity.

> "Indeed, the Muslim men and Muslim women, the believing men and believing women, the obedient men and obedient women... the charitable men and charitable women, the fasting men and fasting women... and the men who remember Allah often and the women who do so — for them Allah has prepared forgiveness and a great reward." Qur'an 33:35

2) <u>All</u> Muslims, male and female, are also obliged to seek <u>education</u>.

3) In the early days of Islam, there were many female <u>religious scholars</u>.

4) But there are also some teachings that might be <u>interpreted</u> as meaning men are <u>superior</u>, e.g.

> "Men are in charge of women by [right of] what Allah has given one over the other and what they spend [for maintenance] from their wealth..." Qur'an 4:34

Although they're usually taken to mean that men and women just have different <u>roles</u> within the community or family — men are responsible for <u>providing</u> for the family, and women are responsible for the <u>home</u>.

WOMEN AND THE MOSQUE

<u>Women</u> aren't encouraged to attend the mosque for prayer, but the Prophet Muhammad did <u>permit</u> it. If they do go to the mosque, they must pray in a <u>separate group</u> — <u>behind</u> (or otherwise out of sight of) the men.

Women are not permitted to <u>lead</u> the prayers of men, but they may lead other women. This is agreed by <u>all</u> traditional schools of Islam, both Sunni and Shi'ah.

Muslim feminist <u>Asra Nomani</u> is leading a campaign to end segregation in the mosque, and allow woman-led <u>mixed-gender</u> prayers. In 2005, <u>Amina Wadud</u> led a mixed-gender prayer in New York. Their actions have been <u>condemned</u> by Muslim scholars as not following the teachings of Islam.

Equal but not the same — don't try that one in maths...

In Islam, a woman's <u>traditional</u> role has been to create a good homelife for the family, while the man went out to work and made sure the children were good Muslims. However, not all Muslims live in this traditional way. In some Islamic cultures there is almost complete equality between men and women.

Christianity, Judaism, Islam & General

Family Roles of Men and Women

As you might have noticed, men and women are a bit... <u>different</u>... in some ways.
Religions have noticed this too...

Roles of Men and Women Have Changed A Lot in Society...

1) In the past, it was seen as a woman's role to take care of the <u>home</u> and raise <u>children</u>, while the man went out to <u>work</u>. The man was the <u>head</u> of the household, and his wife was expected to be <u>obedient</u>.

2) After World War II, these attitudes started to change in the UK (see p.31). Now it's considered perfectly normal for <u>women</u> to go out to work, and <u>men</u> to take part in housework and childcare (although women still do a lot more of this overall).

3) <u>Religious views</u> on the roles of men and women have shifted over time in a similar way.

Charles was a modern man — but he just couldn't find where his wife kept the lumps for the gravy.

...And in Christian Families

> "Wives, submit to your husbands as to the Lord. For the husband is the head of the wife as Christ is the head of the church..."
> Ephesians 5:22-23 NIV

1) The Bible talks about wives <u>submitting</u> to their husbands (doing as they say).

2) But many Christians argue that this just reflects the ideas of society at that time, and doesn't correspond with <u>Jesus's attitude</u> towards women. Women are found among Jesus's followers, and he treated them <u>equally</u>.

3) Nowadays, most Christians believe that men and women should have <u>equal roles</u> in the <u>family</u>.

Jewish Women Must Learn to Run a Jewish Home

1) Jewish women and men have traditional roles in the home. But these expectations are changing, especially for <u>Reform Jews</u> (see p.34).

2) Men and women have <u>clear roles</u> during the <u>Shabbat meal</u> — the mother lights candles and welcomes Shabbat, and the father blesses the children.

There's lots to do to prepare for Shabbat — cleaning the house and preparing food. This is traditionally the woman's job.

Mothers are Very Important in Muslim Families

1) In traditional Muslim families, women are generally expected to take care of the <u>home and the children</u>, and men are expected to <u>support</u> their wives (see p.35).

2) However, it's quite acceptable for women to go <u>out to work</u> if their husbands agree.

3) Even though they're not head of the household, <u>mothers</u> have a very <u>high status</u> in Muslim families.

4) <u>Modern interpretations</u> of the teachings of the Qur'an say that husbands should consider what's <u>normal in society</u> when dealing with their wives, and that family decisions should be taken <u>together</u>.

> "Who amongst the people is most deserving of my good treatment? He said: Your mother, again your mother, again your mother, then your father..."
> Prophet Muhammad (Sahih Muslim)

And in some spider families the male gets eaten...

Religious texts are read within the context of society. As the roles of men and women have gradually changed in society the different religious texts have been interpreted differently.

Religious Help for Immigrants

Christianity, Judaism, Islam & General

Hundreds of thousands of people move to the UK every year — either looking for <u>work</u> or to find <u>refuge</u> from persecution (<u>asylum seekers</u>). And there are plenty of religious organisations out there to help them...

Immigrants Often Face Difficulties

1) Many immigrants arrive with either no, or very poor, <u>English</u> — so they need <u>interpreters</u> while they learn the language.

2) They're often <u>unfamiliar</u> with British <u>customs</u> and <u>laws</u>, so can find themselves in trouble without understanding why.

3) Many asylum seekers have suffered <u>physical</u>, <u>mental</u>, <u>emotional</u> or <u>sexual</u> abuses in their countries, which can leave them seriously <u>traumatised</u>.

4) Without good English and an understanding of the system, it can be <u>very difficult</u> to get good-quality <u>legal advice</u>, register for <u>healthcare</u> or find <u>accommodation</u>.

5) Immigrants are frequently <u>exploited</u> as unofficial, <u>cheap labour</u>, paid well below the minimum wage.

6) Some people accuse immigrants of taking <u>homes</u> and <u>jobs</u> from local people. This attitude can lead to <u>discrimination</u> and abuse (ranging from playground name-calling to physical attacks).

Religious Organisations Offer Practical Help

Christianity, Islam and Judaism agree that <u>all</u> human beings should be treated <u>fairly</u> and <u>humanely</u>. So there are organisations from <u>all three faiths</u> working to improve the lot of immigrants to this country. You need to know some <u>examples</u> of these religious organisations and the <u>work</u> they do:

The Boaz Trust

A <u>Christian</u> charity based in Manchester, set up to help <u>asylum seekers</u> whose initial application to stay in the UK has been <u>turned down</u>. Many of these people aren't allowed to <u>work</u> and get <u>no</u> help from the Government, so they're entirely dependent on charity for food, accommodation and any <u>legal help</u> they might need for an appeal.

The Jesuit Refugee Service

An international <u>Roman Catholic</u> organisation, with bases in over 50 countries worldwide. JRS offers <u>pastoral</u> services (taking care of people's spiritual well-being), <u>counselling</u>, <u>English-language</u> teaching and help with <u>healthcare</u> and <u>legal</u> representation. They also campaign across Europe against the <u>detention</u> of asylum seekers. (Detention means holding asylum seekers in a centre while deciding if they should be allowed into the community or sent back to where they came from.)

The Jewish Council for Racial Equality (JCORE)

A Jewish organisation, based in the UK. They <u>campaign</u> for the rights of asylum seekers, <u>raise awareness</u> of the problems faced by immigrants and offer all sorts of <u>practical help</u>. For example, they have a '<u>refugee doctors project</u>' that gives information and practical help to trained immigrant doctors, to help them re-train to practise in the UK.

Islamic Aid

An international Muslim organisation dedicated to reducing <u>poverty</u> and <u>deprivation</u>. Their work in the UK centres on improving the lives of Muslim immigrants, e.g. by raising awareness of the problem of '<u>ghettos</u>' and tackling <u>unemployment</u> among UK Muslims.

Bienvenue, Willkommen, Witajcie, Swaagatam, Huan yin...

There are tens of thousands of failed asylum seekers in the UK, living off the charity of organisations like Boaz and JCORE. They have no home, no legal way of making money, no access to medicine or education for their children — it's a terrible way to live. But as far as the law's concerned, they have <u>no right to be here</u> at all...

General

The UK as a Multi-Faith Society

All through history, people from different <u>cultures</u> have come to settle in Britain, bringing with them their own <u>beliefs</u> and <u>customs</u>. It makes our society <u>rich</u> and <u>diverse</u>, but can sometimes cause <u>problems</u>.

The UK is a Diverse, Multi-Faith Society

1) Your <u>identity</u> is what makes you <u>you</u>. It's how you see yourself and how others see you. It's made up of <u>basic stuff</u> like your name, age, appearance, as well as '<u>deeper</u>' stuff such as your beliefs and attitudes.

2) The United Kingdom is a <u>diverse</u>, <u>multi-faith</u> society — there are a wide range of Christian denominations. In England and Wales almost 9% of the population say they follow a non-Christian religion.

3) In most major towns and cities you'll find a <u>variety</u> of places of worship
   — including different <u>churches</u>, <u>synagogues</u> and <u>mosques</u>.

Although some Roman Catholic and other church schools limit the amount of time spent looking at other religions.

4) Children in UK schools are taught about <u>all</u> major world faiths in an attempt to increase <u>understanding</u> and <u>tolerance</u>.

5) <u>Religious freedom</u> — the freedom to practise any religion you choose (including no religion at all) — is a legal <u>right</u> in the UK.

6) The religious diversity of the UK provides a great opportunity for increasing <u>understanding</u>, and for finding <u>common ground</u> between the different faiths.

7) But that isn't the <u>only</u> advantage of a multi-faith society. Along with their faiths, these different cultural groups bring their <u>customs</u>, <u>dress</u>, <u>art</u>, <u>music</u>, <u>food</u>, <u>architecture</u>...

8) All this helps to make the UK a really <u>vibrant</u> and <u>interesting</u> place to live.

Conversion and Interfaith Marriages are Issues in the UK

But along with religious diversity and freedom come the issues of <u>conversion</u> and <u>interfaith marriages</u>.

CONVERSION

In the past, Christians often believed they had the <u>right</u> to <u>make</u> people take up their faith. In general, Christians are much more <u>tolerant</u> now, but <u>evangelical</u> Christians still consider it a priority to '<u>win people for Christ</u>'. This is because they don't believe that a person can get to Heaven <u>any</u> other way (see next page).

Muslims are <u>happy</u> to accept converts, but they don't usually go out trying to convert people. However, rejecting Islam to take another faith (<u>apostasy</u>) is a sin that's still punishable by <u>death</u>.

While the <u>early</u> Jews accepted converts to the faith, <u>modern</u> Orthodox Jews aren't very keen to at all. <u>Reform</u> Jews will accept converts after a period of <u>study</u> (usually about 18 months) but they don't encourage conversion either. In the Middle Ages, many Jews were <u>forced</u> to reject Judaism, but encouraging other Jews to do the same carried the <u>death</u> penalty.

INTERFAITH MARRIAGES

As a rule, interfaith marriages are <u>disapproved</u> of — unless either the husband or the wife intends to <u>convert</u> at some point.

<u>Children</u> of a mixed marriage are much <u>less</u> likely to be brought up as <u>observant</u> members of either religion (although the child of a Muslim is considered a Muslim, and the child of a Jewish mother is considered Jewish — whatever the faith of the other parent). And it can be difficult for any member of the family to really stay a part of their <u>own</u> faith community. There are groups like the '<u>Inter-Faith Marriage Network</u>' that offer advice and support for mixed-faith couples.

Pluralists say there's Room for Everyone

1) Most religious believers are happy to live alongside other faiths in the UK. Organisations representing every major faith in the UK belong to the '<u>Inter Faith Network for the UK</u>'.

2) The aim of this network is to promote <u>mutual understanding</u>, combat <u>prejudice</u> and help build <u>community cohesion</u>.

3) This is an example of <u>religious pluralism</u> — the idea that <u>every faith</u> has as much right to exist as any other, and that there's room for everyone.

The <u>Inter Faith Network</u> for the UK describes itself as based "...on the principle that dialogue and cooperation can only prosper if they are rooted in respectful relationships which do not blur or undermine the distinctiveness of different religious traditions".

Pluralism — is that, like, being against more than one of something...

Your <u>identity</u> is <u>influenced</u> by your religion and ethnic background — but they don't have to <u>define</u> you.

Attitudes to Other Religions

Christianity, Judaism & Islam

Christianity, Judaism and Islam have a great deal <u>in common</u>, and their approach to other religions is generally one of <u>tolerance</u> and <u>mutual understanding</u>. Over the years, though, there have been times of misunderstanding, ignorance and intolerance, which have led to <u>discrimination</u> and <u>war</u> (e.g. the Crusades).

Christianity Teaches that Jesus is the Only Path to God

"I am the way and the truth and the life. No one comes to the Father except through me." John 14:6 NIV

1) Christians generally believe that people have the right to practise <u>any</u> faith, although they might argue that only Christianity has the <u>truth</u> about God. This passage stresses the Christian belief that it's only through following the teachings of <u>Jesus Christ</u> that people can reach God.

2) In the Decree "Ad Gentes", the Roman Catholic Church makes it clear that "...the Church still has the <u>obligation</u> and also the <u>sacred right</u> to evangelise all men". 'Evangelise' means <u>spread</u> the Christian message with the aim of <u>converting</u> people (see previous page).

3) There are also Christian <u>missionaries</u> who work all over the world spreading the message of Christianity and trying to <u>convert</u> people.

4) This approach could be described as <u>exclusive</u> — it doesn't really <u>welcome</u> other faiths, and may even <u>reject</u> them because Christianity is seen as the only way.

5) But not all Christians accept this. Christian <u>inclusivists</u> believe that there's at least <u>some truth</u> in what other religions say about God.

> <u>Ecumenism</u> is a principle within Christianity. Its aim is to create unity amongst the <u>different Christian</u> traditions, e.g. Roman Catholics, Anglicans, Methodists, etc.

Jews believe Judaism is the Only True Faith (for Jews)

1) Judaism teaches that it is the only <u>true</u> faith for <u>Jews</u> to follow, but is <u>tolerant</u> of other faiths.

2) Most faiths have similar <u>moral</u> and <u>spiritual</u> laws and so are <u>tolerated</u> by Judaism. Because of this, there's no real desire to <u>convert</u> people.

3) People of <u>any</u> religion are generally deemed to be <u>righteous</u> if they follow the <u>Noahide Code</u> — moral laws given to Noah after the flood that prohibit idolatry, murder, theft, sexual immorality and blasphemy.

...and that whole tearing the flesh from a still-living animal and eating it thing — that's <u>right</u> out.*

Aww... you're joking?

Baaa!!

4) Islam and Judaism have very <u>similar</u> beliefs in one all-powerful God. However, some Jews have difficulties with the <u>Christian</u> belief that <u>Jesus Christ</u> was the <u>incarnation</u> of God. And with the use of <u>statues</u> and <u>icons</u> in Roman Catholic and Orthodox Christianity, which they see as <u>idolatry</u>.

5) But there's still a great deal of mutual <u>respect</u>, and Jewish participation in <u>interfaith</u> groups (see previous page) is common. One example of an interfaith group in the UK is 'The Council of Christians and Jews'.

Muslims believe Islam is the Only True Faith

1) Muslims believe that Islam is the only <u>true</u> faith — although there is an acceptance that all <u>righteous</u> people will be favoured by Allah, as he knows all we do.

> "Indeed, those who believed and those who were Jews or Christians... those [among them] who believed in Allah and the Last Day and did righteousness — will have their reward with their Lord..." Qur'an 2:62

2) Muslims believe that men like Adam, Ibrahim (Abraham), Musa (Moses) and Isa (Jesus) were all <u>Prophets of Allah</u>. So the <u>Torah</u> and the <u>Bible</u> are also holy scriptures revealed by Allah (albeit <u>edited</u> from their original form). This suggests that Islam is an <u>inclusive</u> faith.

3) But some Muslims interpret the scriptures to argue that Islam should be <u>exclusive</u>, and shouldn't have anything to do with other faiths. And like Christians, some Muslims feel they have a <u>mission</u> to lead <u>non-Muslims</u> to Allah.

4) However, many Muslims in the UK live side by side with other religious believers, and some take part in <u>interfaith</u> groups.

E.g. The Centre for the Study of Islam and Christian-Muslim Relations.

I know what you're thinking — this is a righteous page...

So exclusivists believe that their religion is the <u>only</u> way to salvation. Inclusivists believe that other religions have <u>some truth</u> in them. And pluralists believe that all religions are <u>equally valid</u>. And there are followers of all three philosophies in the three main religions. Ooh, it's a tricky subject, is this... make no mistake.

* Noahide Law No. 6 — mmm... lovely

Section Four — Religion and Community Cohesion

The Media: Religion and Society

General

Community cohesion isn't really much of a story until everything goes pear-shaped.
But when it does, it gets everyone's attention.

The Media Raises Sensitive Issues

With community cohesion issues, the media has to strike a balance — drawing
attention to problems that may be of public concern, but without encouraging
racism or xenophobia (fear or hatred of people from other countries).

Immigration is Regularly in the News

The mainstream British press would deny that it ever carries a racist or
discriminatory message, but some people argue that it encourages prejudice.

1) Elements of the British media have described immigration as a big problem and
   have called for stricter controls on who's allowed to settle in the country.
2) They point to the strain placed on social services, the competition for jobs and the fact that
   immigrants often send a large proportion of the money they earn back to their country of origin.
3) Some think this media attention has made life harder for migrants, by turning people against them,
   and ignores the positive impact they have — creating economic activity often in deprived areas.

Islamophobia is a Serious Problem

1) Islam is often portrayed by the media as a violent religion, which
   threatens the security of the nation. This attitude was reinforced
   by the London bombings in 2005, conducted by four Muslims.
2) Many people feel that the influence of the media has
   contributed to Islamophobia — hatred and fear of Islam.

> The Forum Against Islamophobia
> and Racism (FAIR) was set
> up in 2001 to monitor media
> coverage of Islam, and to work
> with media organisations to
> combat misrepresentation.

Rioting in 2001 Highlighted Tensions

1) In 2001, activity by the far-right group, the National Front, sparked off rioting in Oldham and Burnley.
   This unrest spread to Bradford, a city that had seen decades of high immigration, which had developed
   a number of ethnically segregated neighbourhoods.
2) Much of the violence was focused in Manningham, a mainly Pakistani area of the city, where it was
   reported that around one thousand Asian youths confronted riot police.
3) News reports featured local religious leaders — including the Archbishop of Bradford and members of
   local Muslim organisations — expressing their distress and appealing for calm.
4) In the aftermath, the leaders of Bradford's different religious groups met up with the Home Secretary
   to try to end the mistrust between their communities.
5) While some in the media applauded the role played by religious organisations, others complained that
   focusing on religion took attention away from the problem of racism, and the real social and economic
   difficulties faced by the people of Bradford.

> In 2006 Channel 4 made Bradford Riots, a drama which tells the story of Karim, a Muslim student
> from Bradford, who gets caught up in the rioting and ends up being given a harsh prison sentence.
> - Religion plays an important, but background role in the film. The Imam in the mosque offers
>   spiritual guidance rather than practical advice.
> - Religion is seen as an inescapable part of the characters' identities — but one that they are
>   sometimes reduced to. At the end, Karim's cellmate calls him simply 'Muslim-boy'.
> - The film reflects on the uncertainty and vulnerability felt by Britain's Muslim communities in
>   the wake of the 9/11 terrorist attacks.

1.5 MILLION UK MUSLIMS BELIEVE IN PEACE — not a good headline...

The nature of the media means that when religion is covered, it's more likely to be a story about a riot,
or an extreme weirdy cult, than about people practising their faiths quietly, as they have done for years.

Practice Questions

Can't we all just learn to get along? Well, no — you have to learn all the stuff in this section first.
This covers some pretty big issues — prejudice, discrimination, tolerance... and it's your job to pick your
way through this muddle that we call twenty-first century society.

Here are some questions to test what you've learnt so far — remember to think about your spelling,
punctuation and grammar, especially on the long-answer questions.

1) What is:
   a) discrimination?
   b) prejudice?
   c) racism?
   d) sexism?
   e) an ethnic minority?
   f) community cohesion?
   g) religious freedom?
   h) religious pluralism?
   i) Islamophobia? (Islam)

To get the marks for these questions you just have to learn what the key terms mean — it's that simple.

2) a) Name two forms of discrimination.
   b) How might a Christian/Jew/Muslim respond to racism?
   c) How are the roles of women different from those of men in a traditional church/synagogue/mosque?
   d) What do Christians mean by 'missionary work'? (Christianity)

Make sure you've learnt all the basic facts for the religions you're studying and picking getting the marks for these questions will be easy.

3) For each of the following questions, give two reasons for your point of view.
   a) Do you think religions tend to create conflict in mixed communities?
   b) Do you think Christianity/Judaism/Islam is fair to women?
   c) Do you think different religions should have the right to try and convert people in the UK?
   d) Do you think that people with religious faith should ever consider a mixed marriage?

Remember, you're not getting marks here for having the 'right' opinion — only for having the reasons to back it up.

4) For these questions, you need to express yourself as clearly as possible — make sure your writing is correct, accurate and well organised.
   a) Explain how the British Government has sought to combat discrimination and improve community cohesion in recent decades.
   b) Explain Christian/Jewish/Muslim teachings on gender equality in religious matters.
   c) Explain how Christian/Jewish/Muslim teachings might encourage racial harmony.
   d) Explain the difficulties faced by immigrants to the UK and how one religious organisation works to help them.
   e) Explain Christian/Jewish/Muslim teachings on other faiths.

These are worth a fair few marks — so they're worth taking a little bit of time over. And don't forget your spelling, punctuation and grammar.

5) Read the following statements:
   a) "Truly religious people could never be racist."
   b) "The media tends to promote conflict more than cohesion in mixed ethnic communities."
   c) "Religion encourages discrimination against women."
   d) "A religion that teaches that it is the one true faith cannot be tolerant of other religions."
   Discuss each statement. You should include different, supported points of view and a personal viewpoint. You must refer to a religion in your answer.

These questions should remind you that you need to learn both sides of the big arguments — no matter how passionately you believe in your own opinion. You'll only get all the marks if you include your own opinion and other people's.

General & Christianity

Moral Guidance

A <u>moral code</u> is a list of what someone believes to be right and wrong. Different people use different <u>sources</u> of moral guidance. For most religious people, the first place to start is <u>sacred texts</u>.

People Look for Moral Guidance in Different Places

Religious people look in various places to find the 'truth' about what's <u>right</u>, and what <u>God wants</u>.

SACRED TEXTS Believers most commonly look to sacred texts (e.g. the Bible, the Qur'an or the Torah and Talmud) for moral guidance. Some people claim that the religious texts were written for a society with different values, and should be <u>interpreted</u> to suit the times. Others argue that they're the Word of God and so must be obeyed <u>to the letter</u>. (There's loads more about sacred texts on pages 74-76.)

THE EXAMPLE OF TEACHERS/PROPHETS Religious people may also look at the <u>lives</u> and <u>actions</u> of teachers like <u>Jesus</u> and <u>Muhammad</u> to guide them along the right path (more about that later).

CONSCIENCE Your conscience is that <u>little voice</u> in your head telling you what's right or wrong. Some believers argue that this is the <u>voice of God</u>, so we should listen to it very carefully and always trust what it's telling us. Others say that it's just the result of your <u>upbringing</u> — e.g. your parents' opinions, things you've read or heard, religious teachings... If this is true, then your conscience is <u>only</u> as <u>trustworthy</u> as the things it's <u>based</u> on. Some people believe that your conscience has to be <u>schooled</u> in the teachings of your faith, or it might lead you astray.

A little voice told Kevin it was wrong...

"My conscience is clear, but that does not make me innocent. It is the Lord who judges me." 1 Corinthians 4:4 NIV

Jesus Set an Example for Christians Today

Jesus Challenged Laws and Traditions in the Name of Love

1) Jesus's Jewish opponents often accused him of <u>breaking religious laws</u> — for example, he healed people on the Sabbath when Jews were not supposed to do any work.

2) Jesus thought the Jewish authorities had missed the <u>point</u> of God's law, and that the '<u>spirit</u>' of the law was more important than the '<u>letter</u>'. He also criticised the Pharisees for allowing <u>ritual</u> and <u>tradition</u> to become too important, e.g. in Mark 7:1-22 he challenges '<u>ritual washing</u>' and '<u>unclean</u>' things.

3) In fact, he taught that your <u>motivation</u> was even more important than your actions — being <u>angry</u> with someone could be as bad as <u>killing</u> them (Matthew 5:21-22).

4) Above <u>all else</u>, Jesus wanted his followers to <u>love</u>. When asked which was the most important commandment, he gave a pretty neat answer that summed up his beliefs...

➡ "Love the Lord your God with all your heart and with all your soul and with all your mind and with all your strength... love your neighbour as yourself." — Mark 12:30-31 NIV

Jesus Set an Example of Self-Sacrifice

1) Christians believe that in his willingness to suffer and die on their behalf, Jesus <u>set an example</u> which they themselves should be prepared to <u>follow</u>. In Mark 8:34 Jesus says, "If anyone would come after me, he must deny himself and take up his cross and follow me." (NIV)

2) In dying on the cross, Christians believe Jesus paid for <u>all</u> the sin of <u>mankind</u>. The Bible teaches that God is <u>merciful</u>, but he is also <u>just</u>, so our sins have to be paid for.

3) Christians believe that <u>everyone</u> who has died will be <u>judged</u>. Most Christians believe that only those that have followed Jesus's teachings, and have behaved <u>morally</u> (or have repented and sought <u>forgiveness</u> for any immorality) will enter <u>Heaven</u> as a result of his sacrifice.

Moral Guidance: Christianity

Christianity

The <u>main</u> source of moral guidance for most Christians is the <u>Bible</u> (see page 74).

The <u>Ten Commandments</u> are about Showing <u>Respect</u>

The most famous moral laws in the Bible are the <u>Decalogue</u> (i.e. the <u>Ten Commandments</u>):

From Exodus 20 NIV:
You shall have <u>no other gods before me</u>.
You shall not bow down before <u>idols</u>.
You shall not <u>misuse the name of the Lord</u>.
Observe the <u>Sabbath</u> and keep it holy.
Honour your <u>father and mother</u>.

You shall not <u>murder</u>.
You shall not commit <u>adultery</u>.
You shall not <u>steal</u>.
You shall not <u>give false testimony</u> (lie).
You shall not <u>covet</u> (want to possess) someone else's <u>things</u> or <u>wife/husband</u>.

Basically the Ten Commandments are about showing <u>respect</u> — to God, and to other people.

Churches have a <u>Powerful Influence</u> on their Followers

1) Some Christians look to religious <u>leaders</u> (e.g. the Pope or the Archbishop of Canterbury) and religious <u>traditions</u> to find moral truth.

2) Church leaders are <u>respected</u> and <u>trusted</u>, so the teachings of Churches (particularly the Roman Catholic Church) exert a strong <u>influence</u> on issues like medical ethics, war and justice.

> **The Magisterium** — this is the <u>teaching authority</u> of the Pope and bishops of the Roman Catholic Church.
> 1) To Roman Catholics, the authority of the <u>Church</u> rivals that of the Bible itself.
> 2) The Pope is believed to be <u>infallible</u> on questions of faith and morals (i.e. he <u>can't</u> make a mistake).
> 3) <u>Dogmas</u> are firm beliefs of the Catholic church — some come from the Bible, but some are Church <u>traditions</u> (e.g. the belief that the Virgin Mary was born without sin). Most of them are set out in a series of statements called the <u>Catechism</u>, to help its members understand what they should believe.

But religious leaders are <u>human</u>, and humans have <u>failings</u> — so can Christians trust that they speak for God? The same goes for the <u>traditions</u> of the Church. All religious institutions were founded by <u>humans</u>.

Situation Ethics <u>is all about Showing the</u> Greatest Love

1) Situation Ethics is a Christian principle based on the idea that the only <u>intrinsically good</u> thing is <u>Christian love</u> — that is an unselfish, absolute and unconditional love for all people.

2) The principle states that <u>all decisions</u> should be made to achieve the <u>greatest amount</u> of love. So any Biblical or Church law can be broken, if breaking it results in <u>more love</u>.

3) This is quite a <u>hard</u> thing to get your head around, because the sort of love we're talking about isn't <u>cuddly</u> or <u>sentimental</u>. These decisions are usually about causing the <u>least harm overall</u>.

4) Here are a few <u>real examples</u> of where Situation Ethics could come into play:

- A homeless man steals a loaf of bread to feed himself.
- A widow marries someone she doesn't love, but who will care for her children.
- A dictator is murdered to end a harsh regime.
- Tens of thousands of civilians die, to end a war that had killed millions (Hiroshima).

5) In each case, from the perspective of '<u>greatest love</u>', it could be argued that the <u>end</u> justifies the <u>means</u>.

The most loving thing isn't always the nicest...

In practice, most Christians base their moral judgements on a combination of lots of different sources. But respect and love are the <u>basic principles</u> of Christianity, and they're a good place to start when you're looking for answers to complex moral questions. Not that they give any <u>easy</u> answers, mind you...

Moral Guidance: Judaism and Islam

Observant Jews believe they should live in a way that's pleasing to God — this means obeying the 613 mitzvot.

Morality Matters in Judaism

The most famous mitzvot (commandments) are the Ten Commandments (see previous page) — but they're not the only ones. There are 613 mitzvot in total, which can be divided up in different ways...

> 248 of the mitzvot are positive, telling Jews what they should do.
> 365 are negative, telling them what they shouldn't be doing.

> Ritual mitzvot are about Jews' relationship with G-d.
> Moral (ethical) mitzvot are about Jews' dealings with other people.

> The first four of the Ten Commandments are ritual mitzvot, and the last six are moral mitzvot.
>
> The singular of mitzvot is mitzvah.

1) Observant Jews think it's vital to live by a moral code, and will generally regard a moral individual as someone who combines religious observance with concern for other people.

2) In deciding how to behave, Jews look first to the Torah, then to the Talmud (there's more about these on p.75), then to the wider body of traditional Jewish teaching. But an individual Jew can always ask someone who knows more about these things than they do.

> The word 'mitzvah' is sometimes translated as a 'good deed'.

3) Jews realise that no one can live by all 613 mitzvot all of the time. But they believe that God is merciful and will always forgive someone who is truly sorry for his sins. Yom Kippur (see page 86) reminds Jews of this every year.

4) For Reform Jews, the buck stops with the individual conscience. They're expected to use all the traditional sources of authority on moral behaviour, but in the end they must decide for themselves what's right.

5) Orthodox Jews tend to believe that the correct moral judgements are to be found by sticking as close as possible to traditional Jewish teaching — from the Torah, the Talmud or from other respected sources.

Muslims Follow the Qur'an and Muhammad's Example

1) According to the Qur'an (p.76), the prophets bring Allah's message so that people know how to behave.
2) Allah's mercy and compassion mean he can't just leave us to mess up our lives. So Allah gives messages to angels, who then pass on his words to prophets (or rasuls).
3) Allah sent many prophets as messengers, maybe because we seem to forget the plot quite quickly. But Muhammad was the last prophet (the 'seal of the prophets'), and Allah revealed the Qur'an to him.
4) As Allah's last prophet, Muslims regard Muhammad as a very moral, trustworthy man, that they should try to be like. Collections of his sayings (Hadiths) are a source of moral and spiritual guidance for many Muslims — particularly Sunni Muslims.
5) The Sunnah is a record of Muhammad's life and actions. It's seen as the model for a correct Muslim life.

Khalifah — Taking Responsibility in Allah's Name

1) Muslims believe that they have a duty to obey Allah.
2) Allah has laid down rules for living a moral life in the Qur'an (e.g. rules on dress, money and food), so any Muslim who doesn't obey those rules is disobeying Allah.
3) Muslims believe that they will pay for any disobedience on Judgement Day, when Allah will judge us on the basis of our actions.
4) Muslims also believe they have been appointed khalifah (vice-regents or trustees) of the Earth. This is the idea that while we're on Earth we should take responsibility for the world in Allah's name, and make it the sort of place he wants it to be. This sometimes means applying the teachings of the Qur'an to new situations, and relying on our conscience to tell us what's right and wrong.

613 — that's an awful lot of rules...

So sacred texts will tell you generally how you ought to behave, but you need to use your conscience too.

Human Rights

Human rights are the moral, legal and political rights that ought to apply to <u>every</u> human being on Earth. They give basic <u>freedoms</u>, e.g. freedom from violence, and <u>protection</u>, to people around the world.

The <u>United Nations</u> Defined <u>Human Rights</u> in 1948

1) In 1948, the United Nations (UN) published the <u>Universal Declaration of Human Rights</u>. The aim was to lay down <u>minimum</u> rights for every person, in every country in the world.

2) It states that all human beings are born <u>free</u> and <u>equal</u> in dignity and rights. It also contains '<u>articles</u>' that lay down specific rights, e.g. the right to <u>life</u>, freedom from <u>slavery</u>, freedom from <u>imprisonment</u> or <u>exile</u> without good reason, freedom of <u>opinion</u> and <u>expression</u>, the right to seek <u>work</u> and to receive an <u>education</u>.

3) The Universal Declaration of Human Rights is a statement of how things <u>ought</u> to be, but means nothing in a court of law. So in 1953, the Council of Europe brought into effect its European Convention on Human Rights. This is a <u>similar</u> list of rights that's <u>enforceable</u> by the European Court of Human Rights in Strasbourg.

4) These rights became part of the UK's <u>domestic</u> law in 1998, with the <u>Human Rights Act</u>.

The European Court of Human Rights. (I think.)

> This act <u>protects</u> the human rights of <u>UK Citizens</u> under <u>UK law</u>.
> Most of the rights in the Human Rights Act are <u>limited</u>. That means a person's rights can be restricted to <u>prevent a crime</u> or protect the <u>rights of others</u>.
> The rights of the <u>wider community</u> are put before the rights of one individual.

Most <u>Christians</u> Strongly Support <u>Human Rights</u>

Whatever their <u>denomination</u> (Roman Catholic, Anglican, Methodist, etc.) most Christians agree that:

1) <u>All</u> human beings deserve to be treated <u>fairly</u> and with <u>respect</u>, simply because they're human. This is based on a belief in <u>human dignity</u> — the idea that all human life is <u>valuable</u>, because people are created in the <u>image of God</u>.

> "So God created man in his own image, in the image of God he created him; male and female he created them." Genesis 1:27 NIV

> "You, my brothers, were called to be free. But do not use your freedom to indulge the sinful nature; rather, serve one another in love." Galatians 5:13 NIV

2) Everyone is <u>free</u> — to <u>think</u> and to <u>choose</u> how to behave (although Christians hope people will choose to live in love).

<u>Protestant ministers</u> were heavily involved in the drafting of the Universal Declaration of Human Rights.

The <u>Government</u> and <u>Charities</u> Protect People's Rights

1) The Government provides <u>all</u> UK citizens with free <u>healthcare</u>, free <u>education</u> up to the age of 18 and <u>support</u> to help find a home or job (the welfare system). Charities like <u>Barnardo's</u> and <u>Shelter</u> are also there to help people stay <u>alive</u> and <u>healthy</u> if they fall through the gaps in the system.

2) The Government also works to reduce <u>social injustice</u>. This is where groups of people are <u>unfairly disadvantaged</u> (i.e. discriminated against), or there's an <u>uneven</u> distribution of <u>wealth</u> in society.

3) But other rights, such as freedom of <u>opinion</u>, freedom of <u>expression</u> and freedom from <u>imprisonment</u>, <u>aren't</u> universal. The Government will <u>limit</u> these rights if they think it's for the good of the community, e.g. you're not allowed to say anything that might encourage <u>racial or religious hatred</u>, and terrorism suspects can be held for up to <u>14 days</u> without charge.

4) Human rights charities, like <u>Amnesty International</u> and <u>Liberty</u>, constantly <u>challenge</u> these decisions to limit people's rights. They argue that any limitations on freedom of speech are <u>dangerous</u>, since they can restrict debate on important issues.

You've gotta fight... for your right... to RE...

Some governments don't agree with the idea of human rights. They argue that the UN declaration was written by Western countries, reflecting Western values — so it isn't always appropriate for non-Western countries.

General

Democracy

Whether you're interested in politics or not, you can't get away from how <u>important</u> it is and how much it affects <u>everyone's</u> lives — yours included. In fact, it's <u>so</u> important that they've put it on the Religious Studies syllabus... well, obviously... the connection's quite clear... ahem...

Democracy *is 'Rule by the People'*

1) The UK is a <u>democratic society</u> — the <u>people</u> select <u>representatives</u> (e.g. MPs) to run the country.

2) We <u>elect</u> MPs to form a government every five years or so. If a government makes lots of unpopular decisions, they can be kicked out at the next general election. This helps keep their power in <u>check</u>.

3) But democracy is about <u>more</u> than voting — in a democratic society, people can speak out, or take part in <u>peaceful protest</u> if they want something changed.

Democratic Processes *are Important*

A <u>democratic process</u> is <u>any</u> way in which citizens can take part in the running of a country:

- <u>VOTING</u> — This is the most <u>obvious</u> way to affect government. UK citizens can be asked to vote for a <u>representative</u> (e.g. in local council, general or European elections) or on a particular issue in a <u>referendum</u>. A referendum is a "yes" or "no" vote on a question that's considered <u>too important</u> to be decided by representatives, e.g. the UK joining the Euro.

- <u>PROTESTING</u> for or against a government decision — This can take many forms, e.g. <u>writing</u> to your representative, signing a written <u>petition</u> or taking part in a <u>protest march</u>.

- Joining a <u>PRESSURE GROUP</u> — These organisations try to <u>influence</u> government decisions on particular issues, e.g. <u>Greenpeace</u> or the <u>Stop the War Coalition</u>.

- Joining a <u>POLITICAL PARTY</u> — Political parties are groups of (usually) <u>like-minded</u> people who try to get elected based on <u>policies</u>. There are three main parties in the UK — Labour, the Conservatives and the Liberal Democrats. Party members can stand as <u>candidates</u> for election, <u>campaign</u> on behalf of a candidate or just <u>donate money</u> to help pay for election campaigns.

It's <u>really important</u> to take part in these processes, because they give you a <u>say</u> in how the country's run. Decisions that affect <u>your lives</u> are being made <u>every day</u> by the people in power. Democratic processes let you make your <u>opinions</u> known, to help you influence those <u>decisions</u>.

Democracy can bring about real <u>social change</u> — changes in the structure, behaviour and attitudes of society (for better or for worse). And that affects everyone, so make sure you have a voice.

Electoral Processes *— Organising the Voting System*

1) In the UK, <u>every citizen over 18</u> has the right to vote (unless they're in prison).

2) Voting happens at a <u>polling station</u> — somewhere local with easy access, such as a village hall. Voting is secret so it's fair — you're not bullied into voting for one particular candidate.

3) There are two electoral <u>systems</u> used in the UK:

First-past-the-post: This is the system used in most UK elections. The country is divided into voting areas called <u>constituencies</u> (for general elections) and <u>wards</u> (for local elections). The candidate with the most votes in each constituency or ward is elected to represent that area.

Proportional representation: This is only used in European elections, and in elections to the Northern Irish, Scottish and Welsh assemblies. Each person votes for a <u>political party</u>. The number of representatives elected from that party is <u>proportional</u> to the total number of votes they got.

Democracy — power to the people...

Yeah, yeah, politics — how dull, yawn. But free and fair elections and the right to peaceful protest are vital parts of our society, and they should never be taken for granted. Once you get the vote — use it wisely.

Christian Teachings on Responsibility

Christians believe that they have a <u>responsibility</u> to care for other people.

The Golden Rule — a Moral Rule of Thumb

Christian moral teachings on <u>duty</u> and <u>responsibility</u> come down to this one basic rule:

> "So in everything, do to others what you would have them do to you, for this sums up the Law and the Prophets." Matthew 7:12 NIV

1) That means Christians should always think about <u>others</u>, not just themselves.
2) It's the same sort of vibe as "love your neighbour as yourself" (Leviticus 19:18 NIV). But Christians have a <u>responsibility</u> to put this love into <u>practice</u>, e.g. by offering support, shelter, food or clothing to someone in need.
3) Many Christians also believe that they have a duty to be <u>socially responsible</u>. Social responsibility is the idea that we should consider the <u>impact</u> our actions have on the rest of <u>society</u>, not just the impact they have on our <u>own lives</u> — it's basically about not being <u>selfish</u>.

Most Christian denominations remind people to "<u>Go out to love and serve the Lord</u>" at the end of a service.

The Sheep and the Goats is a Parable of Judgement Day

1) In the Gospel of Matthew (Matthew 25:31-46), Jesus tells a story about the <u>end of the world</u> and how everyone will be judged and separated into the <u>good</u> (the <u>sheep</u>) and the <u>bad</u> (the <u>goats</u>).

> "He will put the sheep on his right and the goats on his left. Then the King will say to those on his right, 'Come, you who are blessed by my Father... For I was <u>hungry</u> and you gave me something to eat, I was <u>thirsty</u> and you gave me something to drink, I was a <u>stranger</u> and you invited me in, I needed <u>clothes</u> and you clothed me, I was <u>sick</u> and you looked after me, I was in <u>prison</u> and you came to visit me.'" Matthew 25:33-36 NIV

2) But the people <u>won't remember</u> helping Jesus (and let's face it — it's not the sort of thing you'd forget)...

> "The King will reply, 'I tell you the truth, whatever you did for one of the <u>least of these brothers of mine</u>, you did for <u>me</u>.' Then he will say to those on his left, 'Depart from me, you who are cursed, into the eternal fire... ...whatever you did <u>not</u> do for one of the least of these, you did not do for me.'" Matthew 25:40-41 & 45 NIV

3) Jesus is saying that helping <u>any other person</u> is just as <u>good</u> as helping him. And that if you <u>don't</u> help a starving person, it's <u>as bad</u> as leaving Jesus hungry.

Genesis 4:1-10 NIV — "Am I my Brother's Keeper?"

1) Genesis 4:1-10 is the story of the brothers <u>Cain and Abel</u>.
2) Cain commits <u>three sins</u>: i) he's <u>jealous</u> of his brother Abel; ii) he acts on his jealousy by <u>killing</u> Abel; iii) then he <u>lies</u> to God about it.
3) When God asks Cain where Abel is, he replies: "I don't know... <u>Am I my brother's keeper?</u>" (NIV)
4) The story of Cain is referred to later, in the <u>New Testament</u>, where Cain represents those without love for others. This quote is from the <u>first letter of John</u>.
5) John is saying that it's not enough to go around <u>talking</u> about love and charity and <u>claiming</u> to be Christian. A true Christian <u>acts</u> to help people who need it.

> "...We should <u>love</u> one another. Do not be like Cain, who belonged to the evil one and murdered his brother... We know that we have passed from death to life, because we love our brothers... This is how we know what love is: Jesus Christ laid down his life for us. And we ought to lay down our lives for our brothers. If anyone has material possessions and sees his brother in need but has no pity on him, how can the love of God be in him? Dear children, <u>let us not love with words or tongue but with actions and in truth</u>." 1 John 3: 11-18 NIV

This should sort the sheep from the goats...

Lots of Bible quotes here. For "The Sheep and the Goats" and "Cain and Abel", you need to go away and read the full excerpts — there isn't room to put the whole lot on this page. The main point here is that, for Christians, it's not enough just to <u>feel sorry</u> for people — they have a <u>duty</u> to actively <u>help</u> people.

Environmental Issues

Humans have come up with <u>all sorts</u> of ways of damaging the environment...

Our <u>surroundings</u>, that we <u>depend on</u> for survival.

Global Warming could be Very Serious

1) <u>Gases</u> in the atmosphere, called '<u>greenhouse gases</u>', help keep the Earth <u>warm</u>.
2) Over the past century, the amount of greenhouse gas (e.g. carbon dioxide) in the atmosphere has <u>increased</u>, and measurements show that the Earth has <u>got hotter</u>. This effect is called <u>global warming</u>.
3) There's now a <u>consensus</u> among climate scientists that the increasing levels of greenhouse gases have <u>caused</u> most of the increase in temperature. There are still a <u>few</u> scientists who <u>don't</u> agree with the consensus view. They argue that the warming either <u>isn't significant</u>, or can be explained by <u>natural effects</u>.
4) Nobody knows for <u>sure</u> what'll happen if the Earth keeps getting hotter.
   But if climate scientists are right, there are plenty of reasons to be <u>worried</u> about global warming:

   - As the <u>sea</u> warms up it will <u>expand</u>, making sea levels rise, which could <u>flood</u> low-lying places (e.g. the Maldives, the Netherlands, etc.).
   - Higher temperatures make <u>ice melt</u>. Water that's currently 'trapped' on land (as ice) could run into the sea, causing sea levels to rise even more.
   - Weather patterns could be affected (climate change), leading to more <u>hurricanes</u>, <u>droughts</u> and <u>floods</u>.

5) Governments hope to reduce greenhouse gas emissions and <u>prevent</u> climate change. But it's almost impossible to set <u>worldwide</u> targets.
6) Some governments look to <u>short-term</u> benefits, rather than <u>long-term</u> care for the planet. They may say they're trying to do the best for their <u>people</u>, and that <u>people</u> should be our first priority.
7) Competition means that <u>businesses</u> often feel forced to put <u>profit</u> before the welfare of the planet — if they don't, they may not survive.
8) And <u>developed</u> countries are the worst, but not the only polluters. <u>Developing nations</u> often claim that they're only doing now what richer countries did in the past, and that it's <u>hypocritical</u> to tell them not to.

We Produce Lots of Different Pollutants

In Water <u>Sewage</u>, <u>agricultural chemicals</u> (e.g. fertilisers) and <u>toxic chemicals</u> from industry can pollute lakes, rivers and seas. These pollutants <u>harm</u> the plants and animals that live in and around the water, including humans.

On Land We use <u>toxic chemicals</u> for farming (e.g. pesticides and herbicides). We also bury <u>nuclear waste</u> underground, and we dump a lot of <u>household</u> and <u>industrial waste</u> in landfill sites. These toxic chemicals can <u>kill</u> plants and animals, and cause <u>cancer</u> in humans.

In the Air <u>Smoke</u> and <u>gases</u> from vehicles and industry can pollute the air, e.g. <u>sulfur dioxide</u> and <u>nitrogen oxides</u> can cause <u>acid rain</u>, fine dust called '<u>particulates</u>' can cause health problems in humans and <u>CFCs</u> damage the ozone layer.

And We're Running Out of Natural Resources

1) The Earth's population is <u>increasing</u> — it has more than <u>doubled</u> in the last 50 years. At the same time, our <u>standard of living</u> is improving — particularly in developing nations.
2) We use more <u>raw materials</u> and more <u>energy</u> for manufacturing processes every year. If we carry on as we are, these <u>natural resources</u> will eventually <u>run out</u>.
3) <u>Fertile land</u> for growing crops is also in danger of running out. Each year, overgrazing and irresponsible farming methods turn more fertile land into <u>desert</u>.

A <u>natural resource</u> is just anything found naturally that's useful to humans.

If you've ever fancied seeing the Maldives — do it soon...

You'd be forgiven for thinking you'd stumbled into a science book by mistake (aarrghhh!!!). In fact, you're probably wondering what on earth any of this has to do with Religious Studies. Well, you need to know about the issues before you can learn how religious people react to them. Fret not, all will be revealed...

Stewardship

There are Ways to Reduce Pollution

1) There are now <u>tight restrictions</u> on the types and amounts of chemicals that can be released into waterways.

2) Many <u>farms</u> are moving towards <u>organic</u> solutions, which are less damaging to land and water.

3) Most air pollutants can now be <u>removed</u> from waste gases before they reach the atmosphere.

4) Recycling cuts down on the amount of rubbish that goes to landfill, and helps to <u>conserve</u> natural resources — both by reducing the amount of <u>raw materials</u> (e.g. metal ores) used and the amount of <u>energy</u> needed.

<u>Conservation</u> means protecting and preserving things, particularly natural resources.

Religious Ideas about the Environment — 'Stewardship'

CHRISTIANITY

1) <u>Christians</u> of all denominations believe that the Earth is God's <u>creation</u>. They believe that God <u>gave</u> us the Earth, but expects us to <u>care</u> for it — this idea is called 'stewardship'. We have no right to <u>abuse</u> God's creation, but must act <u>responsibly</u>.

2) There's pressure on governments and companies to sell goods and services, even at the expense of the environment. Although it can be difficult to balance taking care of the <u>Earth</u> with providing for <u>humankind</u>, this is what Christians believe we must <u>try</u> to do.

"We have a responsibility to create a balanced policy between consumption and conservation." Pope John Paul II, 1988

3) Christianity teaches that everything is <u>interdependent</u> (i.e. everything depends on everything else), so driving species of animal or plant to <u>extinction</u>, or harming the <u>planet</u>, eventually ends up harming <u>us</u>.

4) Christian organisations such as <u>CAFOD</u>, <u>Christian Aid</u> and <u>Tearfund</u>® are concerned with putting this responsibility into practice. They put pressure on governments and industry to think more about how we are abusing the planet.

"You made him [humankind] a little lower than the heavenly beings, and crowned him with glory and honour. You made him ruler over the works of your hands; you put everything under his feet." Psalm 8:5-6 NIV

"The earth is the Lord's, and everything in it, the world and all who live in it; for he founded it upon the seas and established it upon the waters." Psalm 24:1-2 NIV

JUDAISM

1) Jews also believe in the concept of <u>stewardship</u>. Concern for the natural world is often seen as being at the <u>heart</u> of Jewish teaching.

2) God's creations should remain as he intended, and we have no right to abuse them. Everything is <u>interdependent</u>, with trees being particularly important. Since the creation of Israel in 1948, millions of trees have been planted to aid the <u>reclamation</u> of the desert and help rebuild the nation.

"The Lord God took the man and put him in the Garden of Eden, to work it and take care of it." Genesis 2:15 NIV

3) Jews also believe that as <u>custodians</u>, they're responsible for making the world <u>better</u> — this is called <u>Tikkun Olam</u> ('mending the world'). Tikkun Olam isn't <u>just</u> about the environment — it's a general <u>ideal</u> that includes helping the <u>poor</u>, and behaving <u>morally</u>.

ISLAM

1) <u>Muslim</u> teaching on environmental issues is very <u>similar</u> to that of Judaism.

2) At the Day of Judgement questions will be asked of us. We will be required to <u>answer</u> for any ill-treatment of the planet and its resources.

3) The Earth is seen as being a product of the love of Allah, so we should treat it with <u>love</u>.

Dr Abdullah Omar Nasseef stated at the 1996 World Wide Fund for Nature conference that, "His [Allah's] trustees are responsible for maintaining the unity of his creation, the integrity of the Earth, its flora and fauna, its wildlife and natural environment."

Look after the planet — or it's eternal damnation, my friend...

Once again, the ideas of all three of these religions are <u>very similar</u>. Which is good for me, since I don't have to <u>write</u> as much. And good for you, since you don't have to <u>remember</u> as much. Huzzah.

Animal Rights

Religions usually say be nice to other people. But what about squirrels...

Christianity says Animals come Below People

Animal rights issues are of interest to many Christians. For example...

i)   Animal experimentation
     (e.g. to develop new medicines),
ii) Factory farming,

iii) Hunting,
iv) Zoos and circuses,
v)   Vegetarianism.

> "...Rule over the fish of the sea and the birds of the air and over every living creature that moves on the ground." Genesis 1:28 NIV

1) One of the major issues for Christians is whether animals have souls or not.
   Many people believe that animals don't have souls, meaning that God created
   us as superior to them. Some people argue that animals are here for our use.

2) Christianity teaches that we should treat animals with kindness, but that they can be used to benefit
   mankind (as long as their suffering is considered). It's also thought that excessive money shouldn't be
   'wasted' on animals when human beings are suffering. So humans are very definitely 'on top'.

3) The Roman Catholic Church tolerates animal experimentation, but only if it brings benefit to mankind
   (e.g. if the experiments lead to the development of life-saving medicines). The Catechism of the
   Catholic Church (paragraph 2417) says that animal experimentation is allowable so long as it "remains
   within reasonable limits and contributes to caring for or saving human lives."

4) But some Christians think that it's always wrong to cause suffering to animals just to increase our scientific
   knowledge, particularly since medicines don't always have the same effect on humans as they do on animals.

5) Some Christians point out that as everything is interdependent, our treatment of animals reflects on us.
   Indeed, the Church of England teaches that the medical and technological use of animals should be
   monitored 'in the light of ethical principles'.

6) Certain denominations are generally opposed to any ill-treatment of animals. For example, the Society
   of Friends (Quakers) are particularly likely to frown on zoos, animal circuses, hunting and wearing fur.

7) Unlike some other religions, there are no specific food laws to be followed in Christianity.
   So vegetarianism (not eating meat) and veganism (not eating or using any animal products)
   are matters for individual Christians to decide about.

Judaism and Islam have Similar Views

> Deuteronomy 5:14 says that animals deserve a day off on the Sabbath, just like people.

JUDAISM

1) The Noahide Laws (see p.39) clearly forbid cruelty to animals. Animals are here to help us,
   and not to be abused. There are many stories in the Torah that demonstrate care for animals.

2) In Judaism, if meat is to be eaten, the animal must be slaughtered in a 'humane' fashion.
   This involves cutting the throat of the animal with a very sharp blade to bring about a quick death.

3) Experiments on animals may be tolerated if they result in a benefit for mankind,
   but only as a last resort. Cruel sports (e.g. bull fighting) are seen as an abuse of God's creatures.

ISLAM

> "...when you slaughter, slaughter in a good way. So every one of you should sharpen his knife, and let the slaughtered animal die comfortably." Prophet Muhammad (Sahih Muslim)

1) Khalifah is the idea that we're responsible for the Earth
   — khalifah means vice-regent, or trustee (see p.44).

2) Cruelty to animals is forbidden, as is their use simply for our pleasure.

3) Muslims believe in demonstrating mercy and compassion for all living
   creatures, and animals used for meat must be slaughtered humanely.

4) Muslims will generally only allow animal testing if it is done to produce
   genuine medical advances for humans. The animals should be treated
   humanely, and no unnecessary pain should be inflicted on them.

So it's OK to kill them as long as you eat them afterwards...

You thought I was just going to say 'all religions say be nice to furry things'. But this is where animal testing
comes in, which means benefits for people at the expense of animals. Which complicates things.

Humanity and Talents

If you're reading this, then you're almost definitely part of <u>humanity</u>.

Humanity — <u>Homo Sapiens</u> and What Makes Them <u>Special</u>

1) The term <u>humanity</u> can be used in different ways:

> It can simply mean all the <u>human beings</u> on the planet — all <u>nearly seven billion</u> of us.

> Or it can mean <u>human nature</u>. In particular, all the good ways of acting and feeling that most humans have in common, such as <u>feeling compassion</u>, and <u>doing altruistic (unselfish) deeds</u>.

2) <u>Humanity</u> is what <u>sets us apart</u> from the animals.

3) Christians, Jews and Muslims all believe that humans are special because they were <u>created by God in his image</u>, and that humans have <u>two parts</u>, a physical <u>body</u> and a <u>soul</u> (see p.9).

The Big Question — <u>Why Are We Here</u>?

This is a <u>huge question</u> — one that people have been debating for thousands of years.

RELIGIOUS VIEWS

1) Christians believe that we were created by God, <u>for him</u>. Quite simply, he <u>enjoyed creating us</u>, and he likes to <u>love</u> us and have a <u>relationship</u> with each of us.

2) Some verses of the Bible suggest that God created us to <u>look after</u> the rest of his creation (see p.49).

3) Many Christians, Jews and Muslims believe that what happens <u>after our deaths</u> (see p.9-12) depends on how we lived. So the purpose of us being here now might be some sort of <u>test</u> — of our morals or faith.

4) Muslims believe that Allah created humans to <u>serve and worship him</u>.

> "And I did not create... mankind except to worship Me." Qur'an 51:56

SCIENTIFIC VIEWS

1) A scientific view is that we're <u>not</u> here for any purpose. No one <u>designed</u> us — we're just the products of <u>evolution</u> (see p.3). Like everything else, we're just 'the way things turned out'.

2) It's argued that <u>'special' human characteristics</u>, e.g. altruism and compassion, are things that have evolved to help our genes <u>survive</u> and be passed on (e.g. if you help someone in need, they're more likely to help you in return).

3) So human beings are simply another type of animal — just a very <u>brainy</u> type.

Talents — <u>It's What We Do With Them That Counts</u>

1) Most religious people believe that <u>talents</u> are given to us <u>by God</u>, so it's our duty to use them to <u>serve God</u>.

2) For example, good <u>singers</u> could use their talent to worship God in a church choir, good <u>bakers</u> could make cakes to sell to raise money for religious projects, good <u>public speakers</u> could preach religious messages...

3) The <u>Parable of the Talents</u> (Matthew 25:14-30) explains the Christian attitude to talents:

> A man was going away, and entrusted some money to each of his three servants. To the first he gave <u>five talents</u>, to the second he gave <u>two talents</u>, and to the third he gave <u>one talent</u>.
>
> You twit.
>
> The first two servants used their talents wisely, and <u>doubled them</u>. When their master came home, he was pleased with them both.
>
> The third servant had simply <u>buried</u> his talent, for safe-keeping. The master was very <u>angry</u> with him, took the talent off him, and threw him out.

The 'talents' in this parable are actually <u>units of currency</u>. But it's been interpreted as talking about any of God's gifts, such as our inborn skills. In fact, this is thought to be where our word 'talent' comes from.

It doesn't matter <u>how many</u> talents you have, it's what you <u>do</u> with them that counts.

It's when you don't even <u>try</u> that God gets angry.

4) There are lots of <u>organisations</u> that'll help you use your talents to <u>care for planet</u>. They won't make you <u>plant trees</u> if you're the type that cries if you break a nail — they'll find something that your talents will <u>suit</u>.

> <u>Faiths4Change</u> is an organisation in the North West of England that helps people from <u>all faiths</u> to improve their local environments. For example, they run projects that help children to grow vegetables in their school grounds.

And the answer is — 42...

Religions teach that <u>God made us</u> to worship him and to care for the world. We do this best by using our <u>talents</u>.

Christianity, Judaism, Islam & General

Fertility Treatment

There are many similarities in the attitudes of Christians, Muslims and Jews towards fertility treatment. All believe that a child is a gift, and therefore all allow some methods of fertility treatment.

Infertility means an Inability to Conceive a Child

Nowadays, there are various kinds of fertility treatment that can be used to help.

Artificial Insemination by the Husband (AIH) — sperm from the husband is injected into the wife's womb.
Artificial Insemination by Donor (AID) — sperm from a sperm bank (i.e. an anonymous donor) is used.
In Vitro Fertilisation (IVF) — eggs are fertilised in a test tube and 1 or 2 are implanted in the mother's womb.
Egg Donation — where an egg from a different woman is used as part of IVF.
Surrogacy — where a different woman bears the child for the couple. This can involve IVF, using the couple's eggs and sperm, or artificially inseminating the surrogate with the husband's sperm.

Christianity sees Children as a Blessing from God

1) Most Christian Churches believe that it's okay for science to help childless couples to conceive — as long as the process doesn't involve anyone else.

2) So AIH is permissible. The couple can be blessed with a child, and the sanctity of marriage isn't interfered with. Many Roman Catholics still aren't keen though, since the sperm comes from an 'unnatural' sex act.

3) Some Christians believe that if AIH fails, a couple should adopt instead. Though many other Christians consider IVF an appropriate treatment if the wife's egg and husband's sperm are used.

4) AID and egg donation are much less favoured methods, since a 'third party' is involved.

5) The Roman Catholic Church is opposed to IVF in all forms, as it often creates 'spare' embryos that are thrown away. Many Catholics argue that life begins at fertilisation, and that even an embryo has rights.

Judaism allows most Methods

1) In Jewish teaching, there's an emphasis on having a family.

2) So it's left to individual married couples to decide whether or not to use scientific methods of conception.

> "Be fruitful and increase in number; fill the earth..."
> Genesis 1:28 NIV

3) A Jewish couple might seek advice on the matter from their rabbi (religious leader).

4) AIH is usually permitted, but not AID, as the use of donated sperm might be seen as a form of adultery.

5) IVF is generally approved of — as long as the egg and the sperm are from the married couple involved.

6) Egg donation is seen as okay, though the couple will often prefer the egg to come from a Jewish woman. This is because, according to Orthodox teachings, you're only a Jew if your mother is a Jew.

Muslims allow some Fertility Treatments

1) Some scientific methods are permissible, as long as all natural methods of conceiving have failed.

2) Artificial insemination and IVF are both okay, as long as the egg of the wife and the sperm of the husband are used. But AID is not acceptable as the sperm is donated. Many Muslims see this as a sin comparable with adultery, as the woman has become pregnant using the sperm of a man other than her husband.

3) There are also concerns about diseases that could be inherited from an anonymous sperm donor (although most sperm banks screen donors for serious genetic disorders).

4) Shi'ite Muslims sometimes allow egg donation, so long as the donor is a Muslim woman, and there's no other way for the couple to have a child.

Putting fertiliser on it won't help...

Not being able to have children can be heartbreaking for a couple. If the technology exists to have a child, but their religion is against using it, what should they do? Tricky...

Transplant Surgery

Christianity, Judaism, Islam & General

Transplant surgery is fairly commonplace nowadays. A lot of people carry a donor card (which says they'd like their organs to be donated to someone else after they die).

Transplant Surgery can *Save Lives*

1) Transplant surgery is the replacement of a faulty organ (or tissue) with a healthy substitute.
2) Transplants can be used to replace organs that have been damaged. They can also be used to cure disorders like leukaemia (with a bone marrow transplant) and diabetes (with a pancreas transplant).
3) Bone marrow (which we can replace) and some organs, e.g. kidneys (which we've got two of), can be donated from living donors. But most organs, e.g. heart, pancreas, eyes, etc. can only be transplanted shortly after the death of the donor.
4) There's a worldwide shortage of organs for transplantation, though, and in the UK up to 1000 people die waiting for an organ transplant each year.

Most *Christians* are *in Favour* of Organ Donation

Many Christian organisations encourage organ donation, but not all Christians feel the same way:

ARGUMENTS FOR ORGAN DONATION
- Christians have a duty to help and care for others.
- Donating your organs (before or after death) to save a life is an act of Christian love and charity.
- Most Christians believe God won't need bodies to be intact to resurrect them at Judgement Day, so there's no harm in donating organs after death.

ARGUMENTS AGAINST ORGAN DONATION
- The human body is sacred and so shouldn't be tampered with after death.
- As a living donor, you put your own life at risk.
- Family members can feel pressurised to allow a loved-one's organs to be donated.
- Transplants could encourage harvesting and sale of organs from developing countries.

The Jehovah's Witnesses used to ban their members from receiving transplants, because they saw it as cannibalism. Transplants are now allowed, so long as the organ is completely drained of blood.

Saving Life *is Very Important to Jews and Muslims*

JEWISH VIEWS
1) Jews believe that the human body is sacred, so it's usually forbidden to mutilate a body, e.g. remove organs.
2) It is also forbidden to benefit from a corpse.
3) But most rabbis are prepared to overrule these objections to save a life.
4) For Orthodox Jews, this usually means organ donation is allowed if there's a specific person who needs the organ right then. Reform Jews will also allow organs to be taken where there isn't a known recipient yet.
5) In all cases, it has to be very clear that the donor is actually dead, beyond resuscitation (i.e. brain dead), before the organs can be taken. The organs must be removed respectfully, with the minimum damage to the body.

MUSLIM VIEWS
1) Muslims have very similar views to Jews about the sanctity of the human body, and the respect that it should be shown. Some Muslims also believe that human organs belong to Allah, so we have no right to give them away.
2) Others argue that, according to Shari'ah (Islamic law), even some forbidden things are allowed when the alternative is death. They also argue that you should always choose the lesser of two evils.

> "...But whoever is forced [by necessity], neither desiring [it] nor transgressing [its limit], there is no sin upon him. Indeed, Allah is Forgiving and Merciful." Qur'an 2:173

This passage is about eating forbidden foods, but some Muslims think that the same principle would apply to transplants.

Save a life — carry a donor card...

A couple of techniques in the pipeline are xenotransplantation (using genetically modified animal organs) and growing organs in the lab. In the future, these methods could solve the organ shortage problem for good, and get rid of the need to take organs from other humans. But they have medical and ethical issues of their own...

General & Christianity

Genetic Engineering

Scientific advances mean we can now alter the genes of any living thing to try to get the features we want. But just because we can, that doesn't necessarily mean we should...

You Need to Know about Genetic Engineering and Cloning

There are ethical issues involved with lots of different biotechnologies.

The two you need to know about are:

> GENETIC ENGINEERING — manipulating genes, e.g. moving genes from one organism to another to make an organism with more useful features. Bacteria can be engineered to produce human insulin for people with diabetes, and crop plants can be made more nutritious or more resistant to disease.
>
> CLONING — producing offspring that are genetically identical to the parent.

1) These technologies have the potential to solve many problems (e.g. helping treat diseases or making food production more efficient).

2) Genetic engineering could be used to create an organism (e.g. a crop plant) with all the right characteristics, then that organism could be cloned to produce as many copies of it as we need.

3) For example, genetically modifying crop plants to increase the nutritional value and yield could mean we can produce more than enough food for everyone.

4) Animals can be engineered to produce medicines in their milk to treat diseases.

5) But not everyone thinks it's such a great idea...

There are Practical Issues with Biotechnology...

Some people disagree with genetic engineering and cloning for practical reasons:

1) Creating very successful crop plants is likely to affect the number and variety of weeds living in and around the crops. This could reduce biodiversity.

2) Not everyone is convinced that genetically modified crops or farm animals will be safe to eat.

3) There's a risk that transplanted genes could get out into the natural environment — e.g. herbicide resistance could be picked up by wild plants, creating 'superweeds'.

4) Some people feel that we don't understand genes well enough to know the full effects of tampering with them. Transplanting a gene could create unforeseen problems.

5) Cloning has the problem of reducing the gene pool. Lots of copies of the same organism mean fewer different genes in the population. That leaves the population more susceptible to disease.

6) Also, cloning animals is a difficult process — embryos formed by cloning often don't develop properly, and the adults produced tend to suffer health problems and die young.

I probably shouldn't be

"I have created the perfect beast!! Mwah ha ha ha..."

...as well as Purely Moral Ones

1) Some people think it's wrong to change the characteristics of an organism purely for human benefit.

2) Others worry that we won't stop at engineering plants and animals. That those who can afford it might decide which characteristics they want their children to have, creating a 'genetic underclass'.

3) Therapeutic cloning means creating an embryo that's a clone of an ill person, then taking stem cells from it to grow new organs. This destroys the embryo, which some Christians feel denies the sanctity of life.

4) Other Christians worry that any clone who lived to adulthood wouldn't have a soul.

5) Many Roman Catholics and other Christians are completely opposed to genetic engineering and cloning — they see them as 'playing God'. Christianity teaches that all creation belongs to God, so by creating new organisms ourselves, some Christians believe we're trying to step into God's shoes.

My mate played God in a play once — I was a sheep...

Cloning humans has the added ethical question of why someone's doing it. Some people might want to achieve immortality that way. But of course, the clone wouldn't be them — it would be like an identical twin.

Practice Questions

This is all really fundamental stuff. It's about what's <u>right</u> and what's <u>wrong</u>. It's about the way <u>all</u> human beings should expect to be treated — for no better reason than that they're human. Deep.

But what it's <u>also</u> about is getting you through your exam. And that's where these questions come in. If there are any you can't answer, go back and look at the relevant pages, then try again. For some questions there'll be extra marks for spelling, punctuation and grammar — so check your writing carefully.

1) What is:
   a) conscience?
   b) the Decalogue?
   c) Situation Ethics?
   d) a human right?
   e) human dignity?
   f) a pressure group?
   g) a natural resource?
   h) conservation?
   i) stewardship?
   j) Tikkun Olam? (Judaism)
   k) humanity?
   l) surrogacy?
   m) cloning?

Every question in your exam will start by asking you to define a key term. <u>Learn</u> the definitions.

2) a) Give two sources of moral guidance for a Christian/Jew/Muslim.
   b) State two environmental problems faced by the world.
   c) State two ways in which animals are used by humans.
   d) Describe the role of conscience in making moral decisions.

These questions just check that you know the basic facts about the religion(s) you're studying.

3) For each of the following questions, give <u>two</u> reasons for your point of view.
   a) Do you think you should trust your conscience?
   b) Do you think human rights are important?
   c) Do you think we should reduce our greenhouse gas emissions?
   d) Do you think it's important to conserve natural resources?
   e) Do you think humans are special?
   f) Do you agree with organ transplants?
   g) Do you think genetic engineering should be used to create better crops?

These questions aren't asking for a balanced argument, just two good reasons for <u>one</u> opinion.

4) For these questions, you need to express yourself as clearly as possible — make sure your writing is correct, accurate and well organised.
   a) Explain why Christians/Muslims try to follow the example of Jesus/Muhammad. (Christianity) (Islam)
   b) Explain why some Christians use Situation Ethics as a basis for making moral decisions.
   c) Explain how "The Sheep and the Goats" parable illustrates Christian teachings on responsibility. (Christianity)
   d) Explain why most Christians/Muslims/Jews believe they should take care of the planet.
   e) Explain, from <u>two</u> different religious traditions, beliefs about our relationship with animals.
   f) Explain Christian/Jewish/Muslim teachings on infertility treatment.
   g) Explain why some Christians/Jews/Muslims are in favour of organ donation and some are not.
   h) Explain why some Christians are in favour of the use of genetic engineering and some are not.

These questions can make a big difference to your grade. Have a look at p.118 for some advice on answering them.

5) Read the following statements:
   a) "Moral judgements should be based only on sacred texts."
   b) "It is important to take part in democratic processes."
   c) "Christians have a duty to care for other people."
   d) "Religious people should treat the planet with respect."
   e) "We were not put here for any purpose. Humans just evolved by chance."
   f) "People should use their talents to serve God."
   g) "People should use whatever fertility treatment they need to help them have children."
   h) "Religious people should carry a donor card."

For these discussion questions, you have to give a balanced argument, with good reasons to back up all your points. But don't forget to put your <u>own opinion</u> in somewhere.

Discuss each statement. You should include different, supported points of view and a personal viewpoint. You must refer to a religion in your answer.

Peace and War

World peace — a pretty tall order, but there are a lot of people <u>striving</u> for it...

The <u>United Nations (UN)</u> works for <u>World Peace</u>

1) The UN works to find <u>peaceful solutions</u> to disputes, to encourage <u>global cooperation</u> on law, security and economic development and to protect people's basic <u>human rights</u>. It has 193 members (the only fully recognised, independent state that <u>isn't</u> a member of the UN is Vatican City).

2) Its main function is to promote <u>world peace</u> — an end to <u>all wars</u>, all over the world.

3) If a country breaks the rules, the UN can impose <u>economic sanctions</u> (stop people trading with them) and send in <u>peacekeeping troops</u>.

> <u>UN Peacekeeping and Conflict Resolution</u>
> - A lot of the UN's work is in <u>conflict resolution</u> — ending wars in a way that leads to <u>lasting peace</u>.
> - The first step, before any negotiations, is a <u>ceasefire</u> (everyone stops fighting while they talk).
> - It's the job of <u>UN Peacekeepers</u> to make sure both sides <u>stick</u> to the ceasefire, to <u>protect</u> aid workers and civilians, and to help people <u>rebuild</u>. The UN currently has about <u>15</u> peacekeeping missions in progress, including those in Kosovo, Darfur and the Democratic Republic of the Congo.

There are <u>Religious</u> Peace Organisations Too

PAX CHRISTI — Roman Catholic

Pax Christi is an international, non-profit organisation working for <u>human rights</u>, <u>disarmament</u>, <u>reconciliation</u> (see page 60) and <u>peaceful</u> conflict resolution. For example, they are currently calling for the protection of civilians from fighting in the Democratic Republic of the Congo.

JEWISH PEACE FELLOWSHIP — Jewish

The JPF is a pacifist organisation, originally founded to help <u>conscientious objectors</u> (see page 57) in World War II. The organisation believes that military action <u>never</u> solves conflicts, and that <u>active non-violence</u> (e.g. negotiations, promoting social justice) is the only way to settle disputes.

MUSLIM PEACE FELLOWSHIP — Muslim

The Muslim Peace Fellowship is dedicated to making the '<u>beauty of Islam</u>' present in the world. It promotes peace <u>through</u> Islam, and works to bring about changes in society to make it fair and compassionate to <u>all</u> people.

Wars can have <u>Many Causes</u>

Most wars have causes that are a <u>combination</u> of loads of different factors:
- <u>RELIGION</u> — see '<u>Holy War</u>' on the next page.
- <u>DEFENCE</u> — e.g. a <u>pre-emptive strike</u> (see p.58).
- <u>TRIBALISM</u> — this tends to trigger wars where a <u>group</u> of people fight for their own <u>independent</u> state.
- <u>HONOUR</u> — wars fought to defend the <u>honour</u> and <u>dignity</u> of a country, or to <u>save face</u>.
- <u>ECONOMICS</u> — <u>acts of aggression</u> (attacking without provocation) are <u>condemned</u> by the UN, so purely economic wars (e.g. raids and invasions to gain territory) are few and far between. Economic factors still have an impact though — <u>poverty</u> and <u>economic imbalances</u> can make wars <u>more likely</u>.

> 1) Some wars have used <u>weapons of mass destruction</u> (WMDs).
> 2) <u>WMDs</u> are weapons that can destroy large areas of land and/or lots of people all at once, e.g. <u>chemical</u>, <u>biological</u> and <u>nuclear</u> weapons. They're <u>indiscriminate</u> — they harm soldiers and civilians alike.
> 3) Chemical and biological weapons are <u>banned</u> by international law — using them is considered a <u>war crime</u>.
> 4) Many organisations, including the Church of England, want countries to reduce the number of nuclear weapons they have. However, it recognises that <u>unilateral disarmament</u> (where just one country gives up its weapons) is a difficult thing for a government to do.

<u>*140 million people died in wars in the 20th century...*</u>

Hard to comprehend. It's like wiping out the populations of the UK, France and Australia. For the exam, it's worth learning about a <u>current</u> conflict, especially why it started, and what efforts are being made to end it.

War: Christianity

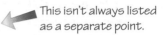

Although Christianity is generally 'anti-war', many denominations accept that a war can be '<u>just</u>' (i.e. justified). <u>Individuals</u> may not agree with this, however. They may be against war <u>under any circumstances</u>.

There are Five Conditions for Declaring a Just War

1) Christianity teaches that <u>peace</u> is the ultimate goal for all human beings.

2) Peace doesn't just mean a lack of war — it's more <u>positive</u> than that. Peace is a total freedom from distress and disturbance that Christians believe can be brought about by '<u>good will</u>' and <u>faith</u>.

3) Although Christians recognise that war goes against the teachings of Jesus, most Christian denominations accept that there can be such a thing as a '<u>just war</u>'. According to the current Catechism of the Catholic Church (see p.43), a just war should satisfy these <u>conditions</u>:

PROPER AUTHORITY   A war must be declared by a <u>proper authority</u>, e.g. an elected government, a president or a monarch.   *This isn't always listed as a separate point.*

JUST CAUSE   A war must be <u>defensive</u>, preventing damage that would be "lasting, grave and certain" (Catechism of the Catholic Church: para 2309). This doesn't always mean <u>self-defence</u> — defending a <u>friendly nation</u> or <u>innocent people</u> is also seen as 'just'. In some versions of 'just war' theory (but not in the Catechism) there's a separate condition of <u>right intention</u>. Even if there <u>is</u> a just cause, it mustn't be used as an <u>excuse</u> to achieve an unjust goal — e.g. to punish an enemy or gain land.

LAST RESORT   <u>All</u> other ways of resolving the conflict <u>must</u> have been tried first.

ACHIEVABLE AIM   A war must have a reasonable chance of <u>success</u>. Fighting a war you have <u>no chance</u> of winning is considered a <u>waste</u> of lives.

PROPORTIONALITY   Any harm caused by fighting the war mustn't be <u>as bad</u> as the harm it's trying to prevent. For example, using <u>weapons of mass destruction</u> (nuclear, biological and chemical weapons) would nearly always violate this condition.

As well as all that, there are conditions for <u>fighting</u> a war justly. These are:

<u>Discrimination</u>: war should <u>discriminate</u> between <u>combatants</u> and <u>civilians</u> — it's not seen as 'just' to deliberately target civilians.

<u>Proportionality</u>: the military <u>advantage</u> gained by an attack must <u>outweigh</u> any harm caused to civilians.

This is different from the 'proportionality' used to <u>justify</u> the war. This is about individual attacks.

A '<u>Holy War</u>' is one where people believe that God is 'on their side' — e.g. in the 11th, 12th and 13th centuries, Christians went on <u>crusades</u> to 'free' the Christian holy places in Palestine.

Pacifists are Opposed to All Violence

1) A <u>pacifist</u> is someone who has strongly held beliefs that war and physical violence are wrong <u>under any circumstances</u>. Pacifists believe that <u>all</u> disputes should be settled <u>peacefully</u>.

2) Some Christians believe that all <u>violence</u> goes against Jesus's teachings to love your enemy and 'turn the other cheek' (Matthew 5:38-48).

3) There were pacifists in Britain who refused to fight in the world wars. These '<u>conscientious objectors</u>' went to prison rather than go against their beliefs — they were <u>prisoners of conscience</u>. They suffered <u>humiliation</u> in prison, and after they'd been released.

"Put your sword back in its place... for all who draw the sword will die by the sword." Matthew 26:52 NIV

The <u>Religious Society of Friends</u> (the <u>Quakers</u>) is a Christian denomination that's opposed to war <u>under all circumstances</u>.

Just war, just cause — just learn it pal...

In the age of weapons of mass destruction, Pope Benedict XVI has questioned whether a 'just war' is possible any more. With these weapons, it's <u>impossible</u> to discriminate between fighters and civilians.

Judaism & Islam

War: Judaism and Islam

Despite the fact that there have been a number of wars between Muslims and Jews, there are many similarities in the way the two religions approach the subject of war.

The Jewish View — Obligatory and Optional Wars

1) The universal greeting amongst Jews is 'shalom' (peace) — this is the ideal. War is hated, but there's a belief that war is sometimes necessary to bring about peace.

2) War is divided into two categories — milchemet mitzvah (obligatory war) and milchemet reshut (optional war).

3) An obligatory war might be:
   i) a war fought in self-defence.
   ii) a pre-emptive strike in order to avoid being attacked — the Six-Day War in 1967 for example.
   iii) a war to help neighbouring countries — so that your own country is not invaded.
   iv) a war commanded by God.

4) An optional war should only take place when all attempts to secure peace have failed.

5) No war should be fought to colonise or take revenge. This is forbidden.

6) Pacifism is considered a good choice when it's the only way to survive, or when using violence would be pointless. This is why Jews generally don't respond violently to anti-Semitism.

7) But at other times, Jewish teaching demands the use of violence. If a Jew sees someone trying to murder someone else, they must do all they can to save the person's life — even if this means killing the murderer.

8) However, using the minimal necessary force is encouraged in Judaism.

> **The Six-Day War**
> In June 1967, Israel launched a series of attacks against its much larger Arab neighbours, destroying the Egyptian Air Force on the ground. After six days' fighting, Israel had won a war against Egypt, Jordan and Syria.

In the Holocaust (see p.6), the Jews were victims.

The Islamic View — 'Hate Your Enemy Mildly'

Muslims believe that war is sometimes necessary, although the concept of jihad is often misunderstood. These passages sum up Muslim teaching:

> "He who fights that Allah's Word should be superior, fights in Allah's Cause."
> Prophet Muhammad (Sahih Bukhari)
> "Hate your enemy mildly; he may be your friend one day." Ali ibn Abi Talib

Jihad — There are Two Kinds

1) There are two kinds of jihad (or 'striving')...

   i) the Greater Jihad (see p.70), which is when a Muslim makes a special effort to be a 'pure' Muslim, or fights against his or her own selfish desires.

   ii) a Lesser Jihad — war is an example of a lesser jihad, but it must be fought only as a last resort. These wars are often thought of as 'Holy Wars'.

2) Military jihad has very strict rules, and is similar to the Christian idea of a 'just war':
   i) It is justified if it will bring about freedom from tyranny, restore peace, combat oppression, or right injustice.
   ii) It must not be used to colonise, suppress or impose Islam on non-believers.
   iii) The sick, the elderly, women and children should not be harmed, the natural world must not be damaged, and indiscriminate killing should be avoided.
   iv) Jihad must be in the name of Allah, and according to his will. It must be declared by a religious leader, not any old politician.
   v) Dying in the service of Allah turns a Muslim into a martyr. True martyrs go straight to paradise as an instant reward — martyrs don't have to wait for the Day of Judgement.

3) There is no real concept of pacifism in Islam, although peace is always the goal of war.

Peace, love and harmony — seems that's what we all want...

Neither religion encourages unwavering pacifism — both religions teach that war is sometimes necessary.

Bullying and Family Conflict

Sadly, bullying happens a lot.

Bullying is Exploitation

1) Exploitation means taking advantage of a weaker person or group. And that's what bullying is all about.

2) A bully intimidates, frightens and controls other people that are weaker than them.

3) Acts of bullying can be: physical (e.g. hitting), social (e.g. enforced isolation) or emotional (e.g. verbal abuse, belittling someone or neglect). Bullies often pick on differences like race, religion or disability.

4) All schools have anti-bullying policies. These include:

- Listening to and supporting the victims of bullying.

- Dealing with those responsible for the bullying. This usually emphasises counselling and reform (see page 62) rather than punishment. Punishing a bully can just make them resentful, and not change their beliefs or behaviour at all. Many bullies are insecure, and pick on other people to make themselves feel strong.

- Encouraging everyone in the school to respect other people (to be considerate of other people and their feelings) and to appreciate their differences, to help prevent bullying.

All Religions are Against Bullying

1) Christians, Muslims and Jews believe that all people are created by God, so mistreating another person is mistreating God's creation.

2) In all three faiths, it's a sin to attack someone else without cause — physically or verbally. Judaism specifically forbids spreading nasty rumours about people.

3) All three religions teach that it's important to protect the weak and to free the oppressed.

4) People of all three faiths believe they will answer to God on Judgement Day for harming, or failing to protect, the innocent.

5) Christians also believe that they have a duty to actively care for others (see page 47).

6) St Paul summed up the Christian attitude to bullying in his letter to the Ephesians.

> "...loose the chains of injustice and untie the cords of the yoke... set the oppressed free and break every yoke..." Isaiah 58:6 NIV

> "Do not let any unwholesome talk come out of your mouths, but only what is helpful for building others up... Get rid of all bitterness, rage and anger, brawling and slander, along with every form of malice. Be kind and compassionate to one another, forgiving each other, just as in Christ God forgave you." Ephesians 4:29-32 NIV

Religion can Cause Conflict within Families

Religion can help to bring families together, but it can also cause conflict. Young people might not want to follow the traditions of their family, particularly in a multicultural, secular (non-religious) country like the UK. Some of the issues that can spark conflict are:

1) SEX/MARRIAGE — this could be sex before marriage, using contraception, homosexuality, marrying outside the faith, etc. Traditionally, Christianity, Judaism and Islam have had very strict teachings on this sort of thing. They say that sex should be between a man and a woman, inside marriage, and with the intention of having children. Mixed-faith marriages are rarely approved of, since children from them are unlikely to be raised as observant members of either faith.

2) RITUALS/WORSHIP — not keeping religious observances, e.g. community worship, food laws, Shabbat (for Jews). Religious observance is generally declining across the country, particularly amongst the young.

3) TRADITIONS — e.g. arranged marriages and the role of women in the family. Modern equal rights legislation means that women now have all the same opportunities as men. Some daughters of conservative families want a good education and a career — they don't want to settle down and have children.

Bullies like to feel strong by making you feel weak...

Being bullied can leave you feeling ashamed. But remember, it's never your choice and it's never your fault.

Christianity, Judaism & Islam

Forgiveness and Reconciliation

Love is all around us — it's everywhere I go. That's good news. But Jesus said forgiveness is also important.

In Christianity Love and Forgiveness go Together

1) Forgiveness means stopping being angry with someone who's done something wrong. Christianity teaches that forgiveness comes from love.

2) Christians believe that Jesus died on the cross to atone for the sins of all those who believed in him, so that God might forgive our sins.

3) Jesus taught that God is always ready to forgive us, but we must accept that forgiveness, and forgive others in turn.

> **Zacchaeus (Luke 19:1-10)**
> A story illustrating Jesus putting forgiveness into practice... Jesus goes as a guest to the home of the hated tax collector Zacchaeus, whose life is completely changed after he decides to repent.

> "For if you forgive men when they sin against you, your heavenly Father will also forgive you. But if you do not forgive men their sins, your Father will not forgive your sins." Matthew 6:14-15 NIV

4) Forgiveness is closely related to repentance. Christians believe that God's forgiveness can only come when we repent of our sins (i.e. say we are sorry, and turn our backs on them).

5) If we repent, and put our faith in God, God forgives us and we are reconciled with him. Christians believe the same sort of reconciliation (coming together and making peace) is needed between people.

Forgive Your Enemies

> "If someone strikes you on the right cheek, turn to him the other also." Matthew 5:39 NIV

1) Jesus taught that people shouldn't seek revenge — he said that they should 'turn the other cheek'.

2) But this doesn't mean being a submissive victim — just that a Christian's response should be based on the principles of love and forgiveness.

3) For example, most Christians believe that if someone commits a crime (anything from petty theft to starting a war), we shouldn't just do nothing. Punishment can be used to reform an offender and to deter others from offending (see page 62).

4) Some people think that it's wrong to keep forgiving people — that if they reoffend they shouldn't be forgiven again (although Jesus said we should forgive "not seven times, but seventy-seven times" — Matthew 18:22 NIV).

5) There are also some evils that are very hard to forgive. Should we forgive Adolf Hitler or Josef Stalin? Many Christians would say 'yes' — it is better to forgive, for the sake of the forgiver, and leave judgement in the hands of God.

Dick's 'turn the other cheek' philosophy seemed somehow inappropriate, given the circumstances.

> "Anyone who hates his brother is a murderer, and you know that no murderer has eternal life in him." 1 John 3:15 NIV

Jews and Muslims have Similar Ideas about Forgiveness

Both Jews and Muslims believe that, just as God is forgiving and merciful towards them, they should forgive other people. They should also seek forgiveness and make atonement for any wrongs they've committed. The Torah and the Qur'an both encourage people to be forgiving and to seek forgiveness.

Specifically Jewish Beliefs About Forgiveness

1) The Medieval rabbi Maimonides wrote in the Mishneh Torah: "It is forbidden to be obdurate... When asked by an offender for forgiveness, one should forgive with a sincere mind and a willing spirit."

2) Jews believe that you can only be forgiven by the one you've injured, so God can only forgive a sin against God, not another person. Each year, before Yom Kippur (the Day of Atonement), Jews seek forgiveness from anyone they feel they've hurt during the year.

3) At Yom Kippur, Jews seek God's forgiveness for their sins at the start of the Jewish Year.

Specifically Muslim Beliefs About Forgiveness

1) The Qur'an allows Muslims to seek retribution for injuries, but encourages them to forgive instead: "And the retribution for an evil act is an evil one like it, but whoever pardons and makes reconciliation — his reward is [due] from Allah..." Qur'an 42:40

2) Muslims believe that injuries should be forgiven if the offender is sorry and tries to make amends.

3) There are also many Hadith describing the Prophet Muhammad's acts of forgiveness, and other Muslims try to follow his example.

4) According to the Qur'an, the only sin Allah will not forgive is idolatry.

Learn it all — the examiner isn't as forgiving as God...

Members of all faiths believe that there can be no true reconciliation without forgiveness on both sides.

The Need for Law and Justice

Religious beliefs about justice centre around the idea of <u>responsibility</u> — both in terms of <u>answering</u> for the things you do wrong, and of taking responsibility for the care of others.

Law and Justice are Essential to Most Societies

1) Most nations believe that the <u>rule of law</u> is the best way of <u>protecting</u> people in society.
2) Without law there's the risk of <u>chaos</u>. With it, people know what they <u>can</u> and <u>cannot</u> do.
3) <u>Laws</u> are rules made by Parliament and <u>enforced</u> by the courts.
4) Christianity, Islam and Judaism all teach that <u>God</u> has commanded us to follow law. But some religious believers think that <u>religious law</u> is more important than the <u>laws of the land</u>.
5) Where religious law and state law <u>disagree</u> some believers think it's better to commit a <u>crime</u> if it means they avoid committing a <u>sin</u> (see below).
6) <u>Justice</u> is the idea of each person getting what they <u>deserve</u>, and maintaining what's <u>right</u>. In the context of the law, that means making sure the <u>guilty</u> are suitably punished, and that the <u>innocent</u> are protected.

Crime or Sin — State Law versus Religious Law

1) For <u>Christians</u>, there's a difference between a <u>sin</u> and a <u>crime</u>. A sin is when <u>religious</u> law is broken, i.e. when God's teaching is disobeyed. A crime is when the <u>state</u> laws are broken.
2) Christians believe that <u>justice</u> is very important, since we are all <u>equal</u> in the eyes of God. Christians have a <u>duty</u> to look after other people, and try to <u>guide</u> them to do what's right and <u>repent</u> of their sins.
3) But Jesus taught that <u>judgement</u> and <u>punishment</u> belong to God:

> "Therefore, it is necessary to submit to the authorities, not only because of possible punishment but also because of conscience." Romans 13:5 NIV

> "Do not judge, or you too will be judged. For in the same way you judge others, you will be judged, and with the measure you use, it will be measured to you." Matthew 7:1-2 NIV

Passing judgement on others is seen as <u>hypocrisy</u>.

Jewish Laws are Called Mitzvot

> "Appoint judges... and they shall judge the people fairly." Deuteronomy 16:18 NIV

1) <u>Judaism</u> teaches that Jews should obey the laws of the land that they live in, as well as following the 613 mitzvot (religious commandments) in the Torah (p.44).
2) <u>Rabbinical courts</u> (<u>Bet Din</u>) exist in many countries to sort out Jewish disputes.
3) Justice is a huge part of Judaism — both in terms of what's <u>due</u> to God, and to fellow Jews. It's sometimes called a '<u>legalistic</u>' religion.
4) The Torah is filled with details of <u>laws</u>, <u>rewards</u> and <u>punishments</u>. But, for many modern Jews, the punishments listed in the Torah are considered <u>too extreme</u>.

Muslims Try to Follow Shari'ah

1) <u>Muslims</u> have a clear and detailed religious law (<u>Shari'ah</u>), and this is often the <u>basis</u> for state law in Islamic countries. Saudi Arabia, for example, is run according to this religious law.
2) Muslims believe strongly in <u>justice</u>. The Qur'an teaches that Allah is <u>just</u> and merciful, and that Muslims should treat all people <u>fairly</u> and <u>equally</u>.
3) Muslims consider maintaining justice to be part of their role as '<u>khalifah</u>' — <u>vice-regents</u> of Allah's creation.

> <u>Muslims</u> believe that Allah sees all. He will know if you have committed a crime and you will be made to answer for it on the <u>Day of Judgement</u>. A truly repentant sinner, however, will be forgiven.

Don't get caught by the long arm of the Shari'ah...

For many religious people, justice doesn't have to come in this life, though. Christians, Muslims and Jews all believe that God is a fair judge, and that the guilty will be punished and the good rewarded in the afterlife.

Theories of Punishment

Punishment can be used to 'get back' at someone for committing a crime, or to prevent crime in the future.

The Courts Force Criminals to Take Responsibility

1) The courts pass judgement in cases of law — they decide whether or not someone is guilty of committing a crime, and what punishment they should face if they are guilty.

2) One goal of the court process is to make people take responsibility for their actions, and acknowledge that they owe a 'debt to society'.

3) This 'debt' can be paid in the form of many different punishments. The punishment given will depend on the severity of the crime, whether or not the criminal has broken the law before and whether or not they show repentance (are sorry for what they've done).

> REPENT!

Punishment can have Various Aims

There are several different theories of what punishment is for.

Deterrence: The idea that if a punishment is sufficiently bad in some way (e.g. expensive, embarrassing, restricting, painful) it will put people off committing the crime.
This is the idea behind telling people in advance what the punishment for a given crime is — so they understand the consequences.
Critics argue that people don't stop to think about punishment before they commit a crime, especially if they've taken drugs or alcohol, so deterrence doesn't work.

Protection: If a criminal is considered dangerous, this is the idea that their punishment should protect the rest of society, e.g. imprisonment. Not many people would disagree with this, but some would argue that you protect society best by reforming offenders.

Reform: The idea that punishment should aim to change criminals so that they won't reoffend once their punishment is over. This theory is based on the idea that nobody is inherently bad — and that with help, criminals can become useful members of society again. Programmes to help criminals reform include counselling sessions, visiting victims of similar crimes and working in the community.

> "Be merciful, just as your Father is merciful."
> Luke 6:36 NIV

Rehabilitation: This is the idea that punishment should prepare the criminal for a return to a normal, useful life. It's closely related to the idea of reform, but a bit more practical. Rehabilitation usually involves the offender improving their education or learning a trade, which helps improve their self-esteem as well as giving them better job prospects.
Some people think this sort of treatment is a waste of money. They argue that criminals will reoffend whatever you do to help them, and that the money would be better spent on hard-working, law-abiding people.

Retribution: Some people think of punishment as a way of taking revenge on a criminal, of making them 'pay' for what they've done.
Critics of this way of thinking argue that revenge doesn't put right the wrong — that it's better to look for a more constructive solution.

> "If anyone injures his neighbour... eye for eye, tooth for tooth. As he has injured the other, so he is to be injured."
> Leviticus 24:19-20 NIV

Crime and Punishment — wasn't that set in Russia...

Not for the first time, I'll say that this is a subject with lots of different shades of grey. Should we just lock people up and throw away the key... or is there something else we should be doing... Ho hum, well you should have known that you don't do RS for an easy life. No, sirree... that's why you have General Studies.

Capital Punishment

General

Capital punishment is <u>killing</u> someone for committing a crime.

There are Lots of Different Ways of Punishing People

1) Punishment can take a variety of forms, including: <u>community service</u>, a <u>fine</u>, <u>probation</u>, a <u>prison</u> sentence, <u>corporal punishment</u> (inflicting pain, e.g. flogging or beating) and <u>capital punishment</u> (death).

2) These different punishments have different <u>aims</u>. For example, <u>fines</u> are designed as <u>deterrents</u>, whereas a <u>prison sentence</u> is primarily to <u>protect society</u>, although most prisons have active reform programmes too.

3) Different countries and religions favour different types of punishment. In general, the punishments given in <u>scripture</u> are fines, corporal punishment or capital punishment.

Capital Punishment Isn't Used Much Nowadays

1) Capital punishment has been used <u>at some time</u> by <u>most</u> societies, for crimes ranging from <u>petty theft</u> to <u>mutiny</u>. Capital punishment has been <u>abolished</u> in many places, including most of Europe and South America. Elsewhere, it only tends to be used for <u>very serious</u> crimes like <u>murder</u>, <u>espionage</u> and <u>treason</u>.

2) There are <u>arguments</u> for and against capital punishment:

FOR CAPITAL PUNISHMENT

- The risk of death might act as a <u>better deterrent</u> to violent criminals than a prison sentence. (Some statistical studies <u>support</u> this view.)
- If you execute a murderer, it's <u>impossible</u> for them to <u>kill again</u>. Imprisoned murderers have been known to <u>order</u> killings from inside jail, or to <u>reoffend</u> when released on parole.

AGAINST CAPITAL PUNISHMENT

- A lot of murders are committed in the heat of the moment (they're not <u>premeditated</u>), so many murderers won't be thinking about the <u>consequences</u> (not an effective deterrent).
- Execution doesn't give the offender the chance to <u>reform</u>.
- There have been cases where someone has been proved <u>innocent after</u> having been executed.

3) There tend to be <u>more</u> murders in countries that <u>use</u> the death penalty than in those that don't. This is often used as an argument against capital punishment, but it's not clear whether one <u>causes</u> the other.

4) Many <u>Christians</u> are opposed to <u>capital punishment</u>, as it doesn't allow for <u>reform</u>, or show <u>mercy</u>. In Matthew 5:38-42, Jesus said that we should set aside 'an eye for an eye', in the name of love and forgiveness. However, some Christians in the United States believe that it's a good thing. They say it <u>protects</u> the innocent.

5) The position of the <u>Torah</u> is very clear on the issue. So <u>Judaism</u> will allow execution for murder if the case is absolutely <u>certain</u> (i.e. there are <u>reliable witnesses</u>). Most Jews are in favour of <u>mercy</u>, though.

"If anyone takes the life of a human being, he must be put to death."
Leviticus 24:17 NIV

The 'Howard League for Penal Reform' was set up by Christians to campaign for punishments that allow offenders to reform.

6) The Qur'an also clearly states the crimes that can be punished by death, but encourages the family of the victim to accept <u>compensation</u> instead.

"...prescribed for you is legal retribution for those murdered — the free for the free, the slave for the slave, and the female for the female. But whoever overlooks from his brother anything, then there should be... payment to him with good conduct. This is an alleviation from your Lord and a mercy..." Qur'an 2:178

For the death penalty to apply in Islam, there must be a <u>confession</u>, or <u>witnesses</u> to the crime.

Wait, wait, he's inno... (bzzzzzz) — oops...

Capital punishment is a very difficult issue for modern religious people. The Bible and Qur'an both say that death is an appropriate punishment for some crimes (have a read of Leviticus chapters 20 and 24 — they're quite scary). But we tend to be a bit more squeamish about killing people these days.

Drugs and Alcohol

Everyone has a <u>view</u> on drugs and drug abuse. But not all drugs are the <u>same</u>.

Most Drugs are Illegal or Age-Restricted

Illegal Drugs: Heroin, Cocaine, Hallucinogens, Cannabis, etc...

1) The <u>Misuse of Drugs Act</u> splits illegal drugs into three categories: Class A (e.g. heroin, cocaine, LSD), Class B (e.g. amphetamines (speed), cannabis) and Class C (e.g. valium, steroids). Some of these drugs can be <u>prescribed</u> by doctors as <u>medicines</u>.

2) The <u>penalties</u> for <u>possessing</u> and <u>supplying</u> Class A drugs are much harsher than those for Class B and Class C drugs. E.g., the police don't usually arrest people for possession of Class C drugs unless they suspect an '<u>intent to supply</u>'. Supplying Class A drugs carries a maximum penalty of <u>life imprisonment</u>.

3) These classifications are because some drugs are more <u>dangerous</u> than others. In general, Class A drugs are highly <u>addictive</u>, cause serious psychological or physical <u>damage</u> and are easy to <u>overdose</u> on (see 'Problems' below).

Age-Restricted Drugs: Alcohol and Tobacco

1) It's illegal to <u>sell tobacco or alcohol</u> to people under the age of 18.

2) That <u>doesn't</u> mean it's illegal for you to drink or smoke under 18 — you're just not allowed to buy them yourself. In theory, that means the decision to let you drink or smoke is made by <u>responsible adults</u>.

3) Campaigners argue that alcohol and tobacco are as <u>addictive</u> and <u>harmful</u> as many illegal drugs, so it's <u>inconsistent</u> for some to be legal and others not. Some people use this as an argument for the <u>criminalisation</u> of tobacco or <u>tighter</u> controls on alcohol. Others use it to argue that other '<u>social</u>' drugs that are currently illegal (e.g. cannabis) should be <u>legalised</u>.

Drugs can Cause Health and Social Problems

Most drugs are <u>addictive</u> — either <u>physically</u> or <u>psychologically</u>, or <u>both</u>. An addiction is a <u>compulsion</u> to keep doing something, even if you know it's harming you. A <u>physical addiction</u> is where your body chemistry has been changed by the drug, so you get <u>withdrawal symptoms</u> if you stop taking it. A <u>psychological addiction</u> is where you <u>crave</u> the feeling the drug gives you, and get anxious or depressed without it.

SOCIAL PROBLEMS

1) Most drugs affect people's <u>judgement</u>, which can make them more likely to take <u>risks</u>.
2) People on a 'high' sometimes feel <u>invincible</u>, and dangerous activities like <u>sharing needles</u> and <u>unprotected sex</u> are more likely to happen under the influence of drink or drugs.
3) Some addicts <u>stop caring</u> about other aspects of their life, and ignore their <u>responsibilities</u>.
4) At the <u>extreme</u>, some addicts turn to <u>crime</u> to help fund their habit.

HEALTH PROBLEMS

1) Different drugs cause different health problems.
2) <u>Alcohol</u>, if drunk in excess, can cause <u>liver disease</u>, <u>brain damage</u>, and <u>heart failure</u>. It also doesn't <u>mix</u> well with other drugs. Even a small dose of some drugs mixed with alcohol can <u>kill</u>.
3) Smoking <u>cannabis</u> can cause <u>lung diseases</u> in a similar way to smoking tobacco. Recent studies have also suggested that it might trigger <u>psychological disorders</u> in vulnerable people.
4) <u>Hallucinogens</u> like LSD and 'magic mushrooms' can cause permanent <u>psychological damage</u>.
5) The biggest health risks with <u>heroin</u> are <u>overdose</u>, <u>diseases transferred by needle sharing</u> (e.g. HIV) and <u>poisoning</u> by other things it's cut (mixed) with. The drug itself doesn't cause much damage in small doses, but <u>deaths</u> from overdose are <u>very common</u>.

Are you feeling lucky — well are you... punk...

One of the biggest dangers in buying drugs off the street is that you never actually know what's in them. A bag of white powder sold as cocaine could be mixed with anything from local anaesthetic to rat poison.

Drugs and Alcohol

General

I suppose we'd better have the <u>religious</u> take on all this now — this is Religious Studies, after all.

Christianity, Judaism and Islam all say <u>Drugs are Bad</u>

1) "Your body is a temple of the Holy Spirit..." — although this is a line from the New Testament (1 Corinthians 6:19 NIV), the message is <u>similar</u> for Christianity, Islam and Judaism. Drugs are seen as <u>bad</u>, as they damage the <u>mind</u>, abuse the <u>body</u> God has given to us, and can lead to <u>poverty</u> or even <u>death</u>.

2) <u>Hard</u> drugs (e.g. heroin and cocaine) and <u>hallucinogens</u> are completely <u>disapproved</u> of by Christianity, Judaism and Islam. They're seen as a way of escaping the <u>realities</u> of life, and existing instead in an artificial <u>fantasy</u> world.

3) They're also <u>illegal</u>, and all religions teach that you should obey the laws of the land you're living in (see page 61).

4) All three religions teach that the mind and the body are <u>gifts</u> from God, and that we do not have the right to <u>abuse</u> them. On a more practical level, drug taking is also seen as leading to <u>irresponsible</u> behaviour (e.g. neglecting your family or responsibilities), and possibly <u>criminal</u> activity.

5) Drugs taken to enhance performance in <u>sport</u> are also disapproved of, as they do not allow a person to properly display the skills they have been given. Again, they create a <u>false</u> world.

6) <u>Islam</u> is <u>against cannabis</u> for the same reasons it's against <u>alcohol</u> (see below). And Sheikh Ibn Taymiyyah (a famous scholar and Islamic teacher) had this to say on the subject: "Sinful people smoke hashish (i.e. cannabis)... it disturbs the mind and temperament... excites sexual desire."

The Religions have <u>Different</u> Views on <u>Alcohol</u>

1) Most Christian denominations <u>allow</u> the consumption of alcohol — it's used in Holy Communion after all. However, <u>drunkenness</u> is frowned on, and some denominations are more disapproving than others.

> <u>MODERATIONISTS</u> (e.g. Roman Catholics, Anglicans and Lutherans) argue that alcohol is a <u>gift</u> from God to be enjoyed in <u>moderation</u> (while being aware of its dangers). Jesus and the Apostles drank wine at the last supper, and wine has always been used in Holy Communion.
>
> <u>ABSTENTIONISTS</u> (e.g. Methodists and the Salvation Army) believe that alcohol can be a <u>bad influence</u>, and so it's <u>not wise</u> to drink it. In Proverbs 31:4-7, the Bible says that alcohol can make you forget your responsibilities. Abstentionists don't believe alcohol is inherently evil though.
>
> <u>PROHIBITIONISTS</u> (e.g. Seventh Day Adventists) believe that drinking alcohol is a <u>sin</u>. They argue that all references in the Bible to Jesus and the Apostles drinking wine referred to grape juice.

2) In Judaism, alcohol is <u>permitted</u>, although drinking to <u>excess</u> is disapproved of. The Midrash (a collection of moral stories) contains the line, "wine enters, sense goes out."

3) Alcohol is <u>forbidden</u> in Islam, as it causes people to lose control — it's seen as a weapon of Shaytan (the Devil). People are more likely to do <u>stupid</u> things when they're <u>drunk</u>, and stop thinking about other people or Allah. A Muslim should have a <u>clear mind</u> when praying, and so there can be no place for alcohol.

So I take it Jimi Hendrix wasn't a Muslim then...

This is a big social issue, so you'd expect every religion to have something to say on the matter. But as with all Religion and Society topics, come exam time, you'll need to give your <u>own opinions</u> too. That's what makes this subject interesting — sometimes there are no right or wrong answers, just different opinions.

Practice Questions

Weeeeeell... war, death, crime, bullying, families falling apart, addicts overdosing...
Now that you're all thoroughly depressed, here are some questions to cheer you up again!
You know the drill by now. Try all the questions. If there are any you can't answer, look back at the
section, and try the glossary if you're stuck for a definition. Then do those questions again until you're
happy with them. And don't forget to use top notch spelling, punctuation and grammar in your answers.

1) What is:
   a) the United Nations?
   b) aggression?
   c) pacifism?
   d) bullying?
   e) exploitation?

   f) reconciliation?
   g) a sin?
   h) justice?
   i) deterrence?
   j) reform?

   k) rehabilitation?
   l) capital punishment?
   m) addiction?

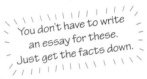
These are just simple definition questions,
so keep your answers short and sweet.

2) a) Describe how <u>one</u> religious organisation works for world peace.
   b) Describe Christian/Jewish/Muslim teachings about peace.
   c) Describe what Christians mean by a 'just war'. (Christianity)
   d) Describe what Jews mean by an 'obligatory war'. (Judaism)
   e) Describe what Muslims mean by a 'lesser jihad'. (Islam)
   f) Describe Christian/Jewish/Muslim teachings about bullying.
   g) State two possible aims of punishment.

You don't have to write
an essay for these.
Just get the facts down.

3) For each of the following questions, give <u>two</u> reasons for your point of view.
   a) Do you think war is always wrong?
   b) Do you think it's important to forgive?
   c) Do you think it's important to follow law?
   d) Do you agree with capital punishment?
   e) Do you think drugs should be illegal?
   f) Do you think drinking alcohol is always bad?

You don't get any marks for just <u>ranting</u>.
Make sure you give two clear reasons
to back up your opinion.

4) For these questions, you need to express yourself as clearly as possible —
   make sure your writing is correct, accurate and well organised.
   a) Explain Christian/Jewish/Muslim teachings about war.
   b) Explain Christian/Jewish/Muslim teachings about pacifism.
   c) Explain why Christians/Jews/Muslims believe that justice is important.
   d) Explain why some Christians/Jews/Muslims support the use of
       capital punishment while others do not.
   e) Explain Christian/Jewish/Muslim teachings on drugs.
   f) Explain why some Christians allow the drinking of alcohol and others do not. (Christianity)

If you're struggling with the
<u>structure</u> of your answer,
have a look at page 118.

5) Read the following statements:
   a) "Religion is the best way to achieve world peace."
   b) "Religious people should never go to war."
   c) "Bullies should always be punished."
   d) "Religious people should always forgive."
   e) "Religious people should always obey the law."
   f) "The aim of punishment should always be rehabilitation."
   g) "Religious people should oppose capital punishment."
   h) "It doesn't matter if religious people drink alcohol."

   Discuss each statement. You should include different, supported points
   of view and a personal viewpoint. You must refer to a religion in your answer.

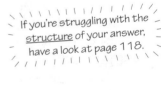
It's easy to get carried away with
your own point of view on these
questions. Make sure you write a
<u>properly balanced</u> argument.

The Nature of God and Religion

General

The question of <u>what God is like</u> has occupied religious thinkers for <u>hundreds of years</u>. There are three main issues:

1) Is God a 'Person' or a 'Force'?

1) The term '<u>personal god</u>' refers to God as a '<u>person</u>' — albeit an almighty and <u>divine person</u>. If this were the case, <u>prayer</u> would become part of our individual relationship — a '<u>conversation</u>' with God.

2) The problem with this is that God is meant to be <u>omnipresent</u> (everywhere at once) — which poses the question of <u>how</u> a <u>personal god</u> can be <u>everywhere at once</u>.

3) The term '<u>impersonal god</u>' refers to God as a <u>concept</u>, a <u>force</u> or an <u>idea</u> of <u>goodness and light</u>.

4) The <u>obvious problem</u> here is how you can have a <u>relationship</u> with a <u>force</u> or an <u>idea</u>.

2) Is God Within or Outside the Universe?

1) An '<u>immanent</u>' God is a God who is <u>in the world</u> with us — a God who has taken an <u>active role</u> in the progress of <u>human history</u> and <u>continues</u> to do so.

2) The <u>problem</u> here is that an immanent God may appear <u>small</u> and <u>fallible</u>.

3) On the other hand, a '<u>transcendent</u>' God is <u>outside the world</u> and <u>doesn't directly act</u> in human history.

4) This view of God makes him <u>remote</u> and <u>separate</u> from our experience on Earth. However, <u>Christians</u> who see God as transcendent might argue that it is <u>they</u> who <u>do the work</u> of God and that he is working <u>through them</u>.

5) Unfortunately, this definition is a bit <u>too abstract</u> for a lot of people to understand.

6) Religious believers (and Christians in particular) often try <u>not</u> to deal with <u>extremes</u> of any of these ideas, preferring instead to draw on <u>different aspects</u> for different occasions. Many would argue that God needs to be a <u>blend</u> of all of the above.

3) Is There Just One God or are There Many Gods?

1) <u>Monotheism</u> is the idea of <u>one God</u>. This exists in <u>Christianity</u>, <u>Judaism</u> and <u>Islam</u>.

2) <u>Polytheism</u> is the belief in <u>more than one</u> god, e.g. in Classical Greek and Roman civilisations, and some forms of Hinduism.

> Although Christianity is monotheistic, there is a belief that God is actually <u>three in one</u> (the <u>Trinity</u> — see next page and p.90-91).

Religion is Important to All Societies

1) Although religion might only seem relevant to people who practise it, it is a fundamental part of all societies. Even <u>secular societies</u>, where religion and government are kept <u>completely separate</u>.

2) People in a secular society are <u>free</u> to follow whichever religious faith they choose, just as they're free to have nothing to do with religion. But the Government <u>won't</u> take religious views into account when setting laws, or fund schools that only take children of a particular faith, etc. Some people believe that this system is <u>fairer</u>, as it gives no advantage to followers of any particular religious faith.

3) But even in a largely secular society, religion can play an important role. Religions continue to provide community <u>traditions</u>, e.g., festivals like <u>Easter</u>, <u>Christmas</u> and <u>Hanukkah</u>.

4) Religion also provides believers with an <u>authority</u> on how they should behave. It can make people more likely to live <u>moral</u> lives and to obey the <u>law</u> — resulting in a more <u>peaceful</u> society.

5) It can bring people <u>together</u> and give them a sense of <u>community</u> — and even non-religious people can enjoy the <u>facilities</u>, <u>events</u> and <u>activities</u> offered by religious groups.

One for sorrow, two for joy... three for a girl... four for a boy...

This is seriously <u>tricky</u> stuff — and not just for Religious Studies. These questions have been worrying <u>loads</u> of people for <u>ages</u>. But, tricky or not, you have to understand all these arguments to do well in that GCSE.

Christianity & Judaism

Beliefs About God

There are many different ideas about what a god is. But Christian, Jewish and Muslim beliefs are quite similar.

Christianity and Judaism say Similar Things about God...

1) As Christianity grew directly from Judaism, the basic concept of God is something the two faiths share.

2) The Judeo-Christian God is usually seen as male (referred to as He or Father) although nowadays many religious believers would argue that this is simply because when these religions were founded society was male-dominated, and that God is actually neither male nor female.

3) Both faiths share the ideas that God is omnipotent (all-powerful), omnipresent (everywhere) and omniscient (all-knowing), that God is divine, supreme, totally good and totally perfect, and that God has given us free will (see p.4).

...but There are Some Big Differences

1) The biggest difference is the Christian belief in the Trinity. Jews never believed Christ was the Son of God.

2) Another key difference between Jewish and Christian teaching is that Jews are forbidden to draw or make images of God.

However, many Jews and Christians believe that our lives are predestined — we control individual actions, but not the ultimate outcome of our lives.

"Hear O Israel: the Lord our God, the Lord is One"

Jews don't all believe exactly the same things. They have many different opinions on many important issues. Most believe these 11 things about God. They believe God is...

...ONE — Jews believe there's only one God. The heading above comes from Deuteronomy 6:4 NIV — it's the opening of a very important Jewish prayer called the Shema.

...A PERSON — i.e. he's not just a 'force', but neither is he an old man with a beard. Human beings were made 'in his image' (but this needn't mean he looks like us).

...THE CREATOR — i.e. he made the Universe and everything in it. Jews don't invent clever arguments for God's existence — they say that creation makes it obvious that he's there.

...THE SUSTAINER — i.e. he didn't just create the Universe and then sit back — his energy keeps it going.

...HOLY — 'Holy' means 'set apart' or 'completely pure'. God (or YHWH in Hebrew) is so holy that some Jews won't even write or say the word 'God' — they write G-d and say Hashem ('the Name') or Adonai ('the Lord', or 'the Master').

...OMNIPOTENT — i.e. all-powerful — although he still allows each person free will.

...OMNISCIENT — i.e. he knows everything, even your darkest secrets and your wildest dreams.

...OMNIPRESENT — i.e. present throughout the whole Universe.

...THE LAWGIVER — Jewish tradition says 'God wrote himself into the Torah'.

...THE TRUE JUDGE — Jews believe they shall all face him one day, for death is not 'the end'.

...THE REDEEMER — Jews believe God is merciful. He will save his people from sin and suffering.

The Trinity — Father, Son and Holy Spirit

1) The Christian idea of the Trinity is that God exists in three 'persons' — the Father, the Son and the Holy Spirit. This is covered in detail on pages 90-91.

2) God the Father might be described as the transcendent part of God, the Son as the immanent and personal part, and the Holy Spirit as the immanent yet impersonal part (see p.67).

Jews and Christians — separated at (the) birth...

I know, it's a jam-packed page, but it's all important stuff. I won't waste your time with stuff you don't need to know. You should be able to close the book and write down a list of similarities and a list of differences.

Beliefs About Allah

Islam

Islam <u>shares</u> a lot of history and beliefs with Judaism and Christianity.
But Muslims believe Islam is the "<u>final word of god</u>".

The Muslim name for God is Allah

1) For Muslims, God is called <u>Allah</u> — and the word '<u>Islam</u>' can be translated as meaning '<u>submission</u>' or '<u>surrender</u>' to Allah.

2) According to Islamic teaching, <u>Allah</u> is the <u>creator</u> of everything.

3) He is referred to by <u>ninety-nine names</u> in the Qur'an — these names tell you what <u>Muslims believe</u> about Allah and his power. They include:
<u>Ar-Khaliq</u> — The <u>Creator</u>, <u>Ar-Rahman</u> — The <u>Merciful</u>, <u>Ar-Aziz</u> — The <u>Almighty</u>.
He is also called The <u>Provider</u>, The <u>Just</u>, The <u>Maintainer</u>, The <u>Hearer</u> and The <u>Real Truth</u>.

'Allah' written in Arabic

"He is Allah, the One, Allah is Eternal and Absolute"

1) This passage is taken from Surah 112 and describes the <u>basic principle</u> that <u>Allah is one</u>.
Islam is a <u>monotheistic</u> religion (see page 67) and this belief in the oneness or the <u>unity of Allah</u> (called <u>Tawhid</u>) is a <u>fundamental</u> principle of Islam.

2) The ninety-nine names sum up much of the nature of Allah. He is <u>loving</u> and <u>compassionate</u>, he is the <u>creator</u> and <u>judge</u> of all humans, and knows <u>everything</u> they do.

3) Muslims believe Allah <u>cannot</u> be thought of in human terms — he is the <u>Supreme Being</u> and has <u>no equal</u>.

4) To Muslims, Allah is <u>both immanent</u> and <u>transcendent</u> (see page 67).
He is <u>transcendent</u> in that he is the <u>power behind the Universe</u> and is <u>outside</u>, above or beyond both <u>his creation</u> and <u>time</u> itself. His <u>immanence</u> is demonstrated in this passage:
"And We have already created man and <u>know</u> what his soul whispers to him, and We are closer to him than [his] <u>jugular vein</u>." Qur'an 50:16
(In this passage 'We' refers to Allah and 'him' or 'his' refers to humankind.)

5) Human lives are <u>predestined</u> by Allah — but humans do have <u>free will</u> (see page 5).

There are Five Main Ways to Know Allah

1) Muslims believe that Allah has <u>intervened</u> in <u>human history</u> and that this is one way of <u>knowing</u> him and <u>his power</u>. His message was delivered by the <u>prophets</u>, of whom twenty-five are mentioned in the Qur'an. These include <u>Musa</u> (<u>Moses</u>) and '<u>Isa</u> (<u>Jesus</u>).
The last was the Prophet <u>Muhammad</u>, who <u>brought Allah's message</u> to the people.

2) Allah has also performed <u>miracles</u> (see p.72).

3) The <u>Five Pillars of Islam</u> also provide opportunities to know and be close to Allah.
These are: <u>Shahadah</u> (a statement of <u>belief</u>)
<u>Salah</u> (<u>prayer</u>) — see p.84
<u>Zakah</u> (<u>charitable</u> duty)
<u>Sawm</u> (<u>fasting</u>) — see p.86
<u>Hajj</u> (<u>pilgrimage</u>)

Muslim prayer ritual — see page 84.

4) Muslims believe that the <u>Qur'an</u> is the <u>word of Allah</u> and allows humans to know him.
Many Muslims learn it off by heart, and all try to live according to the guidelines found within it.

5) Muslims believe Allah is good and kind. However, there is a belief in a <u>devil</u> (called <u>Iblis</u> or <u>Shaytan</u>) who was <u>cast out by Allah</u> and tries to <u>lead people away</u> from him. <u>Some</u> Muslims would argue that Allah <u>allows Shaytan</u> to use this power to <u>test and tempt</u> us — we have the <u>free will to resist</u> (see p5).

Immanent AND transcendent? — I Qur'an't get my head round it...

There's some <u>mind-boggling stuff</u> in these last few pages about what (one or more) god(s) is/are. But at the end of the day, it seems Christians, Jews and Muslims <u>all agree</u> on the <u>fundamentals</u> — that God/Allah is <u>divine</u>, <u>supreme</u>, <u>all-powerful</u> and <u>all-knowing</u>, that our <u>lives are predestined</u> by him/her/it and that we have <u>free will</u>.

Vocation

Christianity, Judaism, Islam & General

A <u>vocation</u> is something God calls someone to do — it's their '<u>calling in life</u>'. It can be a job, but isn't always. God will have created them with special gifts and <u>talents</u> for their mission.

You can Respond to God Through a Vocation

1) You'll probably know if something's your vocation — you'll feel <u>drawn to it</u>, then when you're doing it, you'll feel '<u>at home</u>'.   But vocations are meant to be <u>challenging</u> rather than the easy option. Christians believe you need <u>God's help</u> to do them.

2) There are <u>lots</u> of different vocations a Christian might be called to. Here are a few examples:

- joining a religious order as a <u>monk</u> or a <u>nun</u>, to live a life of prayer and contemplation.
- a life of serving the Church, perhaps by training to be a <u>priest</u>.
- <u>missionary work</u> — trying to convert people to Christianity, maybe in a remote part of the world.
- a non-religious job such as a <u>doctor</u>, <u>teacher</u> or <u>social worker</u>, in order to help people.
- <u>volunteering</u> in the <u>community</u> — e.g. running a youth group.
- <u>charity work</u> — either religion-based (e.g. Christian Aid), or secular (e.g. Greenpeace).
- <u>marriage</u> and <u>raising children</u>.

3) <u>Non-religious people</u> often feel they have a 'vocation' too — they just don't believe that God called them to it.

4) You have to actually <u>choose</u> to follow your vocation — it doesn't just <u>happen</u>.

The Covenant Gave Jewish People Their Chief Vocation

1) The <u>covenant</u> is the <u>contract</u> that God has made with the Jewish people. It commits them to <u>serving God</u> and to living as the <u>Torah</u> says they should. Many Jewish people consider this their <u>vocation</u> in life.

2) The Hebrew phrase '<u>Tikkun Olam</u>' means '<u>mending the world</u>' (see p.49). Jews are all expected to join in this task, although they can't complete it alone.

3) Jewish people may also share many of the same vocations as Christians, e.g. <u>marriage</u> and having <u>children</u> is considered very important in Judaism.

> "Be fruitful and increase in number; fill the earth..." Genesis 1:28 NIV

4) Jewish people can train for religious jobs — for example, as a <u>rabbi</u> or as a <u>chazan</u>. (Although in Orthodox Judaism, only men are allowed in these roles.)

5) Jewish people don't believe that they need to convert people to Judaism — so missionary work <u>wouldn't</u> be a Jewish vocation.

Louise hoped that the 'lemon look' would catch on.

The Greater Jihad is the Vocation of a Muslim

1) <u>The Greater</u> (or <u>Internal</u>) <u>Jihad</u> is the personal <u>struggle</u> of a Muslim to live their faith as best they can — it involves fighting their own desires in order to please Allah.

2) This means following all the rules making up the <u>Five Pillars</u>, being totally devoted to Allah, living as he commanded, and doing everything they can to <u>help other people</u>.

3) For a Muslim, the Greater Jihad may involve anything from learning the Qur'an by heart, to <u>volunteering</u> in the community, or perhaps becoming an <u>imam</u> (an imam is often a community leader as well as a spiritual leader).

4) Pleasing Allah is really important to a Muslim — if someone pleases Allah enough, they'll be sent to <u>Paradise</u> on Judgement Day.

> The Qur'an doesn't cover every detail of how Muslims should live. Extra day-to-day guidance is found in the law code called the <u>Shari'ah</u> (see p.61). This is based on Islamic tradition, as well as religious texts, and covers modern issues, such as drugs.

Can you have a vocation to eat choccy biscuits?...

Don't get <u>vocations</u> muddled up with <u>vacations</u>. God is probably not going to be calling you to go and lounge on a beach in Benidorm for two weeks. Learn all this stuff about how people respond to God.

Belief and Revelations

General

Upbringing, philosophy, comfort and personal religious experiences can all be reasons for belief.

Different People Believe for Different Reasons

1) People brought up by religious parents or in a religious community are more likely to believe in a god (see p.1).

2) The presence of religion in the world gives some people faith, based on the good work that religion does — whether it be for individuals, communities or those who are experiencing suffering.

3) Some people are drawn to the purpose, structure and comfort it provides — or simply to the desire to have something to believe in.

4) Some people are convinced that there's a god by philosophical 'design' or 'causation' arguments (see p.2).

5) Some people's faith is strengthened by the feelings they experience during worship and the way God reveals himself to them (see below).

6) The search for meaning can also spark someone's interest in religion — people want to find answers or find out why life is as it is, and they might believe religion can help.

7) This desire to find out why we are here or why bad things happen in the world might also explain why some people move from one religion to another.

Revelation — God Reveals His Presence

There are loads of ways people claim to experience God. He can reveal his presence in different ways...

Revelation of Sacred Texts

Christians, Muslims and Jews believe that the truth about the world, and their rules for good behaviour were revealed to them by God. These revelations were written down in the scriptures — the Bible (p.74), the Torah (p.75) and the Qur'an (p.76).

Revelation through Mystical and Religious Experiences

The revelation of the scriptures was something that happened a long time ago, but religious people believe that God still reveals himself today, through religious experiences.

1) PRAYER (p.83-84) — This is an attempt to contact God directly. It usually involves words and can be thought of as a conversation with God. A person might feel the presence of God in an answered prayer, e.g. if an ill person they pray for is cured, or if they are filled with a sense of inner peace or wonder.

2) MEDITATION — In meditation, a believer clears their mind of distractions and focuses on God. This could involve repetitive prayer, reading scripture or fasting. It doesn't need to be in a place of worship (you can meditate anywhere) and can result in visions or voices as the believer draws closer to God.

3) MIRACLES — Some people believe miracles occur today (e.g. healing at Lourdes, statues of the Virgin Mary crying blood), and that these miracles show God's power and presence (see p.72).

4) RELIGIOUS ECSTASY — These experiences range from singing, dancing, shaking or crying during worship to 'speaking in tongues' (unknown languages), having visions or prophesying (speaking a message from God).

5) SACRAMENTAL RITUALS — These are the rituals in which Christians believe God makes his presence felt directly. According to Roman Catholics, there are seven sacraments (see p.96) including Holy Communion. In Holy Communion, Catholics believe that bread and wine actually become Christ's body and blood (called transubstantiation) (see p.97).

Revelation through the World

Many believers feel that God reveals himself constantly in the world through numinous experiences. This describes an experience that inspires awe and wonder, where someone can feel God's presence, e.g. a beautiful sunset, a wild sea or a butterfly's wing might convince you there must be a creator.

"I've got a revelation here for a Mr Smith..."

Revelations, eh... Wow. I mean, just imagine. It's just mind-blowing...

Miracles

Christianity, Judaism, Islam & General

Religion is a great source of stories of <u>weird</u> and <u>wonderful</u> events.

Miracles — when Something Extraordinary Happens

1) Christianity, Islam and Judaism all teach that at some points in history the normal course of events was suspended, and something <u>amazing</u> happened.
2) Some believers, such as some Roman Catholics, think miracles <u>continue</u> to happen up to the <u>present day</u> (e.g. healing at <u>Lourdes</u>) — other Christians believe that we don't live in a time of miracles any more.
3) Others argue that the miracles in religious texts should be interpreted <u>symbolically</u> rather than literally.

The New Testament Contains Many Miracles

The miracle stories are some of the <u>best known</u> of the Bible.

Jesus Controls Nature — Inspiring Awe and Wonder

Jesus performs many <u>miracles</u> in the Gospels. He performs them basically for two reasons — to show that he has <u>God's power</u>, and to demonstrate the importance of <u>faith</u>.

Nothing up my sleeves...

> <u>Jesus feeds the 5000</u> (Mark 6:30-44) A crowd has gathered around Jesus and the disciples, but there are only 5 loaves and 2 fish to eat. Jesus gives thanks to God, and breaks the bread. All 5000 people have enough to eat, and there's enough food left over to fill 12 baskets.

> <u>Jesus walks on water</u> (Mark 6:45-52) Jesus catches up with his disciples' boat by walking across the water. Although they have seen him feed the 5000, they are still shocked at his powers.

God has Intervened through Jesus and the Holy Spirit

1) Christians believe that the <u>birth</u>, <u>death</u> and <u>resurrection</u> of Jesus were miracles in their own right (see p.10).
2) At the feast of <u>Pentecost</u> (also known as <u>Whitsun</u>) Christians celebrate the descent of the Holy Spirit on to Jesus's early followers who were instantly able to speak many <u>different languages</u> and were filled with the power to <u>speak out</u> and do <u>amazing things</u> like Jesus did.
3) Many Christians believe that God continues to <u>act</u> in the world <u>today</u> through the Holy Spirit. They believe that the Holy Spirit <u>guides</u> them to do <u>good</u> in this world.

Judaism has Plenty of Miracles of its Own

1) There are many <u>miraculous events</u> described in the <u>Hebrew Bible</u>. Examples include God parting the <u>Red Sea</u> for Moses during the flight from Egypt (Exodus 14) and the fall of the <u>walls of Jericho</u> (Joshua 6).
2) Some Liberal Jews argue that the purpose of the stories of these miracles is to impart a <u>spiritual message</u>, and they don't have to be believed in literally. More orthodox believers might argue that the events actually occurred as described in scripture.
3) More importantly for Jews, God intervened in the world by sending his <u>prophets</u> — such as <u>Isaiah</u> — who they believe <u>represented</u> God's will to the Jews. Jews consider <u>Moses</u> the greatest of the prophets.

The Qur'an is a Miracle in Itself

1) Muslims believe the <u>Qur'an</u> is a miracle — the direct word of Allah, with a <u>style</u> that it's <u>impossible</u> to <u>copy</u>.
2) Some Muslims believe that the Qur'an contains '<u>scientific miracles</u>' — where <u>facts</u> discovered <u>centuries later</u> are described, such as the development of the human embryo (Qur'an 23:12-14). Others argue that the Qur'an is for our <u>spiritual</u> and <u>moral guidance</u>, rather than a source for scientific theories.
3) The Prophet Muhammad didn't work miracles — but many Muslims believe that Allah took him on a <u>journey</u> from <u>Mecca</u> to <u>Jerusalem</u> and on a tour of the heavens in <u>one night</u>. Some Muslims believe it was a <u>spiritual</u> rather than a <u>physical</u> journey. Most Muslims believe that Allah's <u>greatest</u> miracle is <u>creation</u> itself.

You won't need a miracle if you learn it all properly...

Although some religious people seek to distance themselves from the belief in miracles, you have to wonder whether their religion would have been so successful without its tales of bizarre and amazing events.

Revelation Through the Prophets

Jesus Doesn't just Reveal God — He is God

1) Most Christians believe that the Jewish prophets spoke for God (see below), but they believe that God revealed himself fully in the person of Jesus. Christians believe he was both fully God and fully human.

2) Jesus's teachings were written down during his life and passed on in the Gospels. They include the Sermon on the Mount (Matthew 5-7) which many believe is Christ's most important revelation.

3) In his death and resurrection, Christians believe Jesus showed his divine nature to man.

Jews Believe God Spoke to them through the Prophets

In Judaism, prophets are believed to speak for God among the people. A whole section of the Tenakh (p.75), called Nevi'im, is made up of the words of prophets such as Isaiah, Jeremiah and Ezekiel. According to Jewish traditions there have been many thousands of prophets, although not all have been remembered. Here are two of the most important:

Abraham (between 2000 and 1800 BCE)

1) Jews call him Avraham Avinu ('our father Abraham'). He was the first of the patriarchs — the founders of Judaism.

2) Unlike his neighbours in Ur, he believed in one god. God told him to leave Ur and go to Canaan, also known as The Promised Land, The Holy Land, and later Israel. God promised this land to his descendants.

3) God made a covenant with Abraham which forms the basis of Jewish beliefs. God promised Abraham many descendants that God would never abandon. In return they had to be circumcised. The covenant was renewed at Mount Sinai with the giving of the Torah. Jews regard their history as the story of the covenant.

Moses (around 1300 BCE)

1) Abraham's descendants had to leave Canaan and escape to Egypt because of a famine. In Egypt they multiplied and the Egyptians made them slaves for 400 years.

2) With the help of God's direct intervention (sending the Ten Plagues on the Egyptians) Moses then led the Jews to freedom — an event called the Exodus. Their journey back to Canaan took 40 years.

3) On the way back, God revealed the Ten Commandments (Exodus 20) to Moses. Moses is regarded as the greatest of the prophets, and is traditionally believed to have been the divinely inspired author of the Torah (see p.75)

Muslims Believe there were Many Prophets

Muslims also believe that there have been many thousands of prophets in history, across all nations, revealing the nature of Allah and calling people to him. They believe that Muhammad was the final and greatest of these prophets. Muslims have special reverence for Ibrahim (Abraham), Musa (Moses) and Isa (Jesus) who are seen as delivering special messages from Allah to their people, but whose messages later got added to and distorted.

Muhammad was the Final Prophet

Muhammad was around 40 years old when he was called to receive Allah's final revelation.

1) While he was meditating in a cave on Mount Nur, Allah sent the angel Jibril (Gabriel) to him.

2) Although Muhammad was initially frightened, his wife Khadijah helped him realise that Allah was calling him to be a prophet.

3) Muhammad received many revelations from Allah, over 20 years. The Qur'an (p.76) records the exact wording of these revelations.

This was the message that the Prophet Muhammad had to take to the people of Makkah:

i) People were to worship one God, Allah — not many gods.

ii) People were to listen to him, because he was Allah's Prophet.

iii) People were to conduct their business honestly, and to look after the poor.

iv) If they did not do all this, they would be sent to Hell.

Christianity

Sacred Texts — The Bible

The <u>Bible</u> is a <u>collection</u> of books in different styles and languages written over a period of at least 1000 years. It's also the Christian <u>Scripture</u> — meaning that for Christians, it's <u>sacred</u>.

The Bible — the Old and New Testaments

The Bible's divided into two main parts — the <u>Old</u> and <u>New Testaments</u>:

THE OLD TESTAMENT

The Old Testament is the <u>Jewish Scriptures</u> (i.e. it's considered sacred by Jews). Written in Hebrew and Aramaic, its 39 books include the <u>Creation</u> story, the books of the Law (<u>Torah</u>), the <u>10 Commandments</u>, various <u>histories</u> of Ancient Israel, <u>prophecy</u>, <u>poetry</u> and <u>psalms</u>.

THE NEW TESTAMENT

The New Testament is the specifically <u>Christian</u> part of the Bible. Written in Greek in the 1st Century CE, its 27 books include the <u>4 Gospels</u>, the <u>Acts</u> of the Apostles (describing the early years of Christianity), 13 <u>letters</u> by St Paul (giving advice about the Christian life), 8 letters by other early Christian leaders, and the <u>Revelation of St John</u> — an apocalyptic vision.

The 4 Gospels are Matthew, Mark, Luke (called the <u>Synoptic Gospels</u>, as they are all very similar stories of Jesus), and John (which portrays Jesus in a very different way).
The word 'Gospel' means 'good news', and the Gospels tell the good news about Jesus Christ.

The Bible is used as a Christian Faith Guidebook

Christians accept the Bible as <u>authoritative</u> in forming their beliefs and guiding their actions.

1) Christians believe the Bible offers directions for living a <u>moral</u> life. It presents Jesus Christ as our example for <u>godly</u> living, and teaches that we best love <u>God</u> by showing love to <u>others</u>.

2) Both the Old and New Testaments (but especially the New) include <u>rituals</u> for <u>worship</u>, large parts of which are still included in <u>modern</u> worship services (e.g. <u>Holy Communion</u> and <u>baptism</u>).

3) The faith of the Roman Catholic Church is based largely on the <u>Scriptures</u>, but Catholic <u>tradition</u> and the <u>Magisterium</u> (i.e. the teaching of the Pope, his cardinals and bishops) are also very important. The Protestant Churches claim their authority mainly from the Scriptures.

4) Different groups of Christians <u>interpret</u> the Bible in different ways:

(1) **Literalism** Many Christians believe that pretty well everything in the Bible is <u>literally</u> true, e.g. Jesus really did 'walk on water'.

Some people argue that there are <u>contradictions</u> in the Bible, and so it's impossible for everything in it to be <u>literally</u> true.

(2) **Fundamentalism** This is a form of literalism. Fundamentalists believe that it's wrong to <u>question</u> anything in the Bible, since it was <u>dictated</u> by God.

(3) **Conservative View** This view is probably the most common among Christians. They believe that the Bible was <u>inspired</u> by God but not dictated — the writers' own interests also come through. Readers must use their intelligence and the guidance of the Holy Spirit in order to understand the writers' intentions.

(4) **Liberal View** Liberals believe that pretty well everything in the Bible can be interpreted '<u>symbolically</u>', e.g. Jesus didn't really 'walk on water' — the story has some other 'spiritual' meaning.

The Bible has been Influential for Centuries

1) There are many different <u>versions</u> of the Bible in use today, and loads of <u>translations</u> into other languages.

2) The <u>Gospels</u> (which contain the teachings of Jesus) are <u>central</u> to Christian faith.

3) Christians often meet to <u>study</u> the Bible and to <u>pray</u>, and it's also read for <u>guidance</u>, or as an act of <u>devotion</u> towards God.

The Bible — sells more than any revision guide...

The Bible has profoundly affected <u>countless</u> lives (e.g. the saints, missionaries, campaigners for social change), and arguments over its interpretation continue to be a <u>legal</u> matter in some countries — e.g. courts in the USA have had to legislate recently on whether schools should teach the Bible's Creation story as <u>fact</u> or <u>fable</u>.

Sacred Texts — The Torah & Talmud

Judaism

The 'Jewish Bible' is the <u>Tenakh</u> (often just called the <u>Torah</u>). This is basically the same as the Christian <u>Old Testament</u>, except that it's in a different order. The word 'TeNaKh' even helps you remember what's in it.

The Tenakh — its Letters tell you its Contents

T = Torah (Instructions / Law / Teachings)

The <u>Torah</u> is the first <u>five</u> books of the Bible (<u>Genesis</u> to <u>Deuteronomy</u>). It contains 613 commandments (see p.44) which Jews are supposed to live by. Jews regard the Torah as the holiest part of the Tenakh, as it was given to Moses directly by God.

But many people use the word 'Torah' to refer to the whole Tenakh.

N = Nevi'im (Prophets)

This collection of books is divided into two. The <u>Former Prophets</u> trace the history of the <u>Israelites</u> after the death of Moses. The <u>Latter Prophets</u> contain the words of <u>Isaiah</u>, <u>Jeremiah</u>, <u>Ezekiel</u> and <u>12 Minor Prophets</u>. All these men encouraged the Jews to keep their part of the <u>covenant</u>, and their words are believed to have been <u>inspired by God</u>. However, the books in the Nevi'im do not have as high a status as the Torah.

K = Ketuvim (Writings)

This is a hotch-potch of other stuff, chiefly the three 'P's: <u>Psalms</u> (hymns), <u>Proverbs</u> (wise and witty sayings), and <u>Philosophy</u>. This part of the Tenakh is less authoritative than the others.

Torah means Different Things to Different People

Some Jews use the word '<u>Torah</u>' to refer to the whole <u>Tenakh</u>. Others use it to mean the enormous body of <u>teachings</u> which grew up over the centuries to explain how the Torah should be applied in a <u>changing world</u>. Although some of these teachings were originally passed on by word of mouth (and were known as the <u>Oral Torah</u>), they eventually they got written down in a number of <u>collections</u>:

(1) The Mishnah ('Learning' or 'Repetition')
This was a collection of <u>Oral Torah</u> written down by Rabbi Judah the Prince (roughly 200 CE). It ran to 63 volumes.

(2) The Gemara ('Completion')
This is an <u>extended commentary</u> on the Mishnah.

(3) The Talmud (the Mishnah and Gemara combined)
Some Jews think that God gave the entire contents of the <u>Talmud</u> to <u>Moses</u>, so it has a very high status and authority.

(4) The Codes
The Talmud was so huge that summaries had to be made. An important example is the <u>Mishneh Torah</u> written by <u>Maimonides</u> in 1167. Another is the <u>Shulchan Aruch</u> from the 16th century.

(5) The Responsa
New questions arise as technology develops, so panels of rabbis meet to give '<u>responses</u>' to tricky questions, e.g. whether people should drive on the Sabbath.

Orthodox Jews Live Strictly by the Torah

1) <u>Orthodox</u> means 'right belief'. Orthodox Jews think that traditional Jewish beliefs and practices are still important <u>today</u>. Roughly 70% of <u>British</u> Jews belong to Orthodox synagogues, though not all are equally <u>observant</u>.
2) Orthodox Jews believe that the Tenakh and Talmud are of <u>divine origin</u>, and are to be followed to the letter.

Progressive Jews Interpret the Torah Less Rigidly

1) <u>Progressive Jews</u> apply the Torah to <u>modern life</u> in a very different way. They believe that it's merely people's <u>interpretation</u> of the word of God.
2) They consider the <u>moral</u> commandments <u>binding</u> (although open to <u>interpretation</u>), but the <u>ritual laws</u> can be <u>adapted</u> or <u>abandoned</u> in response to changes in society. In <u>Britain</u>, there are two Progressive movements: <u>Reform</u> and <u>Liberal Judaism</u>.

Sacred Texts — The Qur'an

Muslims believe the Qur'an is the most important book in the world, as it records the exact words of Allah. They call these words revelations, because they were revealed by Allah to the Prophet Muhammad.

The Qur'an is Treated with Respect

For Muslims, the Qur'an is...

1 A COMPLETE RECORD OF ALLAH'S WORDS: The Prophet never forgot any revelations, and his followers recorded them at once, and learned them by heart.

2 A TOTALLY ACCURATE AND UNCHANGED RECORD The early Caliph (Muslim ruler) Uthman made sure there was only one version and that it was completely correct.

3 A COMPLETE GUIDE TO ISLAMIC LIFE The Qur'an says what Muslims must believe, and how they must live, in order to get to Paradise. In the Qur'an, Allah tells Muslims what they need to know, so that they can please him. Since Muslims believe the Qur'an came direct from Allah, they trust it completely. Basically, if the Qur'an says 'Do this,' then a Muslim must do it.

4 ALWAYS IN ARABIC Allah gave the Qur'an to the Prophet Muhammad in Arabic. If you read it in another language, you might not get the proper meaning. So all Muslims must learn Arabic to be sure they are reading the real Qur'an.

Because the Qur'an is so important, Muslims treat it with great respect. Many Muslims will:

1) keep their Qur'an wrapped up to keep it clean,
2) wash their hands before touching it,
3) keep it on a higher shelf than all other books,
4) place it on a special stand when they read it.

The Qur'an is also read during private and public prayers, so Muslims get to know it really well. In the month of Ramadan, it's read from beginning to end during worship at the mosque.

The Qur'an is Divided into 114 Surahs

1) The Qur'an is organised into 114 Surahs (chapters).
2) The Surahs are arranged in order of length — longest first, shortest last (apart from Surah 1, the Fatihah, which is a short and punchy statement of central beliefs).
3) Each Surah is made up of Ayat (verses).
4) Most Surahs begin with the Bismillah — an Arabic phrase meaning 'In the name of Allah, the Entirely Merciful, the Especially Merciful'. This means that when Muslims start to read any Surah, they are reminded of the mercy and kindness of Allah.

The Hadith and the Sunnah are also Important Texts

Muslims also pay a lot of attention to the guidance and example they get from the following:

1 THE HADITH — the sayings of the Prophet Muhammad that were not part of the Qur'an. These were Muhammad's words, not Allah's.

2 THE SUNNAH — the actions and way of life of Muhammad.

Because Muhammad was chosen by Allah to be his last Prophet, they regard him as a very remarkable man, and pay special attention to his words and actions.

Are you surah you've learnt all of this...

When Muslims read the Qur'an, they're learning about what Allah's like, how he relates to humans, and how to live the way Allah wants so they can get to Paradise and thus avoid the 'unpleasantness' of Hell. Basically, if it's in the Qur'an, it's important. And if it's important in Islam, it may well be in the Qur'an.

Practice Questions

That section was little short of revelatory (boom, boom). Ah, the old ones are the best, but it's worth remembering that some sort of experience of God/Allah is at the heart of all three religions. Whether it's the direct revelation that the founders of the faiths experienced, or in quiet moments of private prayer, it really is the source of all the other stuff in the book.

And this is where we reveal how much you've remembered and understood. Go through the questions (for those religions you're covering) and try to answer them all. If you can't answer one go back through the section to find the answer. Keep repeating this little ritual till you can answer all the questions without checking back.

Check the spelling, punctuation and grammar of your answers when you've finished.

1) What is:
   a) revelation?
   b) meditation?
   c) a miracle?
   d) literalism? (Christianity)
   e) the Hadith? (Islam)
   f) the Oral Torah? (Judaism)

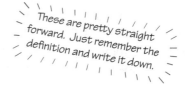
These are pretty straight forward. Just remember the definition and write it down.

2) a) State two beliefs people have about God/Allah.
   b) What is meant by a religious experience?
   c) State two important religious texts for Jews/Muslims. (Judaism) (Islam)
   d) State how two different groups of Christians/Jews interpret scripture. (Christianity) (Judaism)

Get a couple of facts down in short order and move on. Try not to get bogged down with 'em.

3) a) Describe what a believer may think about miracles.
   b) Describe the role of Jesus in the revelation of God to the Christians. (Christianity)
   c) Describe the role of Muhammad in the revelation of Allah to the Muslims. (Islam)
   d) Describe the role of Abraham in the revelation of God to the Jews. (Judaism)

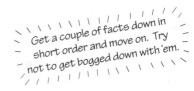
Make sure you cover the key details without going into essay mode.

4) a) Explain in what ways a Christian/Jew/Muslim might feel that God/Allah has revealed himself to them.
   b) Explain, from <u>two</u> religious traditions, beliefs about vocation.
   c) Explain why some Christians/Jews don't believe that everything that is written in their scriptures is literally true. (Christianity) (Judaism)
   d) Explain why Muslims believe that everything in the Qur'an is literally true. (Islam)
   e) Explain why Christians believe that Jesus was more than a prophet. (Christianity)

You can start to stretch your legs with these ones — you'll be judged on how good your writing is for these questions, too.

5) Read the following statements:
   a) "Religion has no value in a secular society."
   b) "God/Allah cannot be defined."
   c) "We don't need any new revelations."
   d) "God/Allah can be found outside scripture."
   e) "Religious people should not believe in miracles."
   f) "Scripture is the literal word of God/Allah."
   g) "Sacred texts can't help to solve today's problems."

   Discuss each statement. You should include different, supported points of view and a personal viewpoint. You must refer to a religion in your answer.

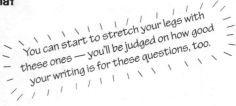
Finally on to the monster sized questions. Aim to give a structured essay-style answer that covers both sides of the argument to slay the beast and score full marks.

Public and Private Christian Worship

Christianity

Worship is the religious person's way of expressing their <u>love</u> of, <u>respect</u> for, and <u>devotion</u> to a god or gods.

Sunday Worship in <u>Church</u> can take *Many Forms*

1) For Christians, Sunday is the '<u>Lord's Day</u>' — this is when they celebrate the <u>Sabbath</u>. Most churches have their main service on a Sunday morning. It may be <u>structured</u> or <u>spontaneous</u>, and will usually include songs, Bible readings, and a sermon. The exact form of Sunday worship will <u>vary</u> between denominations.

2) In Roman Catholic, Orthodox, and most Anglican churches it will be <u>structured</u> and <u>liturgical</u> (i.e. it will follow a pattern laid down in writing — with set <u>prayers</u>, and <u>readings</u>).

3) Methodists and other nonconformists have structured but <u>non-liturgical</u> services, e.g. following the '<u>hymn sandwich</u>' pattern, where the service consists of hymns <u>alternating</u> with things like readings, prayers and a sermon.

> There are several reasons for all this variety. Christians <u>share</u> the same <u>basic beliefs</u> about the importance of Holy Communion, the Bible, the sermon, the Holy Spirit etc., but they <u>differ</u> as to which matters <u>most</u>.

4) Roman Catholic and Orthodox Sunday services <u>always</u> include the <u>Eucharist</u> (called <u>Holy Communion</u> or, in the Roman Catholic tradition, <u>Mass</u> see p.97). Anglican churches <u>usually</u> include the Eucharist.

5) Pentecostals, House Churches and other independent Christian fellowships may have <u>spontaneous</u>, often <u>charismatic</u> worship (see p.91).

6) Some Christians hold church services in their own <u>homes</u>. Some because Christianity is <u>prohibited</u> in their country — others as they believe it's more like the simpler worship described in the New Testament.

7) Many Christians worship informally <u>at home</u> (not just on Sundays). This can be anything from saying <u>Grace</u> before a meal to singing <u>worship songs</u> with family and friends.

Inside *A Typical Parish Church*

Traditional Roman Catholic and Church of England churches are often very similar in layout:

CONFESSIONAL BOX
A Roman Catholic Church will have a <u>partitioned compartment</u> for confession. The priest sits on one side of the partition (usually a pierced wood screen) while the confessant sits or kneels on the other side.

(1) **ALTAR**
The most important place in the church — a table which holds the items for the <u>Communion</u> service. The <u>altar</u> is in the east end.

(2) **EAST WINDOW**
Often of <u>stained glass</u>, it's right behind the altar and draws attention to it.

(3) **PULPIT**
A raised box from which the <u>minister</u> gives the <u>sermon</u> or talks to the congregation.

(4) **REREDOS**
Some churches have a <u>painted</u> or sculpted <u>screen</u> behind the altar. It often has pictures of Jesus, Mary or saints, and it helps to focus attention on the altar.

(5) **SANCTUARY**
A <u>raised platform</u> where the most <u>important</u> parts of a service take place.

(7) **COVERED FONT**
Used to hold <u>water</u> for <u>baptism</u>.

(6) **LECTERN**
A stand for the <u>church Bible</u>. Often made from brass and in the shape of an eagle.

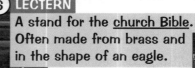

(8) **NAVE**
The main part of the church where the <u>congregation</u> sits (or originally stood).

(9) **AISLE**
Aisles are often used in <u>processions</u>.

There's no sanctuary from revision...

Make sure you spend time learning what each little feature of a church is called and what it's used for.

Symbolism in Christian Worship

Christianity

Symbols are used within the Christian tradition to represent what's believed.
An obvious example is the symbol of the cross — used to represent the sacrificial death of Jesus Christ.

Religious Architecture is often Symbolic

1 Cathedrals can be enormous, demonstrating their importance. They were historically built at the centre of the community to represent God's kingship on Earth. Inside, the focus of attention is always towards the altar (see p.78), where the main act of worship (the celebration of Holy Communion) takes place.

2 Orthodox churches are often in the shape of a cross, with a large dome on top symbolising Christ's presence, eternity and the nearness of heaven. Inside they are richly decorated with friezes and carvings.

3 Free Churches (e.g. Baptists) meet in simple halls where the pulpit is the focus of attention. This shows the importance to them of preaching from the Bible. Also in a Baptist church, the prominence of the Baptistry (a pool for baptism by total immersion) shows the central importance of baptism.

Icons, Statues and Stained-Glass Windows are Symbolic

1 Icons are paintings (mostly of saints) often found in Orthodox churches, and are often greeted with a kiss on entering the building. They're used to represent the presence of saints, and as a means to pray — 'prayers captured on wood'.

Statues also represent the presence of the saints.

In certain festivals a madonna (a statue of Mary) or another saint is paraded through the streets as an appeal to bless the community.

2 Large cathedrals and churches are often decorated with colourful murals or frescoes, and many feature beautiful stained-glass windows depicting biblical stories.

For centuries the finest work of leading artists was made for churches — all to offer to God the highest expression of worship, and to create a sense of awe.

3 The most well known Christian symbol is the cross which represents Jesus's crucifixion. However a cross isn't a crucifix unless it features a representation of Jesus. Crucifixes can be found in Roman Catholic and Orthodox churches, to remind them of Jesus's suffering — but empty crosses are found in Anglican, Baptist and Methodist churches to remind them of the risen Christ.

4 Another important symbol of Christianity from the earliest times is the fish. Jesus called on his followers to be "fishers of men" (Mark 1:17). The Greek word for fish 'ICTHYS' forms an acrostic (each letter becomes the first letter of a new word) for 'Jesus Christ, God's Son, Saviour' in Greek. It was a sign used by early Christians who were being persecuted.

Church Music is also Symbolic

Church music is symbolic as it is used to praise God and to express belief. Mozart, Bach, Beethoven and many other great composers wrote music for worship — e.g. Handel's Messiah, Mozart's Requiem Mass.

1) Hymns have been part of Christian worship for many centuries — they're often derived from passages of scripture.
2) In some Protestant churches, choirs have an important role in leading the singing. There are many types, from Anglican schoolboys to Pentecostal gospel.
3) Many different musical instruments are used in worship — from pipe organs to brass bands and guitars. The music used in worship can be solemn and dignified or loud and lively depending on the type of church.
4) Dancing is common in Charismatic churches (see p.91) — it's seen as a sign of the Holy Spirit's presence.

Who sang that duff note? — hymn...

Don't forget that Christian beliefs are often expressed through worship in ritual form (e.g. baptism), and that this is also a kind of symbolism. Oh, it's all good fun and a whole lot more interesting than maths. So there.

80

 Judaism

Public and Private Jewish Worship

A Jewish place of worship is called a <u>synagogue</u>, although Jews more often use the word '<u>shul</u>', or sometimes even '<u>Bet ha-Knesset</u>' (House of Meeting).

It's not what's on the Outside that matters...

There are <u>no</u> rules stating what a synagogue should look like on the <u>outside</u> — they can be plain or ornate, traditional or ultra modern. But you might recognise a synagogue from <u>symbols</u> on its outside walls, such as a <u>menorah</u> (a seven-branched candlestick), or a <u>magen David</u> (a six-pointed star/shield of David).

...it's what's on the Inside that's Important

The layout of the synagogue's <u>Prayer Hall</u> is based on that of the ancient <u>Temple</u> of the Jews. It faces <u>Jerusalem</u>, where the Temple stood, and is usually <u>rectangular</u>. All synagogues share the following <u>four features</u>:

1 <u>Aron Kodesh</u> (the <u>Ark</u>) — this is the most important item of furniture, since it holds the Torah. It is a large <u>cupboard</u> or <u>alcove</u>, with doors or a screen, set on the wall facing Jerusalem.

2 <u>Ner Tamid</u> (Perpetual Light) — above the ark is a <u>light</u> which <u>never</u> goes out. It represents the menorah which was always kept alight in the <u>Temple</u>.

> There will be no 'pictures of God' (see next page).

3 <u>Sefer Torah</u> (Scroll of the Torah) — parchment <u>scroll</u>. On each end is a wooden pole for winding it to the required passage. It must be <u>handwritten</u> by a <u>sofer</u> (scribe), and is usually decorated. It's kept inside the ark.

4 <u>Bimah</u> or <u>Almemar</u> — a raised <u>platform</u> with a reading desk, normally in the centre of the hall.

Also, some synagogues have a <u>pulpit</u>, and the <u>Ten Commandments</u> above the ark. Some have an <u>organ</u> (but on the Sabbath, all singing should be <u>unaccompanied</u>), and an Orthodox synagogue will have a <u>gallery</u> where women can sit.

Shabbat (Sabbath) is Celebrated in the Synagogue...

The Sabbath is a day of rest to commemorate the <u>7th Day of Creation</u> when God rested after making the Universe. It begins at <u>sunset</u> on Friday, and ends on Saturday evening when <u>stars</u> begin to appear.

There are 3 separate <u>services</u> in the synagogue on the Sabbath.

FRIDAY EVENING Shabbat is welcomed as a <u>queen</u> or a <u>bride</u> with singing led by a <u>chazan</u> (cantor). No instruments are used — in memory of the destruction of the Temple with its instrumental music.

> The <u>4th Commandment</u> instructs Jews to observe the Sabbath.
> "Remember the Sabbath day by keeping it holy." — Exodus 20:8 NIV

SATURDAY MORNING the <u>main</u> service of the week. The <u>rabbi</u> will read from the Torah and give a sermon. Also, seven men are called up to read or recite a blessing, and an eighth reads a portion from the books of the Prophets. In Orthodox synagogues, women sit <u>separately</u> from the men and take little part.

> Much like God, I believe in resting on a Saturday.

SATURDAY AFTERNOON this service includes a reading from the <u>Torah</u>, and three special <u>prayers</u>.

Remember the Sabbath — there might be a question on it...

There are big similarities with all three of the faiths covered in this book. Each religion has a day or more a week set aside for special religious observance. Until the mid 1990s most shops in Britain weren't allowed to open on a Sunday (the Lord's Day). In Israel, government agencies don't open during Shabbat.

Symbolism in Jewish Worship

...and in the Home

1) To prepare for Shabbat, the house is cleaned and tidied, and all the food to be eaten on Shabbat is cooked in advance. Family members bathe or shower. At dusk, the mother of the family will light two candles and welcome the Sabbath by saying a blessing and gesturing with her arms.

2) At the beginning of the Shabbat meal, a sanctifying ceremony called kiddush takes place. It happens at home and at the synagogue, and includes the reciting of Genesis 2:1-3 (God resting after creation). Wine is used to symbolise the sweetness and joy of Shabbat.

> The Mishnah (see p.75) lists 39 kinds of 'work' not allowed on the Sabbath.

 3) Challot are eaten — these are two plaited loaves which commemorate the double portion of 'manna' (miraculous food) which God provided the day before each Shabbat during the Exodus. They are blessed, cut and dipped in salt.

4) After the father has blessed his children, the Shabbat meal is eaten.

5) The havdalah ('division') ceremony marks the end of Shabbat, separating it from the six days ahead. Blessings are said over sweet-smelling spices, a cup of wine, and over a special plaited candle.

Judaism Has Symbols to Remind Them of God

Since God is invisible, symbols are used by believers to help them focus on God in private prayer and in communal worship.

1 The mezuzah is a sign which is put in Jewish houses. It's a tiny parchment scroll containing the words of Deuteronomy 6:4-9 and 11:13-21 in Hebrew. It must be handwritten by a trained scribe, and is put inside a case to keep it safe. There's one on the front door and every other door of the house except the bathroom and toilet. It constantly reminds the family of their duty to God.

2 Many Jewish men and boys wear a small cap called a kippah as a sign of respect to God. It reminds them that God's intelligence is vastly higher than ours.

3 The Tefillin (or Phylacteries) are worn during morning prayers, except on the Sabbath and on festival days. They're two leather boxes, one worn on the upper arm (next to the heart), one on the head. Inside are tiny scrolls containing Torah passages. These remind Jews to serve God with head and heart — the command to wear them comes from Deuteronomy 6:6-9.

But Jews have No Pictures of God

There are two reasons why Jewish art never tries to picture God.
1) No one knows what he looks like.
2) The 2nd of the 10 Commandments forbids it as idolatry.

> "You shall not make for yourself an idol in the form of anything in heaven above or on the earth beneath..." Exodus 20:4 NIV

To avoid idolatry, no images of people are allowed in synagogues, as people are made in the image of God. The ban on idolatry also means three-dimensional sculptures aren't allowed.
Many synagogues won't have images of animals either, although the 'Lion of Judah' (a symbol of Judaism) can sometimes be found.

Some Jews write 'G-d' instead of God

In Deuteronomy (12:1-4) God tells the Jews to tear down the temples and wipe out the names of the gods they find written in the sacred places of other nations in Israel. But verse 4 warns them not to do the same to him. Many Jews take this as a warning never to erase the name of God — so they never write it out fully just in case.

This page must seem like manna from heaven...

Jews don't have pictures of God and won't write down his name so they can't accidentally erase it. But, they do have symbols to help remind them of God. Make sure you know about the mezuzah, kippah and tefillin.

Public and Private Muslim Worship

A mosque (or masjid) is more than a place of worship — it's also a centre of the community for Muslims. Masjid literally means 'place of prostration' (i.e. lying with the face down) — an act of submission to God.

A Mosque (Masjid) is the Muslim House of Prayer

1) The Prophet Muhammad said that any clean place could be used for worship.

2) Some mosques are extremely simple, others are very grand, but all have a dome representing the universe.

3) Most mosques will have at least one minaret. This is a tall tower from where the muezzin (mu'adhin in Arabic) calls the adhan (call to prayer).

Inside the Mosque

1) Beautiful mosaic tiles often decorate both the outside and inside of a mosque.

2) There are no pictures of Muhammad or Allah, since no one is allowed to draw them, and pictures of other living things are usually banned, to avoid idolatry.

3) The ban on images means that richly coloured Arabic calligraphy (writing) is often used to decorate mosques with words from the Qur'an and the names of Allah and Muhammad. The faith of the calligrapher is expressed in writing — this helps the believer focus on the meaning of the words. Calligraphy is one of the most respected arts in the Islamic world.

"Muhammad"

"Allah"

4) The colour green is traditionally used in mosques. This is believed to be because it was Muhammad's favourite colour (he's thought to have had a green turban and banner), and because it symbolises life.

5) Shoes must be left at the door, and every mosque must have somewhere for Muslims to wash before prayer.

6) There are no seats, but the whole floor is usually covered with rich carpet.

7) There is little in the way of furniture, but you will see a pulpit (called a minbar), where the imam (a respected person) will lead prayers from — especially on Fridays.

8) Muslims face Makkah when they pray, and a special niche (called the mihrab) in the 'direction-wall' shows the direction in which Makkah lies.

Apart from prayer, a mosque is used as a Madrasah (a mosque school), where Muslims learn the general principles of Islam, as well as how to carry out Muslim practices and recite the Qur'an.

Regular daily prayer is an important part of being a Muslim (see p.84). It's one of the five Pillars of Islam (see p. 69).

Home life also has an important role in Islam — this is where many of the rules of Islam are kept.
*   Most Muslim households have a copy of the Qur'an.
*   It's where children first learn and witness Islamic values.
*   It is also the centre of religious life for many women, who are not obliged to attend the mosque.

Tawhid is the Belief in the Oneness of Allah

1) Islam teaches that nothing is remotely like Allah, and nothing can be compared to him.

2) The worst sin for a Muslim would be to believe that God was not supreme — this concept is called Shirk. (Shirk is the opposite of Tawhid.)

Muslim beliefs about Allah...
Allah is beyond time and space. He is the Almighty One, the Compassionate and the Merciful. All men and women owe their creation, and continued existence, to Allah — the One and Only Creator.

And see page 69 for more basic Muslim beliefs about God.

This all needs to be learnt — you'd better believe it...

...but only if you're studying Islam. If you have a Mosque near you, see if you can find any calligraphy on the walls. Notice how the words are shaped to be more beautiful and to reflect their meanings. Even if you can't read Arabic, the calligraphy is quite a sight.

Prayer and Meditation

General & Christianity

Prayer is at the centre of many people's faith. Whereas worship involves all the things people do to express their faith, prayer is specifically the 'talking to God/Allah' part.

Prayer Puts People In Touch with their God

1) Prayer is when believers mentally or vocally communicate with their god, or gods.
2) Prayer comes in many different forms: most branches of Christianity, Judaism and Islam have set prayers that people say when they are engaged in their main acts of worship.
3) But prayer also has a private dimension where the individual believer communicates with their god in their own words.
4) Some prayers have set words — these include the Lord's Prayer in Christianity and the Shema in Judaism.
5) Some religions require specific movements for some prayers — such as the Muslim Salah prayers (see next page), which require believers to take various positions including prostrating themselves with their hands, knees and foreheads placed on to the ground.

Prayer can be a Powerful Thing

1) There's a strong tradition in Christian prayer of asking for things from God. When believers feel that God grants their requests this is known as an 'answered prayer'. Some believers think answered prayers are proof that God exists.
2) However this presents the problem of 'unanswered prayers' when God doesn't grant a believer's request.
3) Some Christians argue that God answers all prayers in his own way and in his own time. Others would argue that God has bigger plans that we cannot understand — He moves in mysterious ways.
4) Jesus himself on the night of his arrest prays: "My father, if it is possible, may this cup be taken from me. Yet not as I will, but as you will." (Matthew 26:39 NIV). The "cup" may represent suffering.
5) Roman Catholics and Orthodox believers pray to saints to ask for their 'intercession' (help) with God. They believe that the Saints can join in our prayers to God, making them more effective.
6) Protestant churches believe that Jesus is the only mediator between us and God, so we don't need the Saints' help. Some argue that we shouldn't pray to Saints, as no-one does in the Bible.

Private Prayer draws a Believer Closer to God

Christian prayer is a conversation with God, and should take place both in church and in private. The whole point of prayer is for the believer to draw close to God to communicate with him and hear what he's saying — this deepens their faith. Different Christians use different methods to accomplish this:

The 'Quiet Time' — time spent alone with God, perhaps reading the Bible and praying.

Meditation — a form of prayer where the believer clears his or her mind of distracting thoughts and concentrates on God's nature or work. It may involve repeating a prayer over and over again.

Contemplation — true Christian contemplation is not merely deep thinking — it's intimate wordless prayer in which the believer senses God's presence strongly.

The Rosary — used by Catholics, this is a string of beads arranged in groups. As the beads are moved through the fingers, prayers are said, e.g. the Lord's Prayer, Ave Maria (Hail Mary) and the Gloria.

Icons — Orthodox Christians use icons (sacred pictures of saints) to help them focus on God. Although they may light a candle in front of the icon or kiss it, they don't pray to it.

Many parents pray with their children, believing this encourages them to grow up as praying Christians. And many Christians believe praying while ill brings God's healing or helps them accept their suffering as part of God's plan.

Your prayers are more likely to be answered if you revised first...

Prayer isn't necessarily as straightforward as you might think. People like monks and nuns can devote a whole lifetime to prayer, and it's something they have to work at. If you go to the religion section in your local bookshop you might find books on learning how to pray. But for your exam, you just need to learn this page.

Judaism & Islam

Prayer and Meditation

The Jewish holy day is the <u>Shabbat</u> (<u>Sabbath</u>), but in Judaism, prayer is important every day of the week.

Jews have Three Special Times for Daily Prayer

1) <u>Prescribed</u> daily prayers happen at three special times — in the <u>morning</u>, <u>afternoon</u> and <u>evening</u>.

2) At these times, <u>men</u> will try to attend the <u>synagogue</u> and become part of a <u>minyan</u> — a group of at least ten men, which is the minimum needed for a service. <u>Women</u> (traditionally because of their domestic commitments) are trusted to pray <u>at home</u>.

3) As well as the normal daily prayers, there are also special prayers for getting up, going to bed, before and after eating... in fact, pretty much <u>every</u> event in life, good or bad, can be a reason to pray.

4) The Jewish prayer book is known as the <u>Siddur</u>, which sets out the time of day for different prayers.

5) When praying, Jewish men will often wear a <u>kippah</u> (see p.81).

6) Some Jews wear <u>tefillin</u> (or phylacteries) while praying (see p.81). This fulfils the commandment in Deuteronomy 6:8 — "Tie them [the commandments] as symbols on your hands and bind them on your foreheads." (NIV)

Prayer is a Pillar of Islam

See page 69 for more about the Five Pillars.

You can't be a Muslim without <u>praying</u> in the way Muhammad did. Regular prayer keeps Allah in a Muslim's mind. It also keeps Muslims aware of their <u>duty</u> to obey Allah.

1) Muslims should pray <u>five times</u> a day — at sunrise, early afternoon, late afternoon, after sunset, and late at night.

2) The <u>muezzin</u> makes the call to prayer (<u>adhan</u>) from the <u>minaret</u> of a <u>mosque</u>. The call to prayer begins "Allahu Akbar..." (God is Greatest).

3) Ideally prayer should take place in a <u>mosque</u>. If this isn't possible, a <u>prayer mat</u> should be used to make a prayer place.

Women and men pray separately — so people keep their mind on Allah rather than on the opposite sex.

4) <u>Wudu</u> (washing exposed parts of the body three times before prayer) is important, so that a Muslim is <u>pure</u> and <u>clean</u> when approaching Allah.

5) A Muslim should face <u>Makkah</u> (Muhammad's place of birth) when praying. The direction of Makkah is called the <u>qiblah</u>. A compass can be used to find the qiblah (which in England is roughly southeast).

Salah is <u>compulsory</u> prayer. Extra prayers are called <u>du'a</u>, and Muslims can do these at <u>any time</u>. In Du'a prayers, <u>beads</u> can be used — 99 beads for the 99 names of Allah.

6) There is a set <u>ritual</u> for prayer — each unit of prayer is known as a <u>rak'ah</u> (and the rak'ah may be repeated <u>several</u> times at each prayer session). Each rak'ah involves <u>standing</u>, then <u>kneeling</u>, then putting your <u>forehead</u> to the ground as a sign of submission.

7) If several Muslims are praying in one place, then they all do the ritual <u>together</u> as a sign of <u>unity</u>.

8) <u>Friday</u> prayers are called <u>Salat-al-Jum'ah</u> (or just <u>Jum'ah</u>) — it's a community occasion, and at least 40 people should be there, all praying together.

Benefits of Prayer

1) Keeps you in close <u>contact</u> with Allah and stops you <u>forgetting</u> him.
2) Expression of <u>solidarity</u> — doing exactly the <u>same</u> as all other Muslims.
3) Moral and spiritual <u>discipline</u>.

Problems with Praying in 'non-Muslim' Countries

In <u>non-Muslim</u> countries it can often be hard to pray at the right time, e.g. when you have to go to <u>school</u> or <u>work</u>. This is one of the ways in which life is more <u>complicated</u> for Muslims if they live in a country where Islam is <u>not</u> the way of life of most people.

Five a day — it's not just fruit...

You can see why religion is such a big part of the lives of Jews and Muslims when they have to pray however many times a day. I guess that's one of the main points of prayer — keeping your god in your mind throughout the day. Just don't forget — it's three times for Jews (on ordinary weekdays) and five times for Muslims.

Food and Fasting

Even religious people have got to eat. But not all the time...

Food is Important in Many Religions

1) One of the main ways in which cultures (religious or not) express themselves is through food. This is especially true at special times of year — i.e. during festivals.

2) Christians, Muslims and Jews all believe that God is the creator, and so ultimately, all food comes from Him.

3) Permanent prohibitions (bans) of certain foods are a common feature of many religions, although Christianity is an exception. Most cultures avoid certain food that others may eat anyway, e.g. frogs' legs or dog meat.

4) Fasting (not eating for a period of time) is a part of many religions either as atonement (see below), or as a way to focus the mind on spiritual matters.

Fasting — Not Vital in Christianity

1) Christians believe fasting can help you draw closer to God, but there are no longer any compulsory fasts for Christians, or special foods they must eat or avoid. However Roman Catholics shouldn't eat meat on Ash Wednesday and Good Friday, and they should fast for an hour before the Eucharist (Holy Communion).

2) Lent (February/March) commemorates the 40 days and nights of Jesus' fasting in the wilderness after his baptism. Few Christians today fast during Lent, but many still give up certain luxuries. Lent ends on the day before Easter.

3) Festival foods (e.g. Christmas pudding, hot-cross buns) tend to be more cultural than religious in origin.

- Before Lent begins, rich foods should be eaten up, and Mardi Gras carnivals may be held ('carnival' means 'farewell to meat'). In some countries, like the UK, many people still eat pancakes on Shrove Tuesday (the day before Lent) — so it's often called Pancake Day.
- Whether religious or not, many people celebrate Easter (March/April) with Easter eggs, whether with hard-boiled and decorated versions of the real thing, or with chocolate versions, as a symbol of new life.
- Historically Christian countries often have special meals for Christmas (although some countries eat them on Christmas eve). In the UK 'Christmas Dinner' usually consists of roast turkey with stuffing and then Christmas pudding. *See page 98 for more on Christian festivals.*

4) Don't forget that most Christian denominations celebrate the Eucharist (or Mass or Holy Communion) with bread (usually a communion wafer) and wine. This food and drink represents (and in some denominations is believed to become) the body and blood of Christ.

Kashrut — the Jewish Food Laws

1) Observant Orthodox Jews follow a special diet based on the Kashrut (Jewish food laws).

2) Permitted food is called kosher — everything else is terefah ('torn').

3) These laws are an example of statutes laid down by God to test Jews' obedience, and to mark them out as different from other nations.

4) To be kosher, a mammal must have cloven (split) hooves and chew the cud. Fish with fins and scales are kosher, but no other seafood is. Some birds are also kosher.

5) Animals and birds must be specially slaughtered with one cut across the throat using a razor-sharp blade. Blood must not be eaten, and meat and dairy products must not be eaten together. Foods that aren't meat or dairy may be eaten with either.

In Judaism, food is associated with happiness — so fasting shows grief or repentance.

Judaism teaches that true repentance can atone (i.e. make amends) for any past transgression — 'the gates of repentance are always open'.

Which religion is it that gets the burgers?

Eating is something everyone has to do — so it's no wonder that it pops up as a topic in pretty much every religion. Religious people have lots of special foods and fasts — and you've got to learn 'em all.

Judaism & Islam

Food and Fasting

Jews Fast for Some Festivals...

1) <u>Yom Kippur</u> (the Day of Atonement) is the most important <u>fast</u> in the Jewish calendar. Taking place ten days after the start of the Jewish New Year (Rosh Hashanah), it involves prayer and fasting for 25 hours from half an hour before nightfall on the eve of Yom Kippur, through to half an hour after nightfall on Yom Kippur itself.

2) Not only do Jews refrain from eating during Yom Kippur, they also don't <u>drink</u> — not even water. Yom Kippur is the day when Jews ask God to forgive the sins they committed over the past year. They abstain from food and drink the better to focus on <u>spiritual</u> rather than physical matters.

...and Eat Special Food at Others

1) One of the most important Jewish feasts of the year is <u>Pesach</u> (<u>Passover</u>). It commemorates the night before the <u>Exodus</u> — when <u>Moses</u> led the Israelite slaves from Egypt to freedom. In Egypt, the angel of death killed the first-born sons of the Egyptians, but <u>passed over</u> the Israelites.

2) <u>Yeast</u> is forbidden — all bread must be <u>unleavened</u>. The <u>Seder</u> (Passover meal) involves the symbolic arrangement and eating and drinking of matzah (a cracker-like unleavened bread), wine, salt water, bitter herbs, karpas (a vegetable), roast or hard-boiled egg, and a roasted lamb bone which isn't eaten.

3) During the <u>Shavuot</u> festival in early summer, Jews traditionally eat dairy products like cheesecake.

4) For <u>Hanukkah</u>, a wintertime festival, Jews traditionally eat fried foods like latkes (potato pancakes) and doughnuts, to celebrate the story of a day's worth of oil burning for eight days during the rededication ceremony for the Temple in Jerusalem.

Muslims Fast During Ramadan

1) Muslims must <u>fast</u> between <u>sunrise</u> and <u>sunset</u> during the month of <u>Ramadan</u> in the Muslim calendar.

2) This fasting means no <u>food</u>, no <u>drink</u>, no <u>smoking</u> and no <u>sex</u>. Ramadan is a time of both physical and moral <u>self-discipline</u>, and a time of <u>total</u> obedience to Allah.

3) It's supposed to help Muslims <u>understand</u> hunger, and so makes them more <u>willing</u> to help others.

4) It's also a time to show publicly that Allah matters more than <u>physical</u> needs.

5) <u>Sawm</u> (fasting during Ramadan) is one of the most important obligations for a Muslim.

6) <u>Eid ul-Fitr</u> marks the end of Ramadan. There are special prayers, and Muslims enjoy <u>rich meals</u> with their families.

> There are <u>exceptions</u> to the normal Ramadan rules:
> 1) <u>Children</u> don't have to fast until they're about 12 years old.
> 2) People can be excused for <u>medical</u> reasons. Those who are <u>ill</u> (and women having their <u>period</u>) are excused. And it's okay to take <u>medicine</u> which has to be regular, e.g. antibiotics.
> 3) If you're on a <u>journey</u>, you can be excused. But you have to <u>make up</u> the missed days later.

7) <u>Eid ul-Adha</u> is the <u>festival of sacrifice</u>. It commemorates <u>Ibrahim's</u> willingness to sacrifice his son to Allah. Sheep and goats are sacrificed at the festival, and the meat is <u>shared</u> among the poor.

The Shari'ah says Things are Either Halal or Haram

> HALAL means 'allowed'   HARAM means 'forbidden'

You need to know these two Arabic words. Think of the letter L — ha<u>L</u>a<u>L</u> is a<u>LL</u>owed. And HA<u>R</u>a<u>M</u> can <u>HARM</u>.

Food Laws — No Pork, No Blood at all, No animals that Eat Meat

1) The basic rules are <u>no pork</u>, <u>no blood</u> at all, and <u>no animals that eat meat</u>.

2) This means it's very important how an animal is killed — it must be done by slitting the neck and allowing all the blood to drain out. Meat from animals killed like this is halal, i.e. allowed.

3) Food <u>preparation</u> is also important — <u>no animal fat</u> can be used (but vegetable oil is okay).

4) <u>Intoxicants</u>, e.g. alcohol, are also forbidden (see p.65).

What, no chips?

Remember, some fasts are for a whole day, whereas other fasts last longer, but only during daylight hours.

Christian Funeral Rites

General & Christianity

Every religion has a special way of dealing with the dead.

Funerals are a Way to Say Goodbye

1) While many people never get Christened or have a Bar Mitzvah, nearly everyone gets a funeral.

2) Going back through history, people have always made special provision for their dead — e.g. by mummifying them, burying them, cremating (burning) them or with other rituals, e.g. burial at sea.

3) While UK law only specifies that the body has to be properly disposed of (e.g. buried, cremated) most people, with a religious faith or without, will hold some kind of ceremony.

4) Funerals are seen as a chance to say goodbye to the dead, and to remember and celebrate their lives.

5) Most funerals in Britain are organised by professionals known as funeral directors or undertakers.

6) Mourning is a deep sorrow for someone who has died. Many societies have a period of mourning after a funeral, when loved ones say special prayers for the deceased, remember their lives and forgo pleasures (e.g. music, bright colours, sex). At the end of that period, mourners try to move on with their lives.

Christian Funerals are Sad, but with a Note of Hope

Funeral services vary according to denomination, but all Christian funerals contain a note of hope.
For many this doesn't mean wishful thinking — it means confident expectation based on God's promises.

1) The coffin is carried into the church, and the verses on page 10 from John 11 are often read. There are hymns, other Bible readings and prayers. The priest (or someone else) often gives a short sermon about Christian belief in life after death, and may also talk about the life of the person who has died.

2) Of course there will be sadness too, particularly if the person died young or very suddenly. There are prayers for the bereaved (bereavement is the loss of someone close to you through their death). The congregation will express their sympathy for the family and close friends of the deceased. Black clothes are often worn, though some Christians consider this inappropriate and may even ask guests not to dress in this way.

3) It doesn't matter whether the body's buried or cremated — Christians believe that at the Resurrection they will have new 'spiritual bodies', not their old ones. There's another short service at the graveside or crematorium, then afterwards often a meal for family and friends.

> ### Roman Catholic Requiem Mass
> A Roman Catholic funeral includes Holy Communion (the 'Requiem Mass'). The purpose of a Requiem Mass is to pray for the soul of the dead person. The priest wears white vestments, and the coffin is covered with a white cloth (a pall). The coffin is sprinkled with holy water and the priest says, "In the waters of baptism (name) died with Christ, and rose with him to new life. May s/he now share with him in eternal glory." The coffin is later sprinkled again, and also perfumed with incense.

Funeral Customs help Support the Bereaved

1) Christian funeral services have a great deal to say about the hope of eternal life. The bereaved person is encouraged to believe that one day she or he will be reunited with the deceased.

Hmm... Perhaps a bit premature...

2) In the days following the funeral, family and friends often try to contact those who were closest to the deceased, and encourage them to talk through their grief.

3) Usually the priest or vicar will also try to visit, and may offer counselling, or suggest someone who can. There are several stages to the process of grief, and it can help to talk to someone who understands this.

It's not all bad news...

Funerals — cheery subject. But Christians try not to see death as depressing — after all, they believe the person who died is going to Heaven (probably), which has to be a good thing, if you're a Christian. Of course, it'd be a bit of a downer if you thought they might go to Hell, but let's not dwell on that.

Judaism & Islam

Jewish and Muslim Funeral Rites

Jews and Muslims also have __rituals__ surrounding death.

Judaism has Customs to Comfort the Bereaved

There are many __rituals__ in Judaism concerned with death. They're designed to __help__ bereaved people __accept__ what has happened, give expression to their __grief__, receive __comfort__, and come to terms with their loss.

1) Jewish families __gather together__ to be near a loved one who is dying, while the dying person should spend his/her last moments confessing __sins__ and reciting the __Shema__ (see page 68).

2) After the death, each member of an Orthodox family will make a small __tear__ in their clothing — a symbol of grief and shock. This is less common in Reform Judaism.

3) The dead person must not be left alone, and must be __buried__ (__not__ cremated) as soon as possible, preferably within __24 hours__. Reform Jews often allow longer, so that the family has more time to organise the funeral.

4) The body is __ritually bathed__ and wrapped in a plain linen __shroud__, before being placed in a plain, unpolished, wooden __coffin__ — in death rich and poor are __equal__. This is done by a Chevra Kaddisha (burial society).

5) At the funeral service in the synagogue, __psalms__ are read and a prayer is said praising God for giving life and for taking it away. The rabbi might make a short speech about the deceased.

Mourning Continues for Thirty Days After Death

1) The first week after the funeral is called __shiva__ (seven). The immediate family stay at home and are __visited__ by relatives and friends who pray with them three times a day and offer comfort. They do not cut their hair, shave, listen to music or have sex. The men recite a prayer called the __kaddish__. Everyone is encouraged to talk about the person who has died.

2) The first month after the funeral is called __sheloshim__ (thirty). During this time life returns __gradually__ to normal, and male mourners go to the synagogue to recite the __kaddish__. Anyone who has lost a parent remains in mourning for a whole __year__.

3) The anniversary of death is called __yahrzeit__. It is usually on the first yahrzeit that the __headstone__ is erected above the grave. Every year a candle is lit for 24 hours and men say the __kaddish__.

'Allah' should be the Last Word a Muslim Hears

A Muslim hopes __not__ to die __alone__, but with relatives and friends around, who will:

1) Keep them __company__ and look after them.

2) Ensure last-minute business is settled, so the dying one is not __distracted__ by things to do with this life.

3) __Pray__, and __recite__ 'There is no God but Allah,' so that the person may be helped to __concentrate__ on the name of God. Ideally, the name of Allah should be the __first__ thing a Muslim hears at birth, and the __last__ thing at death.

Bodies are Buried Facing Makkah

1) After a person has died, the body is __washed__, as a sign of respect.

2) The body is then __wrapped__ in a clean white __shroud__.

3) __Funeral prayers__ (__Janazah__ prayers) are said, praying that the dead person may be judged __mercifully__ and gain a place in __Paradise__.

> It's said that graves are visited by two __angels__ to question the deceased and work out whether they're fit for the __next life__.

4) The body is __buried__ in a simple grave, lying on its __right side__ with the face towards __Makkah__.

5) A period of __mourning__ is kept for __three days__, finishing with Qur'an reading and prayers for the dead person. Some Muslims do this after 40 days as well.

Make sure you get this rite in the exam...

Remember that funeral rites and ideas about the afterlife have a big impact on the __living__. They not only help people come to terms with the loss of loved ones, but also give plenty to think about for their own lives — Am I living a moral life? Am I going to make it to paradise? How do I want to be remembered?

Practice Questions

I guess this stuff is getting right down to what being a religious believer is all about — day to day. Here's another set of questions for you to get your teeth into. Make sure you answer them for all of the religions you're studying. Make sure you use correct spelling, punctuation and grammar.

1) What is/are:

   a) a religious symbol?

   b) an icon? (Christianity)

   c) tawhid? (Islam)

   d) prayer?

   e) the Rosary? (Christianity)

   f) the Siddur? (Judaism)

   g) wudu? (Islam)

   h) fasting?

   i) Lent? (Christianity)

   j) Sawm? (Islam)

   k) bereavement?

   l) cremation?

   m) mourning?

The glossary at the end of this book is pretty handy for revising for these definition questions.

2) a) What is meant by 'worship'?

   b) Name two features of a church/synagogue/mosque.

   c) State two things a Christian/Jew/Muslim might believe about prayer.

   d) What is meant by 'kosher'/'halal' food? (Judaism) (Islam)

These questions are just about knowing the basics — don't get carried away.

3) a) What is the difference between liturgical and non-liturgical worship? (Christianity)

   b) How might a Jew observe the Shabbat? (Judaism)

   c) How do Christians/Jews/Muslims pray?

   d) Describe Christian/Jewish/Muslim beliefs about fasting.

   e) How do Christians/Jews/Muslims celebrate a special occasion with food?

   f) What do Christians/Jews/Muslims believe should be done with the bodies of the dead?

   g) Describe what happens at a Christian/Jewish/Muslim funeral.

Make sure you back up your answers to these questions with some facts. If you can use the specialist vocabulary you've learnt, even better.

4) a) Explain why some Christians do not pray to the Saints. (Christianity)

   b) Explain, from two different religious traditions, the use of symbolism.

   c) Explain why some Christian churches are decorated with images. (Christianity)

   d) Explain why there are no pictures of God/Allah in synagogues/mosques. (Judaism) (Islam)

   e) Explain why some Muslims may be excused from fasting. (Islam)

   f) How are Christian/Jewish/Muslim funeral rites designed to comfort the bereaved?

Read these questions carefully, or you may end up giving reasons why people do something when you're supposed to give reasons why they don't. That's an easy way to throw away marks.

5) Read the following statements:

   a) "It should not matter to Christians what their church looks like." (Christianity)

   b) "Symbolism is very important to religious people."

   c) "Unanswered prayers prove that there is no god."

   d) "It doesn't matter what religious people eat."

   e) "It does not matter what happens to someone's body after death."

   f) "Funerals are more for the living than the dead."

   Discuss each statement. You should include different, supported points of view and a personal viewpoint. You must refer to a religion in your answer.

You need to use good spelling, grammar and punctuation for these questions. Write your answer in proper sentences and structure it carefully. Don't waffle.

Beliefs and The Creeds

Worship offered to <u>Jesus</u> is what <u>distinguishes Christianity</u> from all <u>other monotheistic</u> (one-god) religions.

Christians Believe in God as <u>Unity</u> and <u>Trinity</u>

1) <u>Christians</u> believe in <u>one God</u> — God as <u>Unity</u>.

2) They believe that God is <u>omnipotent</u> (all-powerful), <u>omnipresent</u> (everywhere) and <u>omniscient</u> (all-knowing), that God is <u>divine</u>, <u>supreme</u>, <u>totally good</u> and <u>totally perfect</u>, and that God has given us <u>free will</u>.

3) Christians <u>also</u> believe in the <u>Trinity</u>...

The <u>Trinity</u> is Explained Nicely in the <u>Nicene Creed</u>   *no pun intended...*

1) The <u>Christian</u> idea of the <u>Trinity</u> is perhaps best expressed in the <u>Nicene Creed</u>:

> "We believe in one God, the Father, the almighty, maker of heaven and earth... We believe in one Lord, Jesus Christ, the only son of God... Of one being with the Father... We believe in the Holy Spirit... The giver of life... Who proceeds from the Father and the Son..."

A '<u>creed</u>' is a statement of religious beliefs.

2) Christians might describe the <u>Father</u> as the <u>creator</u> and <u>judge</u>, the <u>Son</u> (Jesus) as the <u>human incarnation</u> of God (and the <u>Messiah</u>, or saviour), and the <u>Holy Spirit</u> as the <u>presence of God</u> in the world — inspiring, guiding and comforting them.   *(There's a load more detail about this on the next page.)*

The <u>Apostles' Creed</u> — a *Summary of the Christian Faith*

The <u>Apostles' Creed</u> summarises the basic Christian teachings about Jesus:

① **Jesus is the Christ**   'Christ' isn't a surname — it means the same as '<u>Messiah</u>', i.e. '<u>Anointed One of God</u>'.

② **The Incarnation**   This was the act by which <u>God</u> became a <u>human being</u>. Note that Christians don't believe Jesus was 'half God and half man' — he was <u>fully both</u>.

③ **The Virgin Birth**   The Gospels say that Jesus was born of a <u>virgin</u> — Mary became pregnant through the <u>influence</u> of the <u>Holy Spirit</u>. This is why Christians say "God's Son", or "God the Son".

④ **The Crucifixion**   It was Jesus's death on the cross which won his people <u>forgiveness</u> of sin.

⑤ **The Resurrection**   Jesus rose from the dead on Easter Day, and is still alive <u>today</u>.

⑥ **The Ascension**   After the resurrection Jesus '<u>ascended into Heaven</u>' (not necessarily 'in the sky').

1) The Apostles' Creed also includes important teaching about <u>God the Father</u> and the <u>Holy Spirit</u>.

2) The Holy Spirit is God's <u>influence</u> in the world, and is often pictured as <u>fire</u>, or as a <u>dove</u>, or thought of as a <u>wind</u>.

After the <u>Ascension</u>, God sent his Spirit down upon Jesus's followers in 'tongues of fire'.

At Jesus's <u>baptism</u> the Spirit descended on him in the form of a dove.

For Christians, the statements in the creeds are matters of <u>faith</u> — <u>firmly-held beliefs</u>, without (and without need for) logical proof.

The nature of God — *I thought I'd keep it nice and simple...*

There's a lot of big ideas on this page, and it's really important that you get your head round them. Christians believe in <u>one God</u> who exists as <u>three persons</u> — the Father, the Son (Jesus) and the Holy Spirit. They believe that Jesus was <u>fully God</u> and <u>fully human</u>, that he died, was resurrected and <u>still lives</u> in heaven.

The Trinity

So, back to this Trinity business. It's <u>really important</u> to Christians, so you'd best know a bit more about it.

Christians Believe in the Father...

"In the beginning God created the heavens and the earth." Genesis 1:1 NIV

1) For many Christians, <u>God the Father</u> is the God of the <u>Old Testament</u>.
2) The title 'Father' is a mark of <u>respect</u> for God, and is used by <u>Jesus</u> in the Gospels: "...when you pray... pray to your Father, who is unseen. Then your Father, who sees what is done in secret, will reward you." (Matthew 6:6 NIV).
3) In Genesis 1, the Bible describes God as the <u>Creator</u> of Heaven and Earth, who created the world in six days. Some Christians believe this account <u>literally</u>, while others think that it should be understood <u>symbolically</u>.
4) To most Christians, belief in God as the Creator is <u>important</u> as it means that <u>the world</u> itself must be a <u>good</u> thing since he chose to create it, and that <u>life</u> is God's gift to us. Some Christians take their belief in the Creator to mean that we have a <u>responsibility</u> to look after the environment, as it was made <u>for us</u> (see p.49).
5) Many Christian traditions teach that God the Father will be our <u>Judge</u> after death. Since Christians believe God is <u>all-knowing</u>, everything they say, do or think is important as it will be judged by God.

...the Son...

1) Christians believe that <u>Jesus</u> is the <u>incarnation</u> of God in human form, and that God sending Jesus down to us shows how much he <u>loves</u> the world.
2) They believe Jesus is the <u>Christ</u> or <u>Messiah</u> ('anointed one') <u>prophesied</u> by <u>Isaiah</u> in the Old Testament.
3) Christians believe that Jesus provides a <u>model</u> for Christian behaviour in <u>obedience</u> to God the Father. The <u>Gospels</u> contain a record of his life and teachings, and are an important source of guidance for Christians on how they should live their lives.
4) Jesus is sometimes described as the '<u>lamb of God</u>'. This is a reference to the lambs offered as <u>sacrifices</u> to God in the Jewish Temple. Christ is seen as a sacrifice on behalf of <u>all humanity</u>.

> ### Jesus Offers Christians Salvation from Sin
> Christians believe that through his <u>suffering</u> and <u>death</u>, Jesus won <u>forgiveness</u> for the sins of all people. They believe that Jesus was <u>perfect</u> (without sin), but that God placed <u>all the sins of the world</u> on him at his crucifixion: "...the LORD has laid on him the iniquity of us all." (Isaiah 53:6 NIV). Christianity teaches that his sacrifice <u>paid</u> for our sins, so long as we have <u>faith</u> in him (more about this on page 99). Christians believe that Christ's victory over the power of sin and death was <u>revealed</u> in his <u>resurrection</u>.

As <u>Jesus</u> suffered, many Christians believe they have a <u>duty</u> to help those who are suffering.

...and the Holy Spirit

1) Christians believe that the <u>Holy Spirit</u> is the <u>presence</u> of God in the world, who <u>descended</u> on Christ's disciples after his Ascension and continues to <u>guide</u> the actions of the <u>Church</u>.
2) Some Christians feel that the Holy Spirit also guides them <u>personally</u> in being good Christians.
3) <u>Charismatic</u> Christians believe that the Holy Spirit can descend on them during worship, just as with Christ's disciples. For example they might begin to '<u>speak in tongues</u>' (unknown languages) or <u>shake</u> uncontrollably.
4) <u>Different</u> beliefs about the Holy Spirit are what initially separated the Orthodox and the Roman Catholic Churches during the <u>Great Schism</u>. Catholics (and from them Protestants) believe that the Holy Spirit descended from God the Father <u>and</u> God the Son, whereas the Orthodox Christians believe that the Holy Spirit is the product of the God the Father <u>alone</u>.

<u>Roman Catholic</u> beliefs about the Trinity are detailed in the <u>catechism</u> — a series of statements laying down the <u>official teachings</u> of the Church.

5) For <u>Roman Catholics</u> the most important action of the Holy Spirit is in guiding the <u>Church</u>. They believe that the Holy Spirit is how God continues to <u>influence history</u> through the Church.

Three into one doesn't go in maths — but this is RS...

Remember, Christians don't believe in <u>three Gods</u> — they're just <u>different forms</u> of the <u>same God</u>.

Christian Traditions and the Virgin Mary

There are significant variations among Christians' beliefs, but they share some kind of 'relationship with Christ'.

Three Main Traditions — Roman Catholic, Orthodox and Protestant

There have been a couple of major splits in the history of the Christian Church.

Jesus and the Apostles

The Early Church

East and West split in 1054 — the Great Schism

Western Christianity

Eastern Christianity
The Orthodox Church

Western Church splits in 16th Century — the Reformation

Roman Catholicism

Protestant Churches

Church of England (Has Catholic and Protestant features)

Baptists, Methodists, United Reformed, Quakers, Pentecostal, Salvation Army...

In the Great Schism, the Pope and the Orthodox Patriarch excommunicated each other from their churches.

The Reformation began when Martin Luther challenged the authority of the Pope.

Roman Catholics
1) Roman Catholics are all those Christians who accept the authority of the Pope. They are the largest Christian group in the world.
2) They believe in the 7 sacraments as 'vehicles of God's grace' (see page 96).
3) They respect the authority of the Bible, Church tradition and the Magisterium (p.94).

Protestants

The Church of England has both Roman Catholic and Protestant features. Anglicanism is the worldwide 'communion' of churches in fellowship with the parent Church of England.

1) Protestants base their beliefs and practices on the ideas of the Reformation.
2) The Reformers stressed the importance of the Bible rather than Church tradition or the teachings of the Pope.
3) Members of the Protestant clergy are usually referred to as ministers.
4) The different groupings within Protestantism are known as denominations. In England and Wales, Protestant denominations that are not part of the 'Anglican Communion' are often called 'Nonconformists'. These include Methodists, Baptists, Pentecostals, The Society of Friends (Quakers) and the Salvation Army.

Orthodox Christians
1) Orthodox Christians are found mainly in Eastern Europe, Russia and Greece.
2) They believe that their clergy are in direct succession from the Apostles (see p.94).
3) They also have 7 sacraments, and honour (but don't worship) icons — pictures of saints.

The Virgin Mary is Very Important to Roman Catholics

1) Mary is very important to Christians because she gave birth to Jesus.

2) She is also seen as the model for Christian living, because she cooperated fully with God's will.

3) Roman Catholicism teaches that she was born without original sin, meaning she had none of the flaws that all other humans have — this is known as the Immaculate Conception.

4) Roman Catholics also believe she remained a virgin all her life, and after she died she was taken up to Heaven in the Assumption. They don't believe that Mary died a normal death — instead she's believed to have been taken directly up to Heaven.

5) Catholics don't worship Mary, but they do pray to her and ask her to pray for them (for example in the 'Ave Maria/Hail Mary'). She is also known as 'Mother of God'.

6) Protestants generally believe that Mary is worthy of great respect. But they don't believe in praying to her, as they see this as a form of idolatry — i.e. worshipping something other than God.

Movers and Shakers — Cockney rhyming slang for Quakers... (maybe)

There are at least 20,800 denominations worldwide, so don't think that the above list is all there is to know. But at the same time, don't feel as though you need to know everything about all 20,800 — that would be a pretty tough assignment. Though not for God, obviously, because he's omniscient.

The Role of the Church

The 'Church' traces its roots back to its founder, Jesus Christ. It's basically a community of believers. Those who profess faith in Jesus as God's promised Messiah become part of that community.

The Church — More than a Building

1) The mission of the Church is to expand the community of Christian believers and to help care for those who are already part of the community.

2) The Church teaches that Jesus Christ is our Saviour (see p.91), and that we can be saved by becoming his disciples. Being a disciple is more than just believing in Jesus — the Church teaches that you have to actively follow him by keeping his commandments and trying to be a good person.

3) Many Christians believe that being a member of the Church is necessary for salvation — that you can't win a place in heaven just by performing good deeds. But the Roman Catholic catechism states that someone who's never heard the Gospels can still find salvation through God's mercy.

4) The ceremony of baptism welcomes people into the Church. Roman Catholics believe that baptism is a sacrament (see p.96), and that some form of baptism is necessary to "enter the Kingdom of God".

Saint Paul Called the Church the Body of Christ

1) St Paul taught that the community of believers was the "Body of Christ" on Earth, with Christ as its head.

2) Christians who have died remain part of the faith community. The Church, made up of all Christians living or dead, is referred to as the Communion of Saints.

3) Christians believe the Church is 'holy' — sacred or belonging to God.

4) Despite its fragmentation into various traditions and denominations, the Church claims a spiritual unity. The word 'catholic' (small 'c'), meaning universal, is used to describe the community of all Christian believers.

The Church has Various Functions in the Community

Most communities in the UK have access to at least one church. The role and function of local church communities is to put the Christian faith into action. They do this in the following ways:

i) By providing a regular pattern of worship — most churches hold a Sunday service every week, and may also have other acts of communal worship throughout the week.

ii) By providing 'rites of passage' — e.g. baptisms, confirmations, weddings, funerals...

iii) By teaching Christian beliefs as part of regular services, Sunday schools or Bible classes.

iv) By ministering to the sick, e.g. visiting and praying for parishioners in hospital.

v) By supporting groups that campaign for justice and peace.

The Roman Catholic Church has a Powerful Influence

The Pope has a massive influence over Roman Catholics — e.g. over the issues of abortion and contraception.

©ZUMA/Rex Features

1) The teachings of the Roman Catholic Church on moral issues (such as abortion, sexuality and social responsibility) continue to have a strong influence on its followers.

2) Church leaders are held in respect, and their pronouncements are adhered to by faithful followers.

3) The Church also offers guidance to those who believe they may be called by God into a specific vocation e.g. the ordained ministry.

4) The Church also influences social and political development all around the world, through its involvement in peace and justice movements.

Churches — 'big-C' are communities, 'little-c' are buildings...

Yep — so don't go assuming that when the exam asks a question about the Church, it's talking about that building down the road that rings its bells once a week. There's a wee bit more to it than that.

The Authority of the Church

For Roman Catholics, the <u>only</u> authority higher than the Church is God.

For <u>Roman Catholics</u>, the Church is the <u>Supreme Authority</u>

Roman Catholics consider the authority of the <u>Church</u> to be <u>absolute</u> on matters of faith.
This position of power is based on <u>three main beliefs</u>.

The Apostolic Tradition

'<u>Apostolic</u>' just means 'of, or relating to the Apostles'.
For Roman Catholics, the Church's link to the Apostles is very important.

1) The <u>Apostolic Tradition</u> is a body of teachings and ritual practices, which the Roman Catholic Church believe was <u>handed down</u> through the early Church from the <u>Apostles</u>.
2) The <u>Gospel authors</u> themselves explain that they <u>do not</u> provide a <u>complete record</u> of Jesus's life and teaching: "Jesus did many other things as well. If every one of them were written down, I suppose that even the whole world would not have room for the books that would be written." (John 21:25 NIV).
3) Catholics believe this means that the <u>traditions</u> of the Church have as important a role to play in <u>true</u> Christian faith as the Bible — this means that not everything that Catholics believe will necessarily be taken from the Bible. In contrast, most Protestant denominations try to base <u>everything</u> on <u>scripture</u>.

The Apostolic Succession

1) The <u>Apostolic Succession</u> is what Catholics believe <u>makes</u> a Church. It's the fact that new bishops were ordained by bishops who were ordained by bishops, going back in <u>direct succession</u> to the original Apostles as chosen by Christ.
2) This fact is so important that the Catholic Church does not recognise <u>Protestant</u> Churches as true Churches because of their <u>break</u> with this succession.
3) The Pope is believed to be a direct successor of <u>St Peter</u> — 'the first Pope'. Catholics view the Pope as the most important figure in the Church because Christ singled out St Peter: "And I tell you that you are Peter, and on this rock I will build my church, and the gates of Hades will not overcome it." (Matthew 16:18 NIV)

Churches that believe they were originally founded by the Apostles describe themselves as <u>apostolic</u>.

The Magisterium

1) The <u>Magisterium</u> is the authority of the Pope and his bishops to teach correctly in all matters of <u>faith and morals</u>. Roman Catholics believe this authority is given by the <u>Holy Spirit</u>. The Church has the <u>final say</u> in the interpretation of <u>scripture</u> and <u>tradition</u>.
2) When the Pope and the bishops <u>agree</u> on a point of doctrine it becomes part of <u>official Church teaching</u> — and Catholics are then supposed not only to follow the teaching, but also to <u>believe in it</u> fully.
3) The Pope can make official statements on his <u>own</u> on questions of faith and morals, and these are believed to be <u>infallible</u> (they <u>can't</u> be wrong). But this doesn't happen very often — the last time was in <u>1950</u>.
4) The firm beliefs of the Catholic Church are known as <u>dogmas</u>.
Most of them are set out in the <u>Roman Catholic catechism</u> (see p.91).

Protestant Churches <u>have less</u> Authority

1) Different Protestant Churches hold different views on the importance of Church hierarchy.
2) For example, <u>Congregationalists</u> believe each individual church is responsible for its <u>own organisation</u>. But <u>Presbyterians</u> send <u>elders</u> from each church to form <u>councils</u> which have authority over the churches.
3) Protestants tend to place far greater emphasis on a believer's <u>own faith</u> and <u>understanding of the Bible</u> according to their <u>own conscience</u> — and far less on the authority and teachings of the Church. This is one of the reasons why there are so many <u>different</u> Protestant denominations, as people often left old Churches and set up new ones, because they disagreed on an aspect of Church teaching.

This page is supremely authoritative...

Arguments about the importance and authority of the Church played a key part in the Reformation — when the Protestants split from the Roman Catholic Church. So Protestants will have very different views on this stuff from Catholics. Make sure you know <u>both sides</u>, so you can answer a question about it in the exam.

The Role of the Clergy

This is a page full of <u>bishops</u> and <u>priests</u> and stuff.

The Roman Catholic Church has a Hierarchy...

The Roman Catholic Church is arranged in a <u>hierarchy</u>, with the Pope at the top.

Pope

Cardinals

Bishops

Priests

Deacons

Laity

THE POPE — The <u>Bishop of Rome</u> and head of the worldwide Roman Catholic Church. Jesus is believed to have chosen St Peter as the first Pope, and the current Pope is his spiritual descendant. On matters of faith and morals, the Pope is regarded as <u>infallible</u>, and his teachings are <u>binding</u> on all Roman Catholics (see also page 94). The office of the Pope is known as the <u>papacy</u>.

CARDINALS — The highest rank of bishop next to the Pope. They're appointed by the Pope, and act as his <u>advisors</u>. In turn, they're responsible for electing the Pope's <u>successor</u>.

BISHOPS — Bishops are appointed by the Pope — they each have responsibility for the churches in their <u>diocese</u> (a district made up of several parishes).

PRIESTS — A priest is the head of an individual <u>parish</u> (an area served by a local church). Priests are in charge of Catholic worship and education in their parish.

DEACONS — A deacon may carry out some, but not all of the offices of a priest (see below). <u>Married men</u> can become Roman Catholic deacons, but not priests.

LAITY — all the <u>non-ordained</u> members of the Roman Catholic Church.

1) The office of deacon (and those above it in the hierarchy) can be held by men (and <u>only</u> men) who have been <u>ordained</u>, i.e. officially admitted into the <u>clergy</u>.

2) The rite of ordination is one of the <u>sacraments</u> (see p.96), and it can only be performed by a <u>bishop</u>.

3) A Roman Catholic <u>priest</u> has a number of <u>roles</u> within the parish.

4) His main roles are to lead the celebration of the <u>Mass</u> (only a priest or bishop can perform the Liturgy of the Eucharist, see p.97) and to hear <u>confession</u> (see p.96).

5) It's also his job to <u>preach</u> the Gospel, administer the <u>sacraments</u> of baptism, marriage and anointing the sick (see p.96) and to offer <u>support</u> and <u>guidance</u> to the people of the parish.

6) A Roman Catholic <u>deacon</u> will often assist the priest of a large parish. Deacons may carry out any of the duties of a priest, <u>apart</u> from celebrating Mass, hearing confession or anointing the sick.

Roman Catholic Priests must be Celibate

1) In the Catholic Church, to become a <u>priest</u> a man has to be <u>unmarried</u> and <u>stay celibate</u> (not have <u>sex</u>). Catholics believe that this allows priests to focus fully on their <u>spiritual duties</u>.

2) They base this on the teachings of <u>Paul</u> that "It is good for a man not to marry" (1 Corinthians 7:1 NIV) and Jesus's remark that some "have renounced marriage because of the kingdom of heaven" (Matthew 19:12 NIV).

3) In recent years there has been a <u>fall</u> in the number of men wanting to become priests. Some Catholics <u>blame</u> this on the celibacy rule.

4) Protestants argue that celibacy is <u>not stated</u> as a qualification for priesthood in the Bible. Some have argued that celibacy is too difficult for many and so becomes a <u>distraction</u> rather than an aid to spiritual life.

5) Anglican priests and Protestant ministers are allowed to marry either before or after they're ordained. Some denominations <u>encourage</u> ministers to marry, to set a good example for the congregation.

6) In the <u>Orthodox</u> tradition, married men can be ordained as priests (but not bishops) — but they can't get married once they've been ordained.

It'd be a cardinal sin not to learn this page...

I bet you thought vicars would get a mention. Well, here you are. 'Vicar' is a general title that's come to be used to refer to any parish priest. 'Minister' is also a general title — used to describe anyone who's been ordained. And the clergy consists of anyone who's been ordained. Lots of words for the same kind of thing.

The Seven Sacraments

Roman Catholic and Orthodox Churches believe in <u>seven sacraments</u>.

The Seven Sacraments — Vehicles of God's Grace

God is thought to communicate his <u>grace</u> (unearned favour) <u>directly</u> through sacraments, <u>whether or not</u> the recipient <u>understands</u> what it all means. The sacraments are:

1) **Baptism** Baptism marks a person's official <u>entry</u> into the <u>Church</u>. It symbolises the start of a <u>new life</u> and the washing away of <u>sin</u>. Those who regard baptism as a <u>sacrament</u> see no problem with baptising <u>infants</u>. They believe that this cleanses the baby from <u>original sin</u> (see p.4).

2) **Confirmation** In this ceremony a Christian <u>renews</u> the vows made on his or her behalf at baptism.

3) **Reconciliation** This involves <u>confession</u> of a sin, followed by <u>contrition</u>, <u>penance</u> and <u>absolution</u>.

4) **Eucharist** In Holy Communion (see p.97), the believer <u>receives</u> Christ into him- or herself afresh.

5) **Ordination** This is the rite in which people are made <u>deacons</u>, <u>priests</u> or <u>bishops</u> (see p.95).

6) **Marriage** When a couple are joined in <u>Holy Matrimony</u> they receive a special blessing.

7) **Anointing the Sick** This may be for <u>healing</u>, or to prepare a <u>dying</u> person for the next life.

Confirmation helps Strengthen a Person's Faith

1) Most Churches have a Confirmation rite. For Roman Catholics, it is considered a sacrament. It is believed to strengthen the ties of the confirmed to the Church and to God.

2) In Catholic Confirmations, the bishop anoints the believer's forehead with holy oil called chrism. This oil has been consecrated (made holy) with a blessing from a bishop.

3) Catholics get confirmed around the age of thirteen, when they're old enough to understand what it means. They have to show that they understand their faith — usually by attending a course of religious instruction.

Reconciliation makes up for Sin

1) <u>Reconciliation</u> through <u>confession</u> is how Roman Catholics obtain <u>forgiveness</u> for the sins they commit.

2) Confession is where a believer <u>admits</u> to a priest any <u>sinful</u> things that they've done. To prepare for this, a believer must <u>think seriously</u> about the sins they've committed.

3) The priest will give a <u>penance</u> (a certain number of prayers to be said, or an action to be done) and will then pronounce <u>absolution</u> (God's forgiveness). For confession to be effective the believer needs to be <u>genuinely sorry</u> and make a commitment not to sin again — this is known as <u>contrition</u>.

4) Confession and reconciliation are <u>important</u>. All Catholics are supposed to confess <u>at least once a year</u>, but are recommended to do it more regularly. If a Catholic commits a <u>serious (mortal) sin</u> they should confess as soon as possible — Catholics believe that if they die unreconciled, they will go to Hell.

Catholics Believe in Anointing the Sick

1) Catholics believe in <u>anointing the sick</u> — this is where a priest or a bishop anoints a <u>seriously unwell person</u> with the <u>oil of the sick</u> (oil, usually scented with balsam, that has been blessed by a bishop).

2) If someone is facing death it will be administered as part of the <u>Last Rites</u>, along with a final confession and a final Eucharist (known as the viaticum).

3) Catholics believe that, through this sacrament, the <u>Holy Spirit</u> renews the sick person's <u>faith</u> and <u>strength</u> to <u>cope</u> with their illness and <u>accept</u> their suffering. The anointing is also believed to <u>link</u> the person's suffering to the suffering of <u>Christ</u>, allow their <u>sins</u> to be forgiven and to <u>heal</u> them, if that is <u>God's will</u>.

Big Cats Rarely Eat 'Orrible Maggoty Apples...

Try this way of remembering the <u>initial letters</u> of the <u>seven sacraments</u>. It's a good 'un.

Mass

The <u>Mass</u> is the Roman Catholic service that includes the <u>Eucharist</u> (<u>Holy Communion</u>).

Holy Communion Commemorates the Last Supper

1) At the <u>Last Supper</u>, Jesus said that the bread and wine on the table represented his <u>body</u> and <u>blood</u>. The disciples were to eat and drink in remembrance of him whenever they ate together.
2) Virtually all Christians recognise the importance of <u>Holy Communion</u> (also called the <u>Eucharist</u>), but most see it as largely <u>commemorative</u> — it <u>reminds</u> worshippers of the Last Supper and Jesus's sacrifice.
3) However, Roman Catholics believe that the bread and wine actually <u>become</u> the body and blood of Christ, by the power of the Holy Spirit. This is known as <u>transubstantiation</u>, and it is through this that Jesus takes up <u>residence</u> in his people. This is why it's vital for Roman Catholics to attend Mass regularly.

There are Four Key Features of a Catholic Mass:

Penitential Rite

This is a <u>joint confession</u> of sin and a request for God's mercy and forgiveness in the form of a prayer said by the whole congregation. It's followed by the reciting of the '<u>Kyrie</u>' prayer, either in Greek or in English. "Kyrie, eleison (Lord have mercy) Christe, eleison (Christ have mercy) Kyrie, eleison (Lord have mercy)".

Liturgy of the Word

A '<u>liturgy</u>' is a well-defined <u>pattern</u> of rituals, set prayers and readings.

The penitential rite is followed by the <u>liturgy of the word</u>. This consists of readings from scripture, usually including a section from one of the Gospels, followed by a <u>homily</u> (a short sermon based on the readings). This is followed by a joint recitation of either the <u>Nicene Creed</u> or the <u>Apostles' Creed</u> (see p.90).

Liturgy of the Eucharist

The liturgy of the Eucharist is the most important part of the Roman Catholic Mass — it is the point at which Catholics believe that the bread and wine are <u>transformed</u> into the body and blood of Christ. The bread and wine are usually brought in by a procession, and <u>transubstantiated</u> during a series of prayers including the <u>Institution Narrative</u>, which describes Christ's words and actions during the Last Supper.

Rite of Communion

This begins with everyone saying the <u>Lord's Prayer</u>, followed by the <u>sign of peace</u>, where everyone shakes hands or hugs those around them. Following this, the congregation come forward to receive the bread and wine. Finally there is the <u>concluding rite</u>, which is a series of prayers that brings the Mass to a close. Any leftover consecrated bread and wine must be consumed by a priest, or placed in a <u>ciborium</u> (a lidded chalice) inside a 'safe' called a tabernacle.

On discovering that he had to eat the leftovers, Father Donald quickly made the switch to Communion pizza.

Non-Catholics also have a Eucharist

There are a wide variety of beliefs about the <u>importance</u> of the Eucharist, and what actually occurs during the service, for different denominations.

1) Lutherans, Methodists and most Anglicans believe that Holy Communion is more than just an '<u>intellectual</u>' commemoration of the Last Supper, it's a <u>re-enactment</u>. They believe that there is a '<u>real presence</u>' of Christ in the bread and wine. But they <u>don't</u> believe that transubstantiation occurs.
2) Reformed (Calvinist) Churches believe that the bread and wine are <u>symbolic</u> of a spiritual reality and are <u>physically unchanged</u>, but that the performance of the Eucharist does achieve '<u>spiritual nourishment</u>'.
3) Quakers and the Salvation Army don't celebrate the Eucharist or any other sacraments, seeing them as <u>unnecessary</u> or <u>inessential symbols</u> for the inward acceptance of God's grace.

Mass — it's a weighty subject...

While there are a variety of opinions as to what happens to the bread and wine during the service, Holy Communion is one of the few rites that nearly all Christian Churches have in common.

Festivals and Church Worship

According to the <u>Bible</u>, no time of year is any more sacred than any other. However, certain times of year are used by Christians to commemorate, give thanks for and celebrate specific aspects of their faith.

Christian Festivals Occur Throughout the Year

ADVENT and CHRISTMAS — December

<u>Advent</u> marks the start of the Christian year, and begins <u>4 Sundays before Christmas</u>. It's a period of preparation for Christmas and for Christ's Second Coming. <u>Advent candles</u> are lit in homes and churches, and children may use <u>Advent calendars</u> to count off the days until Christmas.

Christmas celebrates the <u>Incarnation</u> — when God's Son came to Earth as a human being. We don't know the exact date of his birth, but we celebrate it on December 25th.

Customs <u>vary</u> around the world, but often date from <u>pre-Christian</u> times (e.g. Christmas trees). In many Roman Catholic churches there's a 'Midnight Mass' to welcome Christmas Day, and a crib (nativity scene).

But some Christians think that the giving of <u>expensive presents</u> takes away the focus of what Christmas is supposed to be about. And others feel that it has retained too much <u>pagan</u> influence.

> How did I get mixed up in all this?

LENT — February / March

<u>Lent</u> commemorates the 40 days and nights of Jesus's <u>fasting</u> (going without food) in the wilderness after his baptism. On the day before Lent (<u>Shrove Tuesday</u>), Roman Catholics <u>confess</u> their sins and are '<u>shriven</u>' (absolved from sin). Rich foods should be eaten up before the start of the fast and <u>Mardi Gras</u> carnivals may be held.

On <u>Ash Wednesday</u> (the first day of Lent) ash is put on believers' foreheads to show that they are sorry for their sins. Lent ends on the day before Easter.

For Roman Catholics, Lent is traditionally a <u>sombre</u> time where the focus of worship is on the <u>suffering of Jesus</u>. Catholics are <u>obliged</u> to abstain from meat on each Friday of Lent, and to fast (limit themselves to one main meal and two small meals a day) for a minimum of two days — <u>Ash Wednesday</u> and <u>Good Friday</u> (see below).

HOLY WEEK — March / April

This is the final week of Lent, lasting from <u>Palm Sunday</u> (the Sunday before Easter, recalling Jesus's triumphal entry into Jerusalem) until the day before <u>Easter</u>. It commemorates Jesus's final week <u>on Earth</u>.

<u>Maundy Thursday</u> recalls the Last Supper, and <u>Good Friday</u> Jesus's crucifixion. There are special services, especially on Good Friday between noon and 3pm — the hours when Jesus was dying on the cross.

EASTER SUNDAY — March / April

This commemorates Jesus's <u>resurrection</u>. Special <u>services</u> are held — Roman Catholics hold an <u>Easter Vigil</u> the night before. Easter is the most important festival of the year for most Christians, since it celebrates the <u>victory</u> of Jesus over death. It starts a <u>fifty day period</u> of focusing on the actions of the risen Christ.

But some Christians dislike the modern use of <u>symbols</u> (e.g. eggs and Easter bunnies) that are believed to be associated with <u>pre-Christian</u> festivals.

The Altar is the Focus of a Roman Catholic Church

1) The main <u>features</u> of a Roman Catholic Church are on page 78 — go and have a look.

2) In <u>Roman Catholic</u> churches, the <u>focal point</u> of the building is the <u>altar</u>. This reflects the '<u>liturgical</u>' nature of their services and the importance of the Eucharist (see p.97).

3) In Roman Catholic churches, you'll also tend to find <u>statues</u>, e.g. of the Virgin Mary and painted or sculpted scenes called the '<u>Stations of the Cross</u>'. These fourteen scenes depict the last hours before the <u>death</u> of Jesus, and are used to help Catholics pray and meditate on the sufferings of Christ — usually during <u>Lent</u>.

Holy Days or holidays — who cares...

There's huge variety in the way festivals are celebrated, and many customs are <u>cultural</u> rather than <u>Christian</u> (e.g. Easter bunnies). Make sure you learn <u>what</u> the festivals celebrate and <u>why</u>, not <u>how</u> things are done.

Love and the Christian Faith

Love is central to the Christian faith.

God showed his Love by Sending Jesus

One of the most frequently quoted verses from the Bible is:

> "For God so loved the world that he gave his one and only Son, that whoever believes in him shall not perish but have eternal life." John 3:16 NIV

1) Christians believe that God expressed his love for us by sending us his son — who, although he was perfect, was punished so that our sins could be forgiven (see p.91).
2) This reconciliation between God and humanity is known as the atonement.
3) Christians believe that we must trust and love God and accept Christ as our saviour.
4) Then if we repent of our sins (are sorry, seek forgiveness and try hard not to repeat them) we will be forgiven. And doing so will lead to our salvation — we will be accepted into eternal life.

Jesus Taught Us Not Just to Respect — but to Love

1) For Jesus, respect wasn't enough — he wanted his followers to love.
2) When asked which was the most important commandment in Judaism (i.e. all the laws given to the Jews in the first five books of the Bible), he gave this answer...

> "'The most important one,' answered Jesus, 'is this... Love the Lord your God with all your heart and with all your soul and with all your mind and with all your strength. The second is this: Love your neighbour as yourself.'" Mark 12:29-31 NIV

Love is a Key Concept in Christianity

1) Love is what the Christian faith is all about, but this isn't always as simple as it might seem. Christians have developed the concept of agape — a selfless love, unconditional, always serving and always caring.
2) In Matthew 25:31-46, Jesus talks of separating out those who will be saved from those who won't (p.47). He explains that salvation will come to those who demonstrate love by helping people in need.
3) In another example, a man asks Jesus who his 'neighbour' is, since he's commanded to 'love his neighbour'. Jesus replies with the parable of the Good Samaritan (Luke 10:25-37) — see p.32.
4) This parable argues that compassion — the feeling of pity for and the desire to help those who suffer — is more important to God than being high up in the religious hierarchy.

Local Churches Show Love of God and Others

1) Most local churches try to take an active role in the community.
2) A church's main function is to help its congregation express their love of God through regular religious services for people in their local area (parishioners).
3) Some local churches demonstrate their love for others by getting involved in campaigns on social issues, e.g. by raising money to help the poor and underprivileged, or encouraging people to buy Fair Trade products.
4) Many churches have youth groups and Sunday Schools to encourage young people to get involved in the Church and its activities.

Love never ends — I am the walrus, goo, goo, ga joob...

Churches get involved in all sorts of activities: choirs, coffee mornings, Bible study groups, fund-raising... all to express love of God and other people. Who'd have thought a jumble sale could be an expression of love.

Section Nine — Roman Catholic Christianity

The Sermon on the Mount

The <u>Sermon on the Mount</u> is a summary of Jesus's teachings on how Christians are supposed to live.

The Sermon on the Mount — the Christian Ideal

The <u>Sermon on the Mount</u> is one of the most important summaries of Jesus's moral teaching found in the Gospels. It appears as a collection in Matthew 5:1-7:29, but much of the same material is also in <u>Luke</u>. Some say that the Sermon on the Mount preaches an <u>ideal</u>, which no one can live up to. But others argue that Christians can still <u>aspire</u> to this ideal, though no one can be totally perfect (this side of the grave, anyway).

Jesus Reinterprets the Law of Moses (Matthew 5:17-48)

1) In the Sermon, Jesus <u>reinterprets</u> the <u>Law of Moses</u> — the rules given by God in the Old Testament.
2) Jesus takes these laws and makes them more <u>strict</u> and more <u>internal</u>. Where the Law of Moses calls for people not to <u>kill</u>, Jesus orders us to go further and not be <u>angry</u> with each other. Where the Law of Moses orders us not to commit <u>adultery</u>, Jesus warns that looking upon someone <u>lustfully</u> is sinful in itself. Jesus takes commandments about <u>actions</u> and makes them about <u>intentions</u> and <u>emotions</u>.
3) Jesus speaks about anger, adultery, divorce, vows, revenge and <u>love for our enemies</u>: "If someone strikes you on the right cheek, turn to him the other also." (NIV)

Displaying Religion (Matthew 6:1-18)

1) Jesus orders his followers to do their <u>praying</u>, giving to <u>charity</u>, and <u>fasting</u> quietly and without trying to impress other people.

> It's in this part of the Gospel that Jesus teaches his followers the <u>Lord's Prayer</u> — "*Our Father in heaven, hallowed be your name...*" (NIV)

2) Jesus says that those who do good things in <u>secret</u> will be <u>rewarded</u> by God. But that those who deliberately do good work <u>in front of a crowd</u>, known as '<u>displaying religion</u>', have already had their reward in the effect it has on their audience.
3) Jesus calls those who display religion <u>hypocrites</u> — people who act out beliefs they don't really hold, or whose actions don't match what they say.
4) Most modern Christians take this to mean that, while prayers, charity and fasting don't need to be done in private, they should be done for <u>God alone</u>, with no thought of trying to <u>impress others</u>.

Christians and Money (Matthew 6:19-34)

1) Jesus orders his followers not to seek <u>material riches</u> ("treasures on earth"), or even material security, but rather <u>spiritual riches</u> ("treasures in heaven"). He says "You cannot serve both God and Money." (NIV)
2) He tells his followers that it's wrong to even <u>worry</u> about material things : "Look at the birds of the air; they do not sow or reap or store away in barns, and yet your heavenly Father feeds them. Are you not much more valuable than they? Who of you by worrying can add a single hour to his life?" (NIV)
3) Most Christians <u>don't</u> take these verses to mean that we shouldn't save money, but rather that our <u>main concern</u> should be with spiritual things and <u>helping other people</u>.

Christians and Judgement and The Golden Rule (Matthew 7:1-12)

1) Jesus warns his followers "Do not judge, or you too will be judged." (NIV) He uses the image of someone trying to remove a <u>speck of sawdust</u> from another man's eye when they have a <u>plank</u> in their own.
2) Most Christians interpret this as meaning they should strictly judge their <u>own moral state</u> before looking at other people's, and that they must be charitable and forgiving of other people's <u>failings</u>.

And another thing...

3) Jesus then states what's known as the <u>Golden Rule</u>:

> "*do to others what you would have them do to you, for this sums up the Law and the Prophets.*" (NIV)

Many Christians use the Golden Rule as a moral <u>rule of thumb</u> (see p.47).

Don't pass judgement on others — that's the examiner's job...

The Bible's a long book (you've probably noticed) — but Matthew 5, 6 and 7 give you the gist of Jesus's teachings.

Christian Values and Vocation

Jesus was a Jew, so his values were grounded in <u>Jewish</u> belief — the laws found in the <u>Old Testament</u>.

The Ten Commandments were Given to Moses

The most famous laws in the Old Testament are the <u>Ten Commandments</u> given to Moses in Exodus 20. There's a full list of the Commandments on page 43.

Most Christians believe that it's <u>necessary</u> to try to stick to the Ten Commandments.
The <u>Roman Catholic Church</u> teaches that observance of them is necessary for <u>salvation</u>.

Look at my lovely tablets.

The Commandments are about Respecting God...

The <u>first three</u> commandments are about showing <u>respect to God</u>.

1) The first calls for <u>monotheism</u>. Worshippers of God mustn't worship <u>anything else</u> — including <u>idols</u>.

2) The second commandment demands respect for the <u>name</u> of the Lord. Not only does this ban using "God" or "Jesus" as <u>swear words</u>, but also using God's name to back up a <u>lie</u> or in a <u>dishonest manner</u>.

3) Different Christian groups place greater or less emphasis on the third commandment of observing the <u>Sabbath</u>. This is God's instruction to take <u>one day</u> out of the week and keep it <u>holy</u>. Traditionally, the Sabbath was a day dedicated to God and family on which <u>no work</u> was allowed to be done.

4) For most Christians, including Roman Catholics, the Sabbath day is <u>Sunday</u>.
Sunday is the <u>Lord's Day</u>, since this was the day of Christ's resurrection.

5) In the UK, laws against working on a Sunday have gradually been relaxed as society has become less religious. An organisation called <u>Keep Sunday Special</u> campaigns for stricter rules on Sunday trading — both to help religious people keep the Sabbath, and to secure a day that families can spend together.

...and Other People

The <u>last seven</u> commandments are about showing respect for <u>other people</u>.

1) Some Christians believe that the fourth commandment, which calls for the <u>honouring of your father and mother</u>, includes respect not only for extended family members but also for those placed in positions of <u>responsibility</u> and authority, such as teachers.

2) The fifth commandment, <u>not to kill</u>, is interpreted in different ways. The Roman Catholic Church is willing to make exceptions for killing in <u>war</u> — but some groups, like the Religious Society of Friends (Quakers), are <u>pacifists</u> and are against fighting and killing under any circumstances.

3) Many modern Bibles translate the commandment as "You shall not <u>murder</u>", which allows for killing in <u>war</u> and <u>capital punishment</u>. They argue this is more in keeping with the rest of the Old Testament.

4) Roman Catholics take the commandment not to kill to include a ban on <u>abortion</u>.

5) The sixth, seventh and eighth commandments ban <u>adultery</u> (cheating on your partner), <u>theft</u> and <u>lying</u>.

6) The last two are perhaps the <u>subtlest</u> of the commandments. You don't have to actually <u>do</u> anything to break them — you break them just by <u>lusting</u> after a married woman (or man), or <u>yearning</u> for something that belongs to someone else. These commandments are closely linked to the sin of <u>envy</u>.

You can Respond to God Through a Vocation

1) Some people feel that they've experienced a <u>call</u> from God to lead a <u>Christian life</u>.
This 'calling' is known as a <u>vocation</u> (see p.70).

2) It can be a <u>job</u>, but isn't always.

3) For example, some people feel called to serve the <u>Church</u> by taking <u>holy orders</u> (being ordained) as a deacon, priest or bishop. Others are drawn to full-time <u>worship</u> of God as part of a <u>religious order</u> (see next page). Most Christians with a vocation believe that God has created them with the right <u>talents</u> for it.

Number 11 — You shall learn this page...

It's always a good idea to know the rules — that way you won't break them accidentally. But if in doubt, 'respect' is a good place to start. If something feels disrespectful, you probably shouldn't be doing it.

Religious Communities

Christians believe that love is all-important, whatever your vocation, but it can be expressed in different ways.

Religious Communities Worship Full Time

1) A religious order is a group of monks or nuns who live by the same 'rule'.
2) An order who live together in a monastery or convent are called a religious community.
   Religious communities express their love of God by fully committing to a life of worship.
3) Members of religious orders usually make vows dedicating their lives to God (a bit like in a marriage).

> ### Members of most religious orders take three vows
>
> Poverty — Members have no personal possessions. These are given to the community or the poor.
> Chastity — Members abstain from sexual relationships to better focus on a life of prayer.
> Obedience — Members follow the rules of the community, and promise to obey superiors in the order.

4) These three rules are known as the evangelical counsels. They're generally
   believed to be only for those with this specific religious calling.

There are Two Main Types of Religious Community

1) APOSTOLIC orders stress service to the poor, sick or destitute, and their members
   work 'in the world'. Members of these orders are said to live the active life.
   Mother Teresa's 'Missionaries of Charity', and the 'Franciscans' are good examples.

I like to be alone, so I support Millom Athletic.

2) CONTEMPLATIVE orders are dedicated to prayer and study. These orders are usually
   enclosed religious communities, where members live together and rarely (if ever) leave
   their monasteries. 'The Carmelites' and 'Poor Clares' (for women), and the
   'Carthusians' or 'Cistercians' (for men) live the contemplative life.
3) Someone who lives as a monk or nun in a religious community is said to live a monastic life.

Religious Communities Express their Love of God...

1) Those in contemplative orders aim to remove themselves from the world and dedicate their lives to
   God through prayer, and to living together in peace.
2) Monks and nuns pray at a number of specific times during the day — starting from early in the
   morning (around 4:30 a.m.) through into the late evening. The rest of their time will usually be spent
   studying scripture or working — many religious orders make things to sell to fund the community.
3) Members of apostolic orders also dedicate time to prayer and study — but this fits into their work
   'in the world' rather than being their sole focus.
4) Some Protestants don't agree with religious communities based on vows, since this idea isn't
   mentioned in the Bible, so most orders are Roman Catholic.

...and Other People

1) Those in apostolic orders go out into the community to try to help people and to advance their faith.
   For example, the Roman Catholic Society of Jesus (Jesuits) are famous for their work in education.
2) Mother Teresa's Order of the Missionaries of Charity work to relieve the suffering of the poor all over
   the world — see page 17.
3) Members of contemplative orders will pray for other people and offer spiritual guidance to visitors.

Religious orders — learn this Christianity stuff really well...

Most Christians believe that they should seek to discover their vocation — the thing that God's calling them
to do. For some people, that means joining a religious community and dedicating their lives to worship.

Christian Charities in the UK

Christians, like all people with a religious faith, try to act in a way that's consistent with their beliefs. For many this means getting involved in charity — giving time and money to help people in need.

Christians have a Duty to Help Relieve Poverty

> "Rich nations have a grave moral responsibility towards those which are unable to ensure the means of their development by themselves..."
> from the Catechism of the Catholic Church: paragraph 2439

1) All Christian denominations have become more concerned over the last few decades with a fairer distribution of wealth.

2) A key question for all Christians is whether wealth ultimately belongs to God, and should therefore be for the good of everyone.

3) Many Christians are concerned about whether or not they should be wealthy. Jesus spoke of giving up wealth to help the poor, but the Roman Catholic Church is a very wealthy organisation.

4) Financial charity is an important part of Christianity (see p.17).

5) Jesus also said that we have an obligation to love each other, and that if we help those who need it, it is as if we are helping Jesus himself (see p.47).

6) A number of Christian organisations exist to tackle poverty — both in the UK and on a global level. Those who work internationally include Christian Aid (see p.17) and CAFOD.

The Passage Helps the Homeless in London

1) The Passage is a Roman Catholic organisation set up to help the homeless.

2) It was started in 1980 by Westminster Cathedral together with an apostolic religious order (see previous page) called the Daughters of Charity of St Vincent de Paul.

3) The Passage runs a hostel (i.e. temporary accommodation) in London for homeless people, with priority given to the most vulnerable.

4) Although The Passage does provide a Roman Catholic chaplaincy service if requested, it doesn't carry out any deliberate evangelical work — it doesn't try to convert people to Roman Catholic Christianity.

5) It also offers medical care, skills training and advice to help homeless people get jobs and build new lives for themselves.

Church Action on Poverty Campaigns for the Poor

1) Church Action on Poverty is a national ecumenical charity (i.e. made up of representatives from different denominations) that works to reduce poverty in the UK.

2) They encourage churches to get actively involved in helping the poor.

3) They campaign on a number of issues, including securing rights for asylum seekers and trying to get a raise in the minimum wage.

4) They also try to help people in poverty have an influence on the decisions that affect them, e.g. decisions made by local government.

"Let us not love with words... but with actions and in truth..."

(1 John 3:18 NIV) This page is one of the best adverts for Christianity. Regardless of your religious beliefs, it's difficult to argue with any group that gets out into the world and actually spends its time helping people. As Jesus says, "a tree is recognised by its fruit" — and there's some pretty good fruit right here.

Practice Questions

All this stuff should be meat and drink if you're going to get anywhere in your RS exam. Think about it...
how do you expect to be able to answer an exam question about Roman Catholicism if you don't know how
people go about <u>being</u> Catholic... So learn, learn, learn away... and then try <u>all</u> these questions.
Watch out for your spelling, punctuation and grammar along the way.

1) What is:

a) a creed?

b) the Incarnation?

c) the catechism?

d) catholic? (Note the small 'c'.)

e) apostolic?

f) the Magisterium?

g) the papacy?

h) the laity?

i) ordination?

j) celibacy?

k) a sacrament?

l) chrism?

m) absolution?

n) the liturgy of the word?

o) transubstantiation?

p) Holy Week?

q) the atonement?

r) the Sermon on the Mount?

s) displaying religion?

t) holy orders?

u) the evangelical counsels?

Gosh, that's a lot of key terms. Get 'em learnt.

2) For each of the following questions, give <u>two</u> reasons for your point of view.

a) Do you think God should be called the Creator?

b) Do you think being apostolic is important for a Church?

c) Do you think it is important for a community to have a priest?

d) Do you think it's important for a Roman Catholic to be confirmed?

e) Do you think that the Eucharist is the most important sacrament?

f) Do you think Roman Catholics should celebrate Christmas?

g) Do you think being compassionate is important for a Christian?

h) Do you think that being Christian should affect how people live their lives?

i) Do you think Christian religious communities have a positive impact on the world?

Make sure you get two good reasons down for these, and then move on.

3) For these questions, you need to express yourself as clearly as possible —
make sure your writing is correct, accurate and well organised.

a) Explain what Christians believe about the Trinity.

b) Explain what Christians believe about salvation.

c) Explain why Roman Catholics honour the Virgin Mary.

d) Describe the role of a local church or priest in the community.

e) Explain why Roman Catholics do not believe that the Bible is the only source of religious authority.

f) Explain why the sacrament of reconciliation is important to Roman Catholics.

g) Explain why the different elements of the Mass are important to Roman Catholics.

h) Explain why many Roman Catholics think that Easter is the most important event in the year.

i) Explain why Christians think love is important.

j) Explain how Jesus reinterprets the Law of Moses in the Sermon on the Mount.

k) Explain how some Christians use the Ten Commandments as a guide to living.

l) Explain how some Christians fulfil their vocation in a religious order.

m) Explain how one Roman Catholic organisation helps relieve poverty and suffering in the UK.

You have to really get a solid grasp of the facts for these.

4) Read the following statements:

a) "God cannot be three and one at the same time."

b) "To be a Christian you have to go out and help people."

c) "Priests should remain celibate."

d) "The seven sacraments are all vehicles for God's grace."

e) "A child should be baptised as soon as possible."

f) "All Christians should give something up for Lent."

g) "For Christians, helping those in need should be more important than evangelising."

h) "All Ten Commandments are equally important."

i) "You can serve God better in an active life than in a contemplative life."

Discuss each statement. You should include different, supported points
of view and a personal viewpoint. You must refer to Roman Catholic Christianity in your answer.

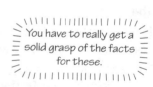
Include relevant technical vocabulary in your answers to impress the examiner.

The Nature of Discipleship

Christianity sees Jesus as the Son of God — and so his story is pretty important.

The Gospels — Good News, but Not Biographies

1) The Gospels were written to preserve the story of Jesus after the apostles died.

2) They also pointed to the coming of the 'kingdom of God'.
The 'kingdom of God' is the rulership of God in people's lives.
In the Gospels, it either refers to the total acceptance of God in
someone's heart, or to the final Kingdom after Judgement Day.

> "Jesus went into Galilee, proclaiming...
> 'The kingdom of God is near. Repent and
> believe the good news!'" Mark 1:14-15 NIV

3) An early Christian wrote that Mark was the 'interpreter of Peter', but that he hadn't known
Jesus personally. Mark may have used early collections of Jesus's words and actions, or
he may have got information from Peter (see pages 107 and 113 for more about Peter.).

The Calling of the Disciples — Jesus Gathered Followers

1) The word 'disciple' means 'follower', and is often used to refer to one of Jesus's followers
from the Gospels. But it can also be used more generally to mean any Christian.

> Follow me!

2) Mark tells us that Jesus called as his first disciples: Simon, Andrew, John, James and Levi.

The Calling of the First Disciples (Mark 1:14-20)
As Jesus walked by the Sea of Galilee, he came across
four fishermen: Simon (who he later called Peter or 'rock'),
Andrew, and the 'sons of Zebedee' — James and John.

> "'Come, follow me,' Jesus said,
> 'and I will make you fishers of men.'"

They all abandoned their nets and followed Jesus.

The Calling of Levi (Mark 2:13-17)
Jesus called a tax collector, Levi, to follow him. He had dinner
with Levi and other people the Pharisees called 'sinners':

> "...they asked his disciples: 'Why does he eat with tax
> collectors and 'sinners'?' On hearing this, Jesus said to
> them, 'It is not the healthy who need a doctor, but the sick.
> I have not come to call the righteous, but sinners.'" (NIV)

3) Jesus didn't choose to call well-educated, religious men, e.g. the Sadducees (Jewish priests) or Pharisees
(teachers of the Law). Instead he called common fishermen to learn from him and serve God.

4) He also called Levi to be a disciple — a tax collector. Tax collectors were strongly disliked by most Jews,
because they worked for the occupying Romans. (According to the Gospel of Matthew, Levi is Matthew the Apostle.)

5) Most modern Christians believe these two passages show that anyone can be a follower of Jesus.
It doesn't matter what your background is, or how much you've sinned in the past. Anyone who repents
and follows Jesus is welcome.

The Mission of the Disciples — Go Out and Preach

1) Over time, Jesus called other disciples to him until he had 'the Twelve' (later known as the apostles).

2) He sent the disciples out in pairs to tell the people of Israel the good news of the kingdom of God.

The Sending Out of the Twelve (Mark 6:7-13)
Jesus sent his disciples out with authority over evil spirits. They
were to take a staff — but should not take bread, money, a bag or
an extra coat. Where they were made welcome, they were to stay in
that place until they left town. Where they were not made welcome,
they were to shake the dust from their feet as a marker to others.

> "They went out and preached that
> people should repent. They drove
> out many demons and anointed
> many sick people with oil and
> healed them." Mark 6:12-13 NIV

3) The disciples were told to trust in God and He would provide for them during their mission (through the
charity of others). Many Christians believe that they should be prepared to do the same.

4) This passage also carries a message to Christians today about giving charity. They should be among the
people who would welcome the apostles, rather than those who turn them away.

This stuff is true — it's all gospel, mate...

'Following' Jesus was a bit more literal back then — the disciples travelled together with Jesus as he preached.

The Costs of Discipleship

Jesus Said there were Costs of Being a Disciple

True Family   ...a disciple's true family is his fellow believers.

> "Then Jesus' mother and brothers arrived. Standing outside, they sent someone in to call him...
> 'Who are my mother and my brothers?' [Jesus] asked.
> Then he looked at those seated in a circle around him and said, 'Here are my mother and my brothers! Whoever does God's will is my brother and sister and mother.'" Mark 3:31-35 NIV

1) Some Christians interpret this as Jesus rejecting his physical family in favour of his 'spiritual' family — that he was telling his disciples to forget blood ties and find a new family in God.

2) Many modern Christians are uncomfortable with these ideas, and feel that you should love and respect your family whatever their beliefs

3) Others interpret the 'true family' teachings as expanding, not replacing, a Christian's family. In following Jesus, you become part of a worldwide family of believers.

True Greatness   ...a disciple must be the servant of all.

1) In Mark 9:33-37, the disciples argue on the road through Galilee to Capernaum about who among them is the greatest.

2) They tried to hide their argument from Jesus, but he responded by saying that true greatness comes through serving others:

> "'If anyone wants to be first, he must be the very last, and the servant of all.'" Mark 9:35 NIV

3) Putting yourself last like this involves a great deal of self-sacrifice (putting other people's needs before your own). Although most Christians see this as an ideal, it can be a very hard teaching to follow.

The Rich Man   ...a disciple must follow the commandments faithfully and give all he has to the poor.

1) In Mark 10:17-31, a wealthy man asks Jesus, "what must I do to inherit eternal life?" (NIV)

2) Jesus said he must do two things: follow the commandments (the ten laws in Exodus 20) and give his wealth to the poor.

> "'...sell everything you have and give to the poor, and you will have treasure in heaven.'" Mark 10:21 NIV

> "'How hard it is for the rich to enter the kingdom of God!... It is easier for a camel to go through the eye of a needle than for a rich man to enter the kingdom of God.'" Mark 10:23-25 NIV

3) He told his disciples that it was desperately hard for a rich person to enter the kingdom of God, although everything is possible for God.

4) He went on to tell the disciples that whatever they gave up now, they'd get a hundred times as much, both now and in the future, i.e. you may face hardship now, but there's eternal life in the end.

5) This story causes big problems for some modern Christians. If a person sells everything they have, they're left with no way of looking after themselves — and so become a burden on other people. And how rich is too rich? In the developed world, are we all too rich to enter the kingdom of God? Also, many modern Christians fail to keep all the commandments (e.g. most Christians do work of some sort (gardening, cleaning, paying bills, etc.) on Sunday, the Christian Sabbath — "Remember the Sabbath day by keeping it holy... On it you shall not do any work..." Exodus 20:8-10 NIV)

The Parable of the Tenants   ...discipleship is dangerous.

1) In Mark 12:1-12, Jesus tells a parable about the dangers and responsibilities faced by God's servants:

> A man left his vineyard in the hands of tenants. He sent servants to collect the rent that was due — but all were beaten or killed by the tenants. In the end he sent his own son, but the tenants killed him too so that the vineyard would become theirs. The owner responded by killing the tenants and giving the vineyard to others.

2) This parable is told to the chief priests and the Pharisees — they are compared to the tenants who would kill the son (Jesus) for their own ends. The vineyard owner represents God.

3) This parable also warned the disciples that they risked persecution and death for carrying God's message. The same warning applies to some Christians today — in some parts of the world, people are still discriminated against, beaten or even killed for their faith.

No one ever said it was gonna be easy...

Jesus expected his disciples to give up everything and risk their lives to be servants of God and men. Hard.

The Problems of Discipleship

Jesus's disciples were only human. They didn't always <u>understand</u>, and sometimes they <u>failed</u>.

The Disciples Couldn't Cast a Spirit from a Boy

1) When the disciples were sent out to preach in Mark 6 (see p.105), Jesus gave them <u>authority</u> over evil spirits. They were <u>expected</u> to heal and perform exorcisms in Jesus's name, just as Jesus did himself.

> <u>The Boy with an Evil Spirit</u> (Mark 9:14-29)
> The disciples attempted to cure a boy with an evil spirit but failed. When Jesus arrived, he called the people an "unbelieving generation", and told the father that the boy could only be healed if he showed faith. The father replied that he believed, but needed help to have enough faith. Jesus cast the spirit out, and told his disciples that the demon could "come out only by prayer". (NIV)

"...the boy's father exclaimed, 'I do believe; help me overcome my unbelief!'" Mark 9:24 NIV

2) So according to Mark, the disciples failed because the <u>people</u> didn't have <u>faith</u>, and hadn't been <u>praying</u> for the miracle. Jesus was able to drive out the demon because the father <u>exercised</u> what little faith he had.

The Sower — Should Only Some People Get It?

Well don't ask me.

1) According to Mark 4:1-20, Jesus told a story about a <u>farmer</u> sowing seed:

> <u>The Parable of the Sower</u> (Mark 4:1-20)
> A farmer scattered seeds across the ground. Some fell on the path and were eaten by birds. Some fell in shallow soil, and grew up quickly, but died because the plants had no roots. Some fell among thorns and the plants were choked. But some fell on good soil and "produced a crop, multiplying thirty, sixty, or even a hundred times". (NIV)

2) This is a rare example of Jesus using <u>allegory</u> in his parables — the story is <u>entirely symbolic</u>, with the seeds and the soils representing the <u>word of God</u> and the <u>hearers of the Gospel</u> respectively.

3) Mark says that Jesus followed the parable with the call, "He who has ears to hear, let him hear" (NIV), and then delivered one of the most <u>controversial</u> passages in the Gospels to the disciples (Mark 4:10-12):
   - He said that he spoke in parables so that the crowds <u>wouldn't understand him</u>.
   - He didn't <u>want</u> the crowds to understand, because "otherwise they might turn and be <u>forgiven</u>!" (NIV)

4) Jesus was <u>disappointed</u> with his disciples, because they needed him to explain the parable — they had <u>failed</u> to understand. But Jesus went on to explain it to them, and <u>only</u> to them (Mark 4:13-20).

More Failures: Rivalry, Gethsemane, Peter's Denial

It <u>wasn't easy</u> being a disciple of Jesus. Mark highlights, in particular, the failings of those <u>closest</u> to Jesus — James and John (the sons of Zebedee) and Simon Peter.

<u>Rivalry and Service</u> (Mark 10:41-45)
James and John asked Jesus to let them sit at his right and left hands in heaven. Jesus told all the disciples that they shouldn't want to "lord it" over other people, and repeated what he'd said earlier about true greatness (see p.106): "...whoever wants to become great among you must be your servant, and whoever wants to be first must be slave of all. For even the Son of Man did not come to be served, but to serve..." (NIV)

<u>Prayers at Gethsemane</u> (Mark 14:27-42)
Jesus told the disciples that they would all abandon him, and he predicted Peter's denial. All the disciples swore they'd never disown him.
Jesus then took Peter, James and John to keep guard while he prayed in the garden of Gethsemane. Three times he went to pray for an hour. Each time, when he returned, he found all three disciples asleep.

<u>Peter's Denial</u> (Mark 14:66-72)
After Jesus was arrested, Peter was asked three times if he was with Jesus. Three times, he denied it: "He began to call down curses on himself, and he swore to them, 'I don't know this man you're talking about.'" (NIV) — then he broke down in tears when he realised that Jesus had been right.

These stories cause <u>problems</u> for some modern Christians. If the <u>disciples</u> (even <u>Peter</u>, the first Bishop of Rome) couldn't obey Jesus, and repeatedly <u>failed</u> him, what chance do they have?

On the other hand, the <u>humanity</u> of the disciples can help Christians to cope with their <u>own</u> failings. Jesus loved his disciples despite their shortcomings — he didn't expect perfection from them, just as he doesn't expect it from us.

Discipleship — is that the one that Jesus walked on water to...

Reading Mark, it's easy to see Peter as a failure. He questioned Jesus, didn't seem to understand a lot of the time, fell asleep at Gethsemane, ran away when Jesus was arrested and denied knowing him three times. But it was Peter who first recognised Jesus as the Christ, and who led the Church following the resurrection.

Jesus in Conflict with Jewish Law

There's evidence of <u>conflict</u> all through Mark's Gospel. And some of the most <u>memorable</u> parts of the Gospel are where Jesus argues about the Law (the laws handed down by God in the Torah) with the <u>Pharisees</u>.

The Pharisees and Scribes were Experts in the Law

1) The <u>Pharisees</u> were a Jewish sect who <u>studied</u> the Law of Moses, and were dedicated to keeping the Jewish faith alive. They believed that obedience to the <u>Law</u> was all important.

2) The <u>scribes</u> were <u>religious lawyers</u>. They made copies of the Torah, and so knew the Law very well.

3) Jesus was often in <u>conflict</u> with the Pharisees and scribes for breaking laws or traditions. For example, Jesus dined with <u>sinners</u> (Mark 2:13-17) and his disciples didn't <u>fast</u> (go without food as sign of devotion to God) (Mark 2:18-20). Jesus explained that his followers would only fast once he was dead.

Jesus Forgave and Healed a Paralysed Man

The Paralysed Man (Mark 2:1-12)
A paralysed man was brought to Jesus. Jesus saw the faith in the man and those who had brought him, and forgave the man for his sins. Some teachers of the Law (scribes) thought this was blasphemy, since they believed only God could forgive sins. Jesus asked whether it was easier to forgive sins or cure a paralysed man. The man then got up and walked, proving that "the Son of Man has authority on earth to forgive sins". (NIV)

"Which is easier: to say to the paralytic, 'Your sins are forgiven,' or to say, 'Get up, take your mat and walk'?" Mark 2:9 NIV

He said People were More Important than the Sabbath...

The <u>Sabbath</u> (Saturday) is the Jewish day of rest, when Jews aren't supposed to do any <u>work</u>.

Picking Grain on the Sabbath (Mark 2:23-28)
The Pharisees accused the disciples of working on the Sabbath when they picked grain. Jesus reminded them that even King David broke the Law when he was hungry and in need, by eating bread meant only for priests. He said "the Sabbath was made for man, not man for the Sabbath" (NIV).

The Man with the Shrivelled Hand (Mark 3:1-6)
Jesus cured a man with a shrivelled hand in a synagogue on the Sabbath — the Pharisees saw this healing as work, and so forbidden. Jesus asked, "Which is lawful on the Sabbath: to do good or to do evil, to save life or to kill?" (NIV). The Pharisees' stubbornness distressed Jesus.

In both cases, Jesus <u>justified</u> working on the Sabbath on the grounds that <u>human need</u> should come before religious laws, and that preventing or repairing harm is <u>always</u> a good thing.

...and Challenged Traditions

Mark tells us that Jesus challenged the traditions of <u>ritual cleanliness</u> (laws on food and washing that prevented anything 'unclean' entering a Jew's body) and <u>corban</u> (a gift dedicated to God).

Ritual Cleanliness (Mark 7:1-8 and 7:14-23)
The Pharisees had elaborate laws about washing before eating in order to stay ritually clean. Jesus argued that it's not what goes into a man that makes him unclean, but rather, what comes out of him.

"What comes out of a man is what makes him 'unclean'. For from within, out of men's hearts, come evil thoughts, sexual immorality, theft, murder, adultery, greed, malice, deceit, lewdness, envy, slander, arrogance and folly." Mark 7:20-22 NIV

These views would have caused <u>major conflict</u> within the Jewish community at the time.

But many Christians believe that putting people's <u>welfare</u> before strict religious rules, and always trying to be a <u>good person</u>, should be the basis for good <u>community cohesion</u>.

Corban (Mark 7:9-13)
Jesus argued that the Jews were more concerned with their own traditions than God's word. The example he gave was that of corban. The priests allowed people to leave their parents destitute, which goes against God's Law, if they were giving everything to the Temple as a gift to God (corban).

Those pesky Pharisees — they just kept turning up...
There isn't room here to put in the full texts from the Gospel, so make sure you go away and read all the relevant bits for yourself. <u>Learning</u> a few of those quotes wouldn't go amiss come exam time, either.

Jesus in Conflict with Authority

It wasn't just lawyers that Jesus fought with — he doesn't seem to have been a fan of authority in general.

The Sadducees were a Group of Priests

1) The Sadducees were a group of priests who ran the Temple in Jerusalem (the building where burnt sacrifices were made to God). They believed in sticking very rigidly to the books of the Torah, and they didn't believe in the resurrection of the dead.

2) The chief priests feared Jesus and wanted him dead.

Jesus Sparked Conflict when he Entered Jerusalem

The Triumphal Entry (Mark 11:1-11)
When Jesus entered Jerusalem at the end of his journeys around Israel, he entered as a King. He was carried on the back of a colt (a young horse) while the people cried: "Hosanna!" and "Blessed is the coming kingdom of our father David!" (NIV). Cloaks and palm branches were spread along the road for his horse to walk on.

This is the event that Christians celebrate on Palm Sunday, the Sunday before Good Friday.

The Cleansing of the Temple (Mark 11:15-18)
In the Temple courtyard in Jerusalem, Jesus found a market, with "money changers" and "those selling doves". He overturned their tables and drove the traders out, saying they'd turned the Temple into "a den of robbers" (NIV).

The Authority of Jesus Questioned (Mark 11:27-33)
The chief priests and elders asked Jesus on who's authority he was acting. He replied with a question about John the Baptist: "Answer me, and I will tell you by what authority... John's baptism — was it from heaven, or from men?" (NIV). Saying "from heaven" meant admitting they were wrong about John, but saying "from men" would anger the people (who believed John was a prophet). So they couldn't answer.

1) In each of these examples, the conflict is about authority. Jesus is implying that his authority is greater than the priests in the Temple, because he's acting for God — but he never actually says that.

2) Instead, he quotes scripture as he clears the Temple (in Mark 11:17 he quotes Isaiah and Jeremiah) and traps his opponents with an unanswerable question.

Jesus Argued about Resurrection and Taxes

Marriage at the Resurrection (Mark 12:18-27)
The Sadducees didn't believe in resurrection of the dead, and they tried to catch Jesus out with an awkward question. The Jews had a custom called levirate marriage, where if a man died childless, his brother must marry his widow. The Sadducees imagined a woman who married seven brothers in turn in this way. They asked Jesus: "At the resurrection whose wife will she be, since the seven were married to her?" Jesus replied that after the resurrection, people would be "like the angels in heaven", and so wouldn't be married at all. In favour of resurrection, Jesus argued: "He is not the God of the dead, but of the living." (NIV)

1) This story is quite significant for modern Christians. It shows that the idea of resurrection was around before Jesus, challenging the belief that life after death depends on a belief in Jesus Christ.

2) It describes life after the resurrection as very different from life on earth.

3) Also, the statement that God is God "of the living" implies that judgement and resurrection come at death, rather than people staying dead until the Last Day.

4) Another time, the authorities tried to catch Jesus out with a question about taxes to Rome:

5) This passage has been used to justify various different positions over the years, e.g., that Church and State should be separate, that Christians are obliged to obey State laws, or that money is an earthly thing that distracts you from God.

Paying Taxes (Mark 12:13-17)
Jesus avoided the trap of some Pharisees and Herod's men when they asked him whether it was right to pay taxes to Caesar. He asked them to bring him a coin and tell him whose picture was on it: "'Caesar's,' they replied. Then Jesus said to them, 'Give to Caesar what is Caesar's and to God what is God's.'" (NIV)

The two things you can be certain of — death and taxes...

Jesus was prepared to challenge authority when he felt it was necessary, but he was no anarchist. He didn't condone not paying taxes, and most of his anger was directed at what he saw as hypocrisy and impiety.

Jesus in Conflict with His Followers

Mark doesn't record <u>many</u> arguments between Jesus and his followers, but there were a few.

Jesus Predicted his Passion Three Times

1) The '<u>Passion</u>' was the <u>suffering</u> of Jesus in the time leading up to his <u>death</u>.

2) He <u>predicted</u> his passion, and according to Mark, he told his disciples about it <u>three times</u>.

> <u>Jesus's Prediction of the Passion</u> (Mark 8:31-33)
> Jesus taught his disciples that he must suffer and die, but would be resurrected on the third day:
> Peter took Jesus to one side "and began to rebuke him" (by telling Jesus it would never happen to him — Mark isn't specific, but Matthew 16:22 is).
> Jesus reacted angrily to Peter: "'Get behind me, Satan!' he said. 'You do not have in mind the things of God, but the things of men.'" (NIV)

> "He then began to teach them that the Son of Man must suffer many things and be rejected by the elders, chief priests and teachers of the law, and that he must be killed and after three days rise again. He spoke plainly about this..." Mark 8:31-32 NIV

3) Jesus's reaction was <u>very strong</u>. Jesus didn't just tell Peter he was <u>wrong</u>, he compared him with <u>Satan</u> tempting Jesus away from his necessary fate.

4) <u>Two</u> more times before entering Jerusalem, Jesus predicted his suffering and death (in Mark 9:30-32 and Mark 10:32-34). On these occasions, the disciples were described as "<u>afraid</u>" and "<u>astonished</u>".

5) Modern Christians accept that the passion was an <u>essential</u> part of Jesus's ministry, and that it's through his sacrifice that Christians find <u>salvation</u>.

The Anointing at Bethany Angered the Disciples

1) This is a <u>slightly odd</u> story — it doesn't <u>fit</u> very well with the rest of Jesus's teachings.

> <u>Jesus Anointed at Bethany</u> (Mark 14:3-9)
> A few days before his arrest, a woman 'anointed' Jesus by pouring an expensive jar of perfume over him. The disciples "rebuked her harshly" for wasting such a valuable thing. It could have been sold for "more than a year's wages and the money given to the poor".
> Jesus's response was unexpected: "'Leave her alone,' said Jesus... 'She has done a beautiful thing to me. The poor you will always have with you, and you can help them any time you want. But you will not always have me... She poured perfume on my body beforehand to prepare for my burial.'" (NIV)

2) 'Messiah' means '<u>anointed one</u>', so some Christians believe she was <u>expressing</u> her faith that Jesus was the Messiah. <u>Kings</u> of Israel were anointed in a similar way, so this could also be a reference to his <u>kingship</u>.

3) Some Christians believe that the disciples' anger showed that they <u>didn't believe</u> Jesus would die — that only <u>Jesus</u> and the <u>woman</u> really understood what was going to happen.

4) But Jesus's response seems surprisingly <u>selfish</u>, particularly given Mark 10:21 ("Go, sell everything you have and give to the poor..." (NIV)).

The Disciple Judas was Part of the Plot to Kill Jesus

1) In Mark 14:1-2, the "chief priests and the teachers of the law" plotted to arrest and kill Jesus in "some sly way" <u>after</u> the <u>Passover</u> feast. They didn't want to take him in public, because he had too many followers. And not during Passover, because the people might "riot".

> "Then Judas Iscariot, one of the Twelve, went to the chief priests to betray Jesus to them. They... promised to give him money. So he watched for an opportunity to hand him over." Mark 14:10-11 NIV

2) One of Jesus's <u>own disciples</u>, <u>Judas Iscariot</u>, decided to betray Jesus to the Jewish authorities.

3) That evening (Mark 14:17-21), Jesus <u>predicted</u> the betrayal:
"'It is one of the Twelve,' he replied, 'one who dips bread into the bowl with me... But woe to that man who betrays the Son of Man! It would be better for him if he had not been born.'" (NIV)

Don't bother arguing with him guys — the man's God...

Some Christians interpret Jesus's response at Bethany to be a reference to <u>worship</u>. The woman was showing her <u>complete devotion</u> to Jesus, and the disciples had no right to question her act of worship.

The Last Supper, Judas and the Trial

It's a fairly famous story... you may just know something about this already.

The Last Supper — Jesus Knew he Would be Betrayed

1) The Last Supper (Mark 14:12-26) is the last meal Jesus and the Twelve ate together. They were celebrating the Feast of Unleavened Bread — the first night of the Jewish Passover festival. Passover commemorates the release of the Jews from slavery in Egypt (Exodus 12), and is a very important festival.

2) During the feast, held in the 'upper room' of a man's house, Jesus predicted that one of the disciples would betray him (see previous page). Each disciple denied that it would be him.

3) Jesus then broke a piece of bread and said, "Take it; this is my body." He passed round a cup of wine and said, "This is my blood of the covenant, which is poured out for many" (NIV).

> This is a very important passage for modern Christians, as it's the origin of the Eucharist (Holy Communion — see p.14). Many Christians believe that they receive the saving power of Jesus into themselves by eating the bread and drinking the wine at the Eucharist.
>
> Holy Communion also reminds Christians of the 'new covenant' made with God through the death of Jesus.
>
> In Luke 22:19, Jesus adds, "do this in remembrance of me" (NIV). This phrase isn't part of Mark's Gospel, though, so there's nothing in Mark's account to suggest that Jesus was beginning a tradition.

4) After the supper (Mark 14:25-31) Jesus felt that his death was near, saying "I will not drink again of the fruit of the vine until that day when I drink it anew in the kingdom of God" (NIV). He then went with the Twelve to the Mount of Olives, where he predicted Peter's denial (see p.107).

Jesus Prayed at Gethsemane

1) That night, after the meal, Jesus went with Peter, John and James to the garden of Gethsemane to pray (Mark 14:32-42). Peter, John and James were to keep watch while he prayed, but failed (see p.107).

2) Mark writes that Jesus was "deeply distressed" saying that his soul was "overwhelmed with sorrow to the point of death". Jesus prayed for God to take the "cup" of his suffering from him, but only if that would fit God's plan. Jesus didn't want to die if he didn't have to, but would obey God.

> "'Abba, Father,' he said, 'everything is possible for you. Take this cup from me. Yet not what I will, but what you will.'" Mark 14:36 NIV

3) These verses show Jesus's humanity, and so cause problems for some Christians. Some feel that if Jesus was God (as part of the Trinity), then he should know what was necessary, and not question his fate. Others think that, by praying to God, Jesus shows that he's separate from him.

He was Betrayed, Arrested and Tried by the Sanhedrin

1) Judas Iscariot arrived at Gethsemane to betray Jesus (Mark 14:43-52), accompanied by "a crowd armed with swords and clubs, sent from the chief priests, the teachers of the law, and the elders" (NIV).

2) Judas had arranged a signal with the crowd — the person he kissed was the one they should arrest.

> The betrayal is a thorny subject for Christians. Many believe that Judas's treachery damned him to hell. He betrayed God and sent a good man to his death. But if Jesus's death was necessary for our salvation, then was the betrayal necessary too? And if Judas was destined to be the betrayer, could he have chosen not to be?

3) In Mark 14:53-65, Jesus was put on trial before the High Priest (the leader of the Temple) and the rest of the Sanhedrin (the Jewish supreme council). According to Mark, the court was simply "looking for evidence against Jesus so that they could put him to death" (NIV).

4) As far as Christians are concerned, this wasn't a real trial, and it had nothing to do with justice. The chief priests felt threatened by Jesus, and this show trial was their opportunity to get rid of him.

5) Various people testified falsely against Jesus, but their stories didn't agree with each other.

6) Jesus stayed silent — he didn't try to defend himself — until the High Priest asked Jesus directly, "Are you the Christ, the Son of the Blessed One?" (NIV)

> "'I am,' said Jesus. 'And you will see the Son of Man sitting at the right hand of the Mighty One and coming on the clouds of heaven.'" Mark 14:62 NIV

7) This was enough to condemn Jesus for the very serious crime of blasphemy — insulting God.

8) Then in the courtyard below, Peter was accused of being a follower of Jesus and denied it three times (see p.107).

The Crucifixion and Resurrection

The Sanhedrin Turned him Over to Pontius Pilate

1) Mark 15:1-15 records the events of the morning after the trial, when Jesus was turned over to Pontius Pilate — the Roman governor of Judea. He had the power to sentence Jesus to death.

2) The priests accused Jesus of "many things" before Pilate, but again Jesus refused to answer the accusations. Pilate was "amazed". The one thing Jesus did reply to was Pilate's question: "Are you the king of the Jews?" Jesus replied, "Yes, it is as you say" (NIV).

3) According to Mark, it was customary to release a prisoner to mark Passover, and Pilate asked the crowd if he should release Jesus. The crowd, having been "stirred up" by the chief priests, called for a man named Barabbas to be released instead. Barabbas had committed murder in a recent uprising.

4) Mark writes that Pilate knew it was "out of envy that the chief priests had handed Jesus over to him" (NIV). He writes that the crowd called for Jesus to be crucified, and that Pilate agreed to it to keep the crowd happy. ▶

> "Why? What crime has he committed?" asked Pilate. But they shouted all the louder, 'Crucify him!'
> Wanting to satisfy the crowd, Pilate released Barabbas to them. He had Jesus flogged, and handed him over to be crucified." Mark 15:14-15 NIV

5) So according to Mark, the priests and the Jewish crowd were responsible for Jesus's death, not Pilate. This view was probably influenced by Mark's background. Mark was most likely living in Rome, where Christians were being persecuted by the Roman authorities. He might have felt it wise to paint the Roman Pilate in a good light.

6) Modern Christians tend to lay some of the blame for Jesus's death with Pilate. As a Roman governor, he had the power to refuse to do what the priests wanted, but he chose to go along with them.

Jesus was Crucified and Died at Golgotha

1) Mark 15:21-39 records that Jesus was led to Golgotha (The Place of the Skull) where he was to be crucified — nailed to a cross to hang until he died. Simon of Cyrene carried his cross.

2) Jesus refused the drugged wine he was offered, and was crucified next to two robbers. A sign was fixed to Jesus's cross that read "The King of the Jews", to record the charge against him. Passers-by threw insults at Jesus, saying that he could save others, but couldn't save himself.

3) Christians believe that it was by dying on the cross that Jesus truly saved his followers from death.

4) They believe that God had placed all the sins of the world on Jesus while he hung on the cross. In his suffering, Jesus cried out, "My God, my God, why have you forsaken me?" (NIV)

5) As he died, the curtain of the Temple tore in two. (This would have been a symbol of mourning to the Jews, who ritually tear their clothes when a loved one dies.) A Roman soldier said, "Surely this man was the Son of God!" (NIV)

6) Joseph of Arimathea was allowed to take Jesus's body down from the cross for a decent burial (bodies were usually left on the cross). Joseph placed it in a tomb cut from the rock and rolled a stone over the entrance. Mark implies that this was done in a hurry, because it was getting close to the Sabbath.

Then on the Third Day he was Resurrected

1) As soon as the Sabbath was over, Mark 16:1-8 tells us that Mary Magdalene, Mary the mother of James and Salome went to Jesus's tomb to anoint his body.

2) They got there to find the stone rolled back and the tomb empty. A young man dressed in white was there who told them: "He has risen! He is not here. See the place where they laid him. But go, tell his disciples and Peter, 'He is going ahead of you into Galilee...'" (NIV)

3) The three women fled in terror and didn't say anything to anyone. The oldest copies of Mark end here.

4) Later copies of Mark go on to say that the resurrected Jesus appeared to Mary Magdalene, and then to the eleven remaining apostles. He told them to "preach the good news to all creation" (NIV).

5) Christians believe that Jesus's resurrection was physical, not just spiritual. The risen Jesus wasn't a ghost — he rose again in the flesh, showing his power over death (see Luke 24:36-49).

The examiners won't be impressed if you don't know this...

Like I said, it's a fairly famous story. But it's not enough to just know what happened — you need to know the significance to Christians of all the events leading up to Jesus's death and resurrection.

Jesus's Baptism and Transfiguration

The start of Jesus's ministry was marked by his baptism by John the Baptist.

Jesus was Baptised by John the Baptist

1) The first few verses of Mark describe the ministry of John the Baptist. John was baptising people in the river Jordan "for the forgiveness of sins". The people confessed their sins and John immersed them in the river to symbolise the sins being washed away.

2) Mark 1:9-11 describes Jesus going to John for baptism. This causes problems for some Christians, since if Jesus was really the son of God and without sin, why did he need to be baptised?

3) But whatever the reason was for him going to John — to encourage his followers to be baptised, or just to mark the start of his ministry — this is where Mark tells us that Jesus was the Son of God.

> "As Jesus was coming up out of the water, he saw heaven being torn open and the Spirit descending on him like a dove. And a voice came from heaven: 'You are my Son, whom I love; with you I am well pleased.'" Mark 1:10-11 NIV

Peter Confessed his Faith at Caesarea Philippi

1) 'Confession' in this sense just means acknowledging something — Peter made a statement of belief.

2) In Mark 8:27-33, Jesus and his disciples were travelling towards the city of Caesarea Philippi when Jesus asked them, "Who do you say I am?" Peter replied, "You are the Christ".

3) This was the first time one of Jesus's disciples had openly declared him to be the Christ or Messiah (see p.115). Jesus told them not to tell anyone who he was (this is often called the Messianic Secret).

Matthew's Account of Peter's Confession is Important for Roman Catholics (16:13-20)

In Matthew, Jesus responds to Peter's confession by offering him the "keys of the kingdom of heaven":

For Roman Catholics, this passage marks the foundation of their Church, with Peter as the first Pope (Bishop of Rome).

> "Blessed are you, Simon son of Jonah... I tell you that you are Peter, and on this rock I will build my church, and the gates of Hades will not overcome it. I will give you the keys of the kingdom of heaven; whatever you bind on earth will be bound in heaven, and whatever you loose on earth will be loosed in heaven." Matthew 16:17-19 NIV

'Peter' means 'rock' in Greek.

Mark's account of the event doesn't include any mention of this, so Matthew's record is more important for Roman Catholic Christians today.

Jesus Met with Elijah and Moses at his Transfiguration

1) Mark 9:1-10 describes a miraculous event called the transfiguration, in which Jesus's appearance changed in front of Peter, John and James.

2) The prophets Moses and Elijah appeared, and were talking to Jesus. Elijah is the Old Testament prophet who is prophesied to return before the Messiah.

> "...he was transfigured before them. His clothes became dazzling white..." Mark 9:2-3 NIV

3) This is the most openly 'god-like' thing that Jesus is recorded as having done in Mark's Gospel. Some Christians are uneasy about it — they find it hard to reconcile Jesus the man with this sort of transformation.

4) While the disciples stood there terrified, a cloud came down and enveloped them. A voice from the cloud said, "This is my Son, whom I love. Listen to him!" (NIV), and then everything returned to normal.

5) As at the baptism, this is the voice of God himself declaring Jesus to be his son.

6) Jesus again told Peter, James and John not to tell anyone what they'd seen until after he'd risen from the dead.

7) But if Peter, James and John had witnessed this transfiguration, seen the prophets, and heard the voice of God, it's hard to understand why they struggled to accept the idea of Jesus's resurrection (Mark 16:11-12).

The clues are there — as we go throooough the Gospel...

So the big question in these pages is, 'who exactly was this Jesus chappy?' The stuff on this page seems to point quite firmly to Jesus being the Messiah, the Son of God. But Jesus never actually says so until his trial.

Jesus's Miracles

According to Mark's Gospel, Jesus performed many miracles. These miracles showed that he had God's power, but they also demonstrated the importance of faith.

Healing Miracles and Faith are Linked

Jesus exercised his own faith every time he performed a miracle. And he showed that people could be cured miraculously of both physical and mental illness — as long as they had faith.

The Raising of Jairus's Daughter (Mark 5:21-43)
Jairus, a synagogue ruler, begged Jesus to heal his daughter. When Jesus arrived, the girl was apparently dead already, but Jesus revived her. As in most of the healing miracles, faith is crucial. The sick girl's father demonstrated faith by asking Jesus for help.

"Jesus told the synagogue ruler, 'Don't be afraid; just believe.'" Mark 5:36 NIV

The Healing of a Man with Evil Spirits (Mark 5:1-20)
A man was possessed by many evil spirits that caused him to hurt himself: "he would cry out and cut himself with stones" (NIV). The spirits were so strong that the man could break the chains put on his wrists and ankles. The man ran to Jesus and fell on his knees in front of him, but the demons spoke through the man. They called Jesus "Son of the Most High God" and referred to themselves as "Legion... for we are many". the demons begged Jesus to send them into a herd of pigs, rather than driving them from the country altogether. When the demons entered the 2000 pigs, they ran to the lake and drowned. Jesus told the man to spread the word about what he had done.

Mark never tells us the name of the man, but you'll often hear him called "Legion" after the demons that possessed him.

1) There are two ways of looking at these healing miracle stories — either as descriptions of real events, or as symbolic of Christian teachings.
2) Where the miracles seem to be treating what we'd now consider mental illness (e.g. Legion), most Christians see how faith could have a profound effect. But healing physical illness, or even death, through faith alone is harder for some modern Christians to accept.
3) Many Christians believe that the story of Legion is symbolic, where the man represents the whole of humanity being plagued by the many demons of sin.

Jesus Controlled Nature — Inspiring Awe and Wonder

Mark also describes several nature miracles, in which Jesus shows his power over nature.

Calming the storm (Mark 4:35-41)
A storm broke out and threatened to sink the boat that Jesus and the disciples were in. Jesus calmly instructed the wind to die down, which it did. The disciples were filled with awe at what they saw: "They were terrified and asked each other, 'Who is this? Even the wind and the waves obey him!'" (NIV)

Walking on water (Mark 6:45-52)
Jesus caught up with his disciples' boat by walking across the water. Although they'd just seen him feed the 5000, they were still shocked at his powers.

"Then he climbed into the boat with them... They were completely amazed, for they had not understood about the loaves; their hearts were hardened." Mark 6:51-52 NIV

Feeding the 5000 (Mark 6:32-44)
A crowd had gathered around Jesus and the disciples, but there were only 5 loaves and 2 fish to eat. Jesus gave thanks to God, broke the bread and the disciples passed the food round. All 5000 people had enough to eat, and there was enough food left over to fill 12 baskets.

1) Taken at face value, these stories cause problems for some modern Christians.
2) In a world that follows the normal physical laws, you can't turn 5 loaves and 2 fish into enough food to feed thousands of people, or walk on water as though it was solid ground.
3) Some Christians believe that physical laws didn't bind Jesus, because he was the Son of God, and had God's power within him. Others prefer to view the stories symbolically. For example, the feeding of the five thousand can be seen to represent God providing for those who trust and have faith in him.

Faith is good — but revision helps too...

In the story of Legion, the demons call Jesus the "Son of the Most High God". So Mark describes the demons as recognising Jesus for who he was, even if the people he was ministering to didn't.

The Titles of Jesus

In Mark's Gospel, Jesus is called by a number of titles, each of which gives a clue as to Jesus's identity.

His Followers Called Jesus the Messiah

1) The words 'Messiah' in Hebrew, and 'Christ' in Greek, both mean 'anointed one'.

2) They come from the practice of consecrating kings and priests to God by anointing them with blessed oil.

3) In the Jewish scriptures, the Messiah is the promised King of Israel who will deliver the Jews from suffering, and usher in the 'messianic age' — an age of peace when everyone will worship God.

4) Christians believe that Jesus was the Messiah promised in the books of Isaiah and Zechariah.

5) The Gospels pick out events and actions that show Jesus fulfilling many of the messianic prophecies during his time on Earth. There aren't many examples of this in Mark's Gospel, but there are lots in Matthew, e.g. Matthew 21:5 describes the Triumphal Entry (see p.109) as a fulfilment of Zechariah 9:9.

6) Christians believe that, during his life, Jesus only fulfilled some of the prophecies about the Messiah. And that he will return (the Second Coming) to bring in the messianic age, or the Kingdom of God.

Jesus Called Himself the Son of Man

1) When Jesus refers to himself in Mark's Gospel, he uses the title 'Son of Man', e.g.

- healing the paralysed man (see p.108): "...the Son of Man has authority on earth to forgive sins..." (NIV)
- in response to the request of James and John to sit at his side in glory (see p.107): "...the Son of Man did not come to be served, but to serve..." (NIV)
- the prediction of his passion (see p.110): "...the Son of Man must suffer many things...". (NIV)
- at his trial before the Sanhedrin (see p.111): "...you will see the Son of Man sitting at the right hand of the Mighty One and coming on the clouds of heaven." (NIV)

2) Many Christians see the title as a reference to Jesus's humanity. They believe that he lived, suffered and died as a man.

3) As a human, Jesus could atone for the sins of humanity (p.91).

4) It's likely that the title was also a reference to the prophet Daniel:

"In my vision... there before me was one like a son of man, coming with the clouds of heaven... He was given authority, glory and sovereign power... His dominion is an everlasting dominion that will not pass away..." Daniel 7:13-14 NIV

Christians Believe Jesus is the Son of God

1) Christians believe that Jesus is the second person of the Trinity (see p.91) and the Son of God.

2) There's evidence for this in Mark's Gospel:

The clearest evidence comes from Jesus's baptism and transfiguration, where the voice of God declared Jesus to be his Son (see p.113).

Jesus prayed to God as his "Father".

Jesus's miracles (see previous page) showed that he had the power of God.

Jesus confirmed that he was the Son of God at his trial before the Sanhedrin (see p.111).

Jesus rose from the dead (see p.112) — demonstrating his divinity.

3) But not everyone is convinced from Mark's account that Jesus was divine. He showed normal, human emotions at Gethsemane (see p.111), and up until his trial, he never claimed to be the Son of God.

4) Others don't trust the evidence of Mark's Gospel. It was probably written some time after Jesus's death, by someone who wasn't a first-hand witness of the things he's describing.

Son of Man — or Son of God...

No person called Jesus the Son of God until his trial, because connecting yourself with God in that way was considered blasphemous by the Jews. But if you believe Mark's account, a supernatural voice said it twice.

Practice Questions

Oooh... lots of questions. And I know what you're thinking — "I could just... skip... it." But there's NO WAY you could possibly remember everything first time through, so use these questions to fill in the gaps... Watch out for your spelling, punctuation and grammar — they can get you extra marks in your exams.

1) What is/are:

   a) a disciple?
   b) the kingdom?
   c) true greatness?
   d) Peter's denial?
   e) the Law?

   f) corban?
   g) ritual cleanliness?
   h) the Sabbath?
   i) Gethsemane?
   j) Golgotha?

   k) the Sanhedrin?
   l) the transfiguration?
   m) confession?

   To get the marks for these questions you just have to learn the key terms.

   Who was/were:

   n) Levi?
   o) the Sons of Zebedee?
   p) the Pharisees?

   q) the scribes?
   r) the Sadducees?
   s) Pontius Pilate?

   t) Elijah?
   u) Jairus?

2) For each of the following questions, give two reasons for your point of view.

   a) Do you think Jesus was right to call Levi as a disciple?
   b) Do you think Christians should serve others?

   Your marks here come from the reasons you use to back up your opinion.

   c) Do you think Christians should keep the Sabbath?
   d) Do you think the woman at Bethany was right to anoint Jesus with perfume?
   e) Do you think Pontius Pilate was responsible for Jesus's death?
   f) Do you think Jesus was the Messiah?

3) For these questions, you need to express yourself as clearly as possible — make sure your writing is correct, accurate and well organised.

   a) Explain why the calling and sending out of the first disciples is important to Christians today.
   b) Explain why Jesus's teachings about true family might cause problems for some Christians today.
   c) Explain why the healing of the paralysed man led to conflict.
   d) Explain the significance to modern Christians of Jesus's disagreements with the Jews over the meaning of the Law.

   These are the big mark questions — so they're worth taking a little bit of time over. And don't forget your spelling, punctuation and grammar.

   e) Explain why the Last Supper is important to Christians.
   f) Explain the significance of Jesus's death and resurrection to Christians.
   g) Explain why Matthew's account of Peter's confession at Caesarea Philippi is important to Roman Catholics.
   h) Explain why Jesus's healing miracles might cause problems for some Christians today.

4) Read the following statements:

   a) "The disciples failed Jesus."
   b) "Helping people is more important than religious traditions."
   c) "Judas was evil."
   d) "Jesus rose from the dead."

   To get all the marks for these questions you need to remember to include both sides of the big arguments.

   e) "Jesus fed 5000 people with 5 loaves and 2 fishes."
   f) "Jesus was the Son of God."

   Discuss each statement. You should include different, supported points of view and a personal viewpoint. In your answers you should refer to Christianity.

Do Well in Your Exam

You've learnt all the facts — now it's time to get those grades.

The Basics — Read the Questions

1) Read the questions carefully. If you've got a choice of questions, make sure you read them all before you pick one of them. Remember, you've got to answer all the parts of the questions you pick.

2) Be aware of how much time you're using. Leave plenty of time for the long-answer questions. The more marks a question's worth, the longer you should be spending on it. Try to leave yourself 5 minutes at the end to check your work.

3) Some questions will have extra marks available for Spelling, Punctuation and Grammar (SPaG). These will add up to 5% of the total marks. The exam paper will tell you which questions offer SPaG marks — so make your writing for these the best it can be (see pages 120-123 for more).

You get Marks for What you Know and How you Express It

In GCSE Religious Studies there are two Assessment Objectives — these are the skills you'll need to show to get marks in the exams. You get half your marks for each.

1) Describing and explaining what you know.
2) Making arguments backed up with well-thought-out reasoning — and understanding and explaining other people's opinions.

The exact format of your questions will depend on your exam board, but they're all along the same lines...

There are Easy Marks for Knowing What Things Mean

You'll probably get questions asking you what important terms mean. They'll only be worth a mark or two, so keep your answers short and to the point — but make sure you define the term properly. Learn the terms from the glossary (see pages 120-122) that relate to the unit (or units) you're doing.

What is meant by **displaying religion**?

GOOD ANSWER: *Making a show of good deeds or religious observance to impress other people.*

Try to answer this sort of question in one sentence.

NOT-SO-GOOD ANSWERS:

In the Sermon on the Mount, Jesus says that we are to carry out acts of charity and worship in private, rather than in public. He says that praying loudly on street corners, or making sure people know when we give to charity is wrong, because we should be doing it for the benefit of God rather than an audience. We describe this fault as displaying religion.

This is too long. You don't have time to write an essay on questions that don't offer many marks. Keep your answer short and to the point.

But this is just an example, not a definition, so it wouldn't get full marks.

Praying in public.

You Might be Asked to Describe Religious Teachings

These are generally worth 3 or 4 marks, so you need to give a bit more detail than in the definition questions, but don't get carried away. They're not expecting you to write an essay.

Describe Islamic teachings about charity.

Muslims are expected to help those in need. Zakah is one of the Five Pillars of Islam, which states that all Muslims should give a percentage of their yearly savings to the poor, regardless of how wealthy they are. Additional charitable acts, called Sadaqah, are also encouraged.

Muslims believe that all possessions in the end belong to Allah, and so should be used for the benefit of everyone.

Most religions teach that it's important to help the poor. Make sure you write about the teachings that are specific to your chosen religion.

Do Well in Your Exam

Descriptions and definitions are all well and good, but it's when you start to explain things that the marks come thick and fast...

You Might Have to Explain the Impact of Faith

These are still fairly quick questions — worth about 4 marks each — but they take a bit more thinking about than the ones on the previous page. You get marks for explaining how religious beliefs might influence a person's actions, views and practices.

> Explain how having a religious faith might encourage a person to get married.

Islam places great importance on procreation and teaches that marriage is the best foundation for starting a family. Muslims also teach that the only right context for a sexual relationship is marriage — cohabiting is considered very sinful.
So a Muslim who wants to have children is likely to get married first.

Try to include some of the specialist language you've learnt.

Use Good English for Longer-Answer Questions

1) For long-answer questions, you're still marked first and foremost on your understanding of the religion. However, you can get a better mark if you use better English. (On Edexcel exams, these questions are marked with an *.)

2) Structure your answer and write in paragraphs — you might want to sketch out a plan before you start.

3) The best marks will go to those who put in a number of reasons and/or develop their reasons well.

4) You'll also get marks for using the specialist language that you'll find in the glossary — learn what the words mean, how to use them, and how to spell them.

> Choose **one** religion and explain its teachings about religious tolerance.

It won't hurt to remember a bit of scripture.

It says in the Qur'an that Allah created everyone from a single soul so that we could "know each other", not so we could "despise each other." This suggests that there is a requirement for Muslims to be friendly to other faiths.

Muslims believe that Islam is the only true faith, and as such they may feel a responsibility to convert non-Muslims.

However the Qur'an states that those who follow other religions faithfully, especially Judaism and Christianity, shall be rewarded in the next life. This suggests that Muslims should respect people of other faiths.

Perhaps the most important reason why Muslims should want to live in harmony with Christians and Jews is the fact that they believe that they all worship the same God.

Best break out the best handwriting for this one.

Put your best point last.

> Explain the use of symbolism in **two** different religious traditions.

Remember — all Christian traditions are not the same. Say which ones you're referring too.

The most common Christian symbol is the cross. It reminds believers of Jesus's suffering and resurrection. Christians will often put a fish symbol on the back of their cars to demonstrate their faith to others.

In Orthodox Christianity, churches are filled with icons that represent Jesus, Mary, angels and saints. Worshippers kiss the images, which they believe brings the presence of those who they represent into the church.

You have to explain why religious people do what they do.

In Islam, images of Muhammad or Allah are not allowed. This is because such images are seen as creating the temptation to commit idolatry. For this reason Arabic characters are used to represent them.

All mosques have a dome to symbolise the Universe. Green is a commonly used colour in Islam, as it was believed to be Muhammad's favourite colour and represents life.

Thou shalt write clearly...

A large chunk of how well you do in the exam will come down to, well... how good you are at exams. Make sure you spend enough time practising doing exam-style questions under timed conditions. It'll all pay off in the end.

Do Well in Your Exam

For these questions, you have to have an <u>opinion</u>, and understand those of <u>other people</u>.

If You're Asked for Your Opinion You'll Need to Back It Up

There's <u>no right answer</u> to this kind of question — only <u>good answers</u> that'll get you <u>lots of marks</u> and <u>bad answers</u> that <u>won't</u>. The difference between the two is that good answers give <u>clearly developed reasons</u>.

> Do you agree with the UK ban on euthanasia? Give **two** reasons for your point of view.

I don't believe that euthanasia is wrong in all circumstances because in cases where people have no quality of life, forcing them to continue living is just forcing them to suffer.
As a Christian I believe that we have a duty to help those who are suffering. In some cases, helping them end their suffering may be the best we can do.

Both of these answers are pretty good despite arguing different things from different perspectives.

Your reasons don't have to be <u>religious</u>, unless the <u>question</u> says they do.

As a Muslim I believe that euthanasia is wrong in all circumstances because suffering is a test of our faith, and those who remain faithful will be rewarded after death.
Doctors and nurses have a duty to protect life, and to never harm their patients. They do not have the authority to decide when it is right for their patients to die.

You Have to Know Both Sides of the Big Arguments

1) In discussion questions, you get marks for writing what <u>you think</u> and for writing what people who <u>disagree</u> with you think. Aim to spend the <u>same time</u> and <u>effort</u> on each.

2) They're long-answer questions, so you'll usually be marked on your <u>writing skills</u> too (see p.118).

3) You'll be told to refer to a <u>religion</u>, so make sure you do or you'll lose marks.

> "Scientific advances make the existence of God less likely."
> Discuss this statement. You should include different, supported points of view and a personal viewpoint. You must refer to at least one religion in your answer.

You might be asked to refer to a specific religion, e.g. Christianity, but that doesn't mean you should only write about Christian views.

Remember to include your own <u>personal</u> response.

I do not believe that scientific discoveries show that God is less likely to exist. I would argue that, although scientific discoveries have made it difficult to believe in some of the scriptures literally, they should be interpreted symbolically.

Some people would argue that the Big Bang theory removes the need to believe in God as a 'first cause', or creator, of the Universe.

Many Christians do not find the scientific explanation of creation a problem. They would argue that although the Universe was not created exactly as described in the Bible, it does not mean that God was not involved. They believe that we should look for the spiritual lessons of the creation story, rather than treating it as if it were a scientific theory about the Universe.

Make a <u>clear reference</u> to the religion(s) you're discussing.

Try to make the reasons why people disagree with you as <u>good</u> as the reasons for your own opinion.

People who believe that science has made the existence of God less likely, would argue that one of the most important proofs of God has been disproved. The argument from design — that the world is so complex it had to have a designer — could be said to have been disproved by the theory of evolution, which shows how complexity could have arisen without being externally guided.

Some Christians, known as creationists, reject scientific theories about evolution and geology, which go against the literal meaning of scripture. For them, no scientific discovery can make God's existence less likely, as any discovery that threatened to do so would be rejected.

Don't <u>waffle</u> — it just makes life harder for the person doing the marking.

"I think exams are rubbish" — "I think exams are great..."

...but that's just because they pay me to put revision guides together. Make sure you learn the different arguments for all sides of the key issues. It's not a bad lesson to take away from the exam — even if you believe something strongly, it's worthwhile knowing why other people don't. You might even change your mind...

Spelling, Punctuation and Grammar

You get marks in your exams for having good SPaG (Spelling, Punctuation and Grammar). This stuff might not be particularly thrilling but if you can get it right, it's easy marks. This page is about checking your work...

Remember to Check what you've Written

1) Leave 5 minutes at the end of the exam to check your work.

2) 5 minutes isn't long, so there won't be time to check everything thoroughly. Look for the most obvious spelling, punctuation and grammar mistakes.

3) Start by checking your answers to the questions which award SPaG marks. Only check the rest of your answers if you've got time.

Check for common Spelling Mistakes

When you're writing under pressure, it's easy to let spelling mistakes creep in, but there are a few things you can watch out for:

Check for missing words as well as misspelt words.

1) Look out for words which sound the same but mean different things and are spelt differently. Make sure you've used the correct one. For example, 'their', 'there' and 'they're':

The Bible talks about wives submitting to their husbands.	There is no real concept of pacifism in Islam.	A lot of murders are committed in the heat of the moment — they're not premeditated.

2) Don't use text speak, and always write words out in full. For example, use 'and' instead of '&' or '+'. Don't use 'etc.' when you could give more examples or a better explanation.

3) Make sure you've used the appropriate technical terms (like 'euthanasia', 'sacrament' or 'Shari'ah'). If they're spelt correctly, it'll really impress the examiner.

Make sure your Grammar and Punctuation are Correct

1) Check you've used capital letters, full stops and question marks correctly (see p.123).

2) Make sure your writing isn't too chatty and doesn't use slang words. It should be formal.

3) Watch out for sentences where your writing switches between different tenses. You should usually stick to one tense throughout your answer (don't worry if you've used a quote that's in a different tense though).

4) Check that you've started a new paragraph every time you make a new point. It's important that your answer isn't just one long block of text (see p.123).

5) Watch out for tricksy little grammar mistakes:
   - Remember — 'it's' (with an apostrophe) is short for 'it is' or 'it has'. 'Its' (without an apostrophe) means 'belonging to it'.
   - It's always 'should have', not 'should of' (the same goes for 'could have' and 'would have' too).

   If you know that you often confuse two words, like 'it's' and 'its', watch out for them when you're checking your work in the exam.

Check, check, check, goose, check, check, check...

Blimey, there's a lot of stuff to check... which is why it's really important to practise it all before the exam. That way it'll be second nature, so you'll do it all automatically and make fewer errors in the first place.

Spelling, Punctuation and Grammar

Making a mistake in your exam is <u>not</u> the end of the world, so don't panic if you find one.
If you just cross it out <u>neatly</u> and correct the mistake, you <u>won't</u> lose any marks at all — excellent.

Make your Corrections Neatly

1) If the mistake is just <u>one word</u> or a <u>short phrase</u>, cross it out <u>neatly</u> and write the correct word <u>above</u> it.

> A stable family can give a child a sense of identity and a feeling of security, teaching
> him or her how to behave in different social situations and how to give and ~~recieve~~ ^{receive} love.

2) If you've <u>forgotten</u> to start a <u>new paragraph</u>, use a <u>double strike</u>
(like this '//') to show where the new paragraph should <u>begin</u>:

See p.123 for more on paragraphs.

> The Third Pillar of Islam commands that Muslims give 2.5% of their yearly savings to
> charity. The money is collected and distributed by the mosque. **//** Christians feel it is
> their duty to be charitable. This doesn't always mean donating money, but could mean
> giving time (e.g. by visiting the sick), or effort (e.g. helping on a volunteer building project).

If only someone had told Graham about the double strike.

Use an Asterisk to add Extra Information

1) If you've <u>missed something out</u>, think about whether you have space to write the missing bit <u>above</u>
the line you've already written. If you <u>can</u>, use a '∧' to show <u>exactly where</u> it should go.

> Jews greet each other by saying 'shalom', which means 'peace'. Generally, they
> believe that war ^{is a} ∧ bad thing, but may be necessary in some circumstances, for
> example in self-defence, to help neighbouring countries, or if all other attempts
> for peace have failed. They believe war should never be fought for revenge.

2) If the bit you've missed out <u>won't</u> fit above the line, use an <u>asterisk</u> (like this '*') to show the examiner
<u>where</u> the missing bit should go.

3) Write the <u>missing words</u> at the <u>end</u> of your answer with another asterisk next to them.

> Christianity teaches that animals should be treated kindly.* Some Christians
> believe that animal testing is wrong because they think it is unhelpful.
>
> * and shouldn't be made to suffer unnecessarily.

Cross Out anything you Don't want to be Marked

1) If you've written something that you <u>don't</u> want the examiner to mark, <u>cross it out neatly</u>.

2) Cross out any <u>notes</u>. If you don't <u>finish</u> your answer <u>in time</u>, don't cross out your <u>plan</u> —
the examiner might look at it to see what you were <u>going to write</u>.

3) Don't <u>scribble things out</u> without thinking — it'll make your answers look <u>messy</u>.

When making corrections, neatness is the name of ^{the} ∧game

Examiners love it if your answer is neat and tidy — it makes it super easy for them to read. This means they
can spend more time giving you lots of marks for the great stuff you've written. So neatness is win-win.

Spelling, Punctuation and Grammar

Some words are darn tricky to spell. The <u>only way</u> to be sure you'll get them right is to <u>learn</u> them off by heart. This page has some of the most common ones you'll need to <u>know</u> for your <u>RS exams</u>.

Learn these Useful Words

The underlined words are useful in a lot of <u>answers</u>, so you need to know <u>how</u> to <u>spell</u> them.

> There are complicated <u>arguments</u> for and against capital punishment.

> People listened to Muhammad <u>because</u> he was Allah's Prophet.

> Religious leaders often appear in the news giving their <u>opinions</u> on current affairs.

> Islam has very <u>definite</u> teachings about life after death.

> A moral code is a list of what a person <u>believes</u> is right or wrong.

> A court decides <u>whether</u> a person is guilty of a crime or not.

> The Church is <u>basically</u> a community of believers.

> In a mosque, men and women pray <u>separately</u>.

Spell Technical Words Correctly

There are a lot of <u>technical words</u> in RS. You need to be able to <u>spell</u> them <u>correctly</u>.
<u>Learn</u> these examples to start you off. The <u>coloured letters</u> are the tricky bits to watch out for.

conscience	euthanasia	celibacy	sacrament
immoral	omnipotence	promiscuity	prejudice
bereavement	pacifism	deterrence	adultery
resurrection	justice	agnosticism	omniscience
surrogacy	procreation	reconciliation	suicide

Make sure you know the <u>specific</u> technical words for your topics. For example, if you're studying the Islamic view on marriage, you would need to know words like '<u>mahr</u>' (a dowry) and '<u>nikah</u>' (the Muslim marriage contract). There's a list of technical terms in the glossary on p.124-126.

You might think revision is immoral — you'd be wrong...

You could always try to make up rhymes to remember how to spell key words. For example, for 'conscience' you could have 'Mrs C, Mrs O, Mrs N S C, Mrs I, Mrs E, Mrs N C E'. Hmm, well it's a work in progress...

Spelling, Punctuation and Grammar

This page is full of tips for good <u>punctuation</u> and <u>grammar</u> to help you avoid making any silly mistakes, hurrah!

You need to Punctuate Properly...

1) Always use a <u>capital letter</u> at the start of a <u>sentence</u>.
   Use capital letters for <u>names</u> of <u>particular people</u>, <u>places</u> and <u>things</u>. For example:

   All sentences start with capital letters. → <u>M</u>any <u>J</u>ews live in <u>I</u>srael, where the official language is <u>H</u>ebrew.

   The name of a group of religious believers.   A country.   The name of a language.

2) <u>Full stops</u> go at the end of <u>sentences</u>, e.g. 'Muslims worship Allah<u>.</u>'
   <u>Question marks</u> go at the end of <u>questions</u>, e.g. 'What is divorce<u>?</u>'

3) Use <u>commas</u> when you use <u>more than one adjective</u> to describe something or to separate items in a <u>list</u>:

   In a <u>diverse</u>, <u>multi-faith</u> city you are likely to find a variety of places of worship, including <u>mosques</u>, <u>churches</u>, <u>synagogues</u> and Hindu temples.

4) <u>Commas</u> can also <u>join two points</u> into one sentence with a joining word (such as '<u>and</u>', '<u>or</u>', '<u>so</u>' or '<u>but</u>'):

   Muslims are happy to accept converts, <u>but</u> they don't usually try to convert people themselves.

   The Earth is seen as being a product of the love of Allah, <u>so</u> we should treat it with love.

5) <u>Commas</u> can also be used to separate <u>extra information</u> in a sentence:

   The Jewish marriage ceremony takes place beneath a wedding canopy, <u>a piece of cloth supported by four poles</u>, called a chuppah.

   Many farms are moving towards organic practices, <u>which are less damaging to land and water</u>.

   When you use commas like this, the sentence should still make sense when the extra bit is taken out.

...and use Grammar Correctly

1) <u>Don't change tenses</u> in your writing by mistake:

   Some schools of Islam <u>allow</u> abortion before 120 days if there <u>is</u> a good reason for it.

   This sentence is correct because the verbs are <u>both</u> in the <u>present tense</u>. Writing 'was' instead of 'is' would be wrong.

2) <u>Don't</u> use <u>double negatives</u>. You should only use a negative <u>once</u> in a sentence:

   Don't put 'nothing' here.

   Some Muslims argue that Islam should be exclusive and should <u>not</u> have <u>anything</u> to do with other faiths.

3) Write your longer answers in <u>paragraphs</u>. A paragraph is a <u>group of sentences</u> which talk about the <u>same thing</u> or <u>follow on</u> from each other. You need to start a <u>new paragraph</u> when you start making a <u>new point</u>. You show a <u>new paragraph</u> by starting a <u>new line</u> and leaving a <u>gap</u> (an <u>indent</u>) before you start writing:

   This gap shows a new paragraph. →

   Weapons of Mass Destruction (WMDs) are weapons that can destroy large areas of land or lots of people at once. They harm anyone in their path, both soldiers and civilians.
   　　Nuclear weapons are one type of WMD. Many religious organisations, for example the Church of England, want countries to reduce the number of weapons they have.

   When you <u>plan</u> long answers, remember that you should write a <u>new paragraph</u> for each of your main points.

Phew, now you're fully SPaG-ed and ready to go...

Having good SPaG is a great way to get marks in RS exams, and having bad SPaG is a great way to lose marks. Which is why it's dead important to learn all the stuff on this page (and all the other pages too).

Glossary

The purple definitions are only for those studying Christianity or St Mark's Gospel. The blue ones are for Judaism only. The green ones are for Islam only. The red ones are for everyone.

abortion	Removing a foetus from the womb before it is able to survive, ending the pregnancy.
absolution	Forgiveness of sins granted by God through a priest, following confession and penance.
addiction	A compulsion to keep doing something, even if you know it's harming you.
adultery	A married person having sex with someone who isn't their husband or wife.
aggression	In war, this means attacking someone without provocation.
agnosticism	A belief that it's impossible to know whether or not there's a god. Not knowing if God exists.
akhirah	The concept of life after death. This is a key Islamic belief.
al'Jannah	The afterlife paradise — described as 'gardens of delight' in the Qur'an.
apostolic	A belief that the Church was founded by, and receives its authority from, Jesus's Apostles.
assisted suicide	Ending your own life with the help of someone else, e.g. asking for a fatal dose of pills.
atheism	A complete denial of the existence of a god.
atonement	Reconciliation with God. This often refers to Jesus's sacrifice on the cross to pay for our sin.
barzakh	The "cold sleep" that the soul enters after death while it waits for the Day of Judgement.
bereavement	The loss of someone close to you through their death.
bullying	Intimidating, frightening and controlling people who are weaker than you.
capital punishment	The death penalty as punishment for a crime.
catechism	A series of statements laying down the official teachings of the Roman Catholic Church.
catholic	Universal. Used to describe the community of all Christian believers.
celibacy	Not taking part in any sexual activities.
chrism	The blessed oil used in the sacraments of confirmation and ordination.
civil partnership	The joining of a same-sex couple with the same rights and responsibilities as in a civil marriage.
cloning	Creating children who are genetically identical to one parent.
cohabitation	Living together in a sexual relationship without being married.
community cohesion	The bonds holding a community together, e.g. shared values, shared culture.
conscience	An inner feeling of what's right and what's wrong.
confession	Acknowledging something. In the case of Peter at Caesarea Philippi, acknowledging faith.
conservation	Protecting and preserving resources, particularly natural resources.
conversion	When someone's life is first changed by becoming a follower of a faith.
corban	A gift dedicated to God (and so not usable for anything else).
creed	Statement of religious beliefs.
cremation	The burning of dead bodies.
Decalogue	The Ten Commandments, as listed in Exodus 20.
deterrence	The idea that potential punishment will put people off (or deter them from) committing a crime.
discrimination	Treating different people, or groups of people, differently (usually unfairly).
disciples	Followers of Jesus. This can refer to just his followers in the Bible or to all Christians.
displaying religion	Making a show of good deeds or religious observance to impress other people.
Elijah	The Old Testament prophet who is prophesied to return before the Messiah.
ethnic minority	A group of people who have a different ethnic background from most of the population.
euthanasia	Ending someone's life to relieve their suffering, especially from an incurable, painful illness.
evangelical counsels	The three vows taken by members of religious orders — poverty, chastity and obedience.
exploitation	Taking advantage of a weaker person or group of people.
fasting	Not eating and/or drinking for a set time. Used in religion for atonement or to focus the mind.
free will	The ability to choose how to behave. All three religions believe humans have free will.

Glossary

Gemilut Hasadim	Kind and compassionate actions towards those in need.
Gethsemane	The garden where Jesus prayed before his arrest.
Golgotha	The 'place of the skull' where Jesus was crucified.
Hadith	Islamic scripture containing a collection of things the Prophet Muhammad said.
holy orders	Ordination to a deacon, priest or bishop.
Holy Week	The last week of Lent, lasting from Palm Sunday until the day before Easter Sunday.
humanity	Either the human race or the caring nature of humans towards each other.
human dignity	The idea that all human life is valuable and everyone has the right to be treated with respect.
human rights	The moral, legal and political rights that every human being on Earth is entitled to.
icon	Paintings of religious figures, used in the Orthodox Christian tradition to help believers pray.
immortality of the soul	The belief that the soul of a person lives on after the death of the body.
Islamaphobia	Fear and/or hatred of all Muslims.
Jairus	A synagogue ruler whose daughter was brought back to life by Jesus.
justice	The idea of each person getting what they deserve, and maintaining what's right.
ketubah	The marriage contract, which sets out the couple's rights and responsibilities.
kiddushin	Betrothal — the first part of the marriage ceremony.
Incarnation	The act by which Christians believe God became human, in the form of Jesus.
the kingdom	The rulership of God in people's lives.
laity	All non-ordained members of the Church — those who aren't bishops, priests or deacons.
the Law	The Jewish laws of the Torah, handed down by God.
Lent	The period spent remembering Christ's 40 days of fasting in the desert.
Levi	A tax collector who was called to be one of Jesus's disciples.
literalism	The belief that everything in religious scripture is literally true.
liturgy of the word	The second part of Mass. Bible readings, a short sermon and a recitation of the creed.
Magisterium	The ability and authority of the Pope and bishops to teach on matters of faith and morals.
mahr	A dowry paid by a groom to the bride when they get married.
meditation	A form of religious discipline that involves clearing the mind of distractions.
miracle	An event believed to be the work of God, that can't be explained by the laws of science.
moral evil	Suffering caused by human beings, e.g. war, murder, rape, torture.
mourning	A period of deep sorrow for someone who has died.
natural evil	Suffering caused by the world we live in, e.g. disease, floods, earthquakes, hurricanes.
natural resource	Anything found naturally that's useful to humans, e.g. metals, oil, fertile land, etc.
near-death experience	A vision experienced by someone close to death, usually an 'out-of-body' experience.
nuclear family	A family made up of a mother, a father and their children living together.
numinous experience	An experience that inspires awe and wonder, in which someone can feel God's presence.
omni-benevolence	Showing unlimited love and compassion.
omnipotence	Having unlimited powers — all things are possible.
omniscience	Knowing everything — in the past, present and future.
Oral Torah	Jewish teachings passed down orally and recorded in the Talmud.
ordination	The sacrament of holy orders, by which someone is made a deacon, priest or bishop.
pacifism	The idea that war and physical violence are wrong under any circumstances.
papacy	The office of the Pope.
paranormal	Things that science can't explain, which are thought to have spiritual causes, e.g. ghosts.
Peter's denial	Peter denying that he knew Jesus after Jesus's trial by the Sanhedrin.

Glossary

Pharisees	A Jewish group who studied the Law and were dedicated to keeping the Jewish faith alive.
Pontius Pilate	The Roman governor of Judea who sentenced Jesus to death.
prayer	An attempt to contact God, often in the form of a conversation.
prejudice	Judging something or someone with no good reason, or without full knowledge of a situation.
pressure group	An organisation that tries to influence government policy on particular issues, e.g. Greenpeace.
procreation	Having children.
promiscuity	Having many sexual partners.
racism	Discrimination against people of other races — often based on unfair stereotypes.
reconciliation	Returning to harmony and friendship after conflict.
reform	The idea that punishment should aim to change criminals so that they won't reoffend.
rehabilitation	Preparing someone for a return to a normal life.
religious freedom	The freedom to openly practise and teach a religion, change religion or not follow a religion at all.
religious pluralism	Accepting that more than one religious view is valid, and that all faiths have the same right to exist.
religious symbol	An object that represents aspects of religious belief.
reincarnation	The rebirth of a soul in a new body after death.
resurrection	Being brought back to life after death. This could be the resurrection of the body or the soul.
revelation	An experience that reveals a god's presence.
ritual cleanliness	Laws on food and washing that prevented anything spiritually 'unclean' entering a Jew's body.
the Rosary	A string of beads used by Catholics, and the set of prayers that goes with them.
the Sabbath	The Jewish day of rest (Saturday).
Sadaqah	Aid given in addition to the compulsory Zakah, e.g. money or an act of compassion.
Sadducees	A group of priests who ran the Temple in Jerusalem and believed in sticking rigidly to the Torah.
sacrament	A ceremony, or outward sign, of the direct communication of God's saving grace.
Sanhedrin	The supreme Jewish council, who tried Jesus for blasphemy.
Sawm	The Muslim obligation to fast during daylight hours through the month of Ramadan.
scribes	Religious lawyers who made copies of the Torah, and so knew it very well.
Sermon on the Mount	A summary of Jesus's teachings on how to live a Christian life — Matthew 5-7.
sexism	Discrimination based on someone's gender (male or female).
the Siddur	The Jewish prayer book, which gives details of set prayers for specific times.
sin	An act that breaks a religious law, i.e. when God's teaching is disobeyed.
Situation Ethics	A Christian ethical principle based on the idea that we should always do the most loving thing.
Sons of Zebedee	John and James, two of the first disciples to be called.
stewardship	Taking care of the Earth as custodians of creation, so it can be passed on to the next generation.
surrogacy	When a woman bears a child for another woman.
tawhid	Belief in the oneness and incomparability of Allah.
Tikkun Olam	The belief that Jews should 'mend the world', e.g. by caring for the environment and the poor.
transfiguration	An event in which Jesus's appearance changed miraculously, making his clothes 'dazzling white'.
transubstantiation	Transformation of the Eucharistic bread and wine into the flesh and blood of Christ.
true greatness	Jesus's teaching that greatness in the eyes of God comes from serving others.
Tzedakah	The practice of giving 10% of your wealth to the poor.
United Nations	An international organisation set up to promote peace, global cooperation and human rights.
usury	Charging high rates of interest on a loan.
wudu	The ritual washing of exposed parts of the body three times before prayer in Islam.
Zakah	A Pillar of Islam — all Muslims must donate 2.5% of their yearly savings to the poor.

Index

Index